Internet Child Pornography

Recent Titles in
Global Crime and Justice

Outsmarting the Terrorists
Ronald V. Clarke and Graeme R. Newman

Human Trafficking, Human Misery: The Global Trade in Human Beings
Alexis A. Aronowitz

Police Use of Force: A Global Perspective
Joseph B. Kuhns and Johannes Knutsson, Editors

Beyond Suppression: Global Perspectives on Youth Violence
Joan Serra Hoffman, Lyndee Knox, and Robert Cohen, Editors

Identity Theft in Today's World
Megan McNally

Sold into Extinction: The Global Trade in Endangered Species
Jacqueline L. Schneider

Corporal Punishment around the World
Matthew Pate and Laurie A. Gould

Internet Child Pornography

Causes, Investigation, and Prevention

RICHARD WORTLEY AND STEPHEN SMALLBONE

Global Crime and Justice

Graeme R. Newman, Series Editor

 PRAEGER

AN IMPRINT OF ABC-CLIO, LLC
Santa Barbara, California • Denver, Colorado • Oxford, England

Library of Congress Cataloging-in-Publication Data

Wortley, Richard.
    Internet child pornography : causes, investigation, and prevention / Richard Wortley and Stephen Smallbone.
        p. cm. — (Global crime and justice)
    Includes bibliographical references and index.
    ISBN 978–0–313–38179–9 (hardcopy : alk. paper) — ISBN 978–0–313–38180–5 (ebook)
1. Child pornography. 2. Internet pornography. 3. Child pornography—Law and legislation.
I. Smallbone, Stephen. II. Title.
HQ471.W67   2012
363.4′702854678—dc23   2012022332

ISBN: 978–0–313–38179–9
EISBN: 978–0–313–38180–5

16 15 14 13 12   1 2 3 4 5

This book is also available on the World Wide Web as an eBook.
Visit www.abc-clio.com for details.

Praeger
An Imprint of ABC-CLIO, LLC

ABC-CLIO, LLC
130 Cremona Drive, P.O. Box 1911
Santa Barbara, California 93116-1911

This book is printed on acid-free paper (∞)

Manufactured in the United States of America

Contents

Series Foreword by Graeme R. Newman   vii

1.   Before the Internet   1

2.   Enter the Internet   16

3.   Who Are the Offenders?   34

4.   Investigating Child Pornography   50

5.   Impacts of Internet Child Pornography   71

6.   Prevention: Offenders and Victims   89

7.   Prevention: The Internet and Related Technologies   106

8.   Conclusion   123

References   131

Index   151

Series Foreword

THE INTERNET HAS OPENED UP A NEW WORLD—a world of seemingly endless opportunity. It is an exciting world where everyone who has an Internet connection can have his or her say, find information more easily than his or her socks, and share with the world even his or her most private thoughts and predilections. In this, the seventh book in the Global Crime and Justice series, Wortley and Smallbone uncover the dark opportunities the information age offers those who would consume or purvey child pornography. They begin by acknowledging that sexual exploitation was around long before the information revolution and that all humans, especially males, were and continue to be capable of it. Nor is the idea of children as sexual objects new. The difference today is that the availability and access to child pornography is so much easier in the information age that the old supply and demand relationship has been turned on its head. The supply leads the demand, not the other way around. Thus, they argue, the key to prevention is to choke off the supply.

Easier said than done! We see from the authors' outstanding review of who the offenders and victims are and how they are connected through the Internet and other technologies that Internet child pornography is the quintessential global crime, bringing with it the increasingly familiar problems of policing—crimes defined differently across multiple countries and jurisdictions, the labyrinthine and decentralized nature of the Internet, the capability to transmit images across borders around the world instantaneously, and the availability of smartphones and other mobile devices to children and those who would exploit them. They remind us that at the shocking end of the continuum of child pornography, it is essentially local because the actual, original production of child pornographic images most often results from contact sexual abuse by adults with close familial or social relationships to the children. It is the international distribution and consumption of images that convert the local crimes into global ones.

Wortley and Smallbone carefully and dispassionately chart a course for the reader through the vast tentacles of this global crime. They show how to neutralize its moral threat but caution against overreaction. There are rational and measured ways to reduce—if not prevent—the many forms and varieties of Internet child pornography, but these require the coordination of efforts on the part of businesses and law enforcement at the local and international levels. If you are a parent, police officer, teacher, community organizer, or IT worker, you will benefit greatly from the insights offered in this book and find many common sense steps you can take to help prevent this crime.

Graeme R. Newman
Anglesea, Australia, 2012

Before the Internet

INTERNET CHILD PORNOGRAPHY (ICP) is a new phenomenon, but the sexual exploitation of children is not. The treatment of children as sexual objects is as old as humanity, and there is a long history of the production of erotic literature and drawings involving children. In more recent times, the proliferation of sexual material involving children has depended on the technologies available to create and disseminate it. The ready availability of the camera by the mid-nineteenth century permitted the creation of child pornography as we know it today. Almost immediately, pornographic images of children were produced, traded, and collected. Even so, child pornography remained a restricted activity throughout most of the twentieth century. Images were generally locally produced, of poor quality, expensive, and difficult to obtain, traded furtively in hard copy form among small, closely knit networks of dedicated consumers. From the 1960s, there was a mini-boom in the availability of child pornography images, in large part fueled by the relaxation of obscenity laws in Scandinavia, which saw an increase in the smuggling of pornographic magazines and films into the United States and other Western countries. As a result, there was also increased public concern about child pornography and a greater commitment by governments to control the problem. For the first time in the United States, laws specifically outlawing child pornography were enacted, and law enforcement officers from various agencies redoubled efforts to stop the importation of images. By the early 1980s, U.S. law enforcement agencies were confident they were on top of the problem. In April 1982, the U.S. General Accounting Office was able to report to the Subcommittee on Juvenile Justice of the House Committee on Education and Labor that

> . . . discussions with Federal, State and local officials indicated that commercially produced (child) pornography has declined. The factors responsible for this decline were (1) the Protection of Children Against Sexual Exploitation Act of 1977, (2) tougher State laws covering child pornography, (3) stricter enforcement of obscenity laws involving child pornography, (4) media attention, (5) the tendency of juries to convict child pornographers more readily than adult pornographers, and (6) the banning in 1979 of child pornography in Sweden and Denmark, which has been the major overseas supplier of child pornography. As a result of the decline in commercial child pornography, the principal Federal agencies responsible for enforcing laws

covering the distribution of child pornography—the U.S. Customs Service and the U.S. Postal Service—do not consider child pornography a high priority. (Ahart 1982, 7)

On January 1, 1983, the first standardized protocols for the Internet were implemented and changed everything. While estimates of the amount of child pornography currently available via the Internet and the number of individuals who now access that pornography are notoriously rubbery—typically involving little more than someone's best guess—all commentators agree that the problem has increased exponentially since the 1980s. The Internet has dramatically increased the amount of material available, the efficiency of its distribution, and the ease by which it can be accessed. It has made vast quantities of technically high-quality images instantly available, at any time, and with (apparent) anonymity. Alone and in the comfort of their own homes, individuals are able to satisfy their secret curiosities and desires conveniently, cheaply, and relatively risk free.

The Internet has also made the distribution of child pornography a truly international enterprise. An image may be created in one country, held on a server in another, and accessed by an offender in yet another. The global nature of ICP creates challenges that demand new methods of investigation and control. An investigation that begins in one police district will almost certainly cross over jurisdictional boundaries. Different countries, in turn, have different laws pertaining to child pornography and different levels of capacity and commitment to tackle the problem within their borders. Perhaps more than any other offense, the investigation and control of ICP requires international cooperation and coordination among law enforcement bodies and other agencies.

This book provides a comprehensive overview of the problem of ICP. In this chapter, we trace the history of child pornography and society's reaction to it. In Chapter 2, we examine the development of the Internet and the impact it has had on the distribution of and access to child pornography. In Chapter 3, we profile ICP offenders and seek to understand the psychological bases of their behavior. In Chapter 4, we examine tactics used by law enforcement agencies to investigate ICP. In Chapter 5, we assess the impact of ICP on the victims, offenders, and investigators. And finally, in Chapters 6 and 7, we consider strategies to prevent ICP.

Across these topics is a recurring theme. The central argument developed in this book is that the problem of ICP must be understood as the product of a person-situation interaction. We need to examine the contributions to the problem of the psychological characteristics of those who offend and the technological characteristics of the Internet that facilitate offending as well as how these two factors interact with one another.

On the one hand, the consumption of ICP ultimately derives from an individual's desire for sexual gratification through viewing sexualized images of children. Without this basic motivation, there would be no demand for child pornography. Therefore, we need to understand the psychological origins of these sexual desires. We will argue that the *potential* to view children as sexual objects is common in humans—and in males in particular. Under certain conditions, many men may experience sexual arousal to children, and the consumption of child pornography is probably more widespread in the community than is usually assumed. Those arrested for online pornography crimes have come from all walks of life and include judges, soldiers, dentists, teachers, academics, and police officers. At the same time, individuals also differ markedly in their propensity to become sexually attracted to children. Most males will go through life having never having viewed child pornography nor feeling any driving desire to do so; some will have a transient encounter with child pornography but not develop an enduring interest in it; while others will repeatedly seek out opportunities to access child pornography images and their behavior will become compulsive and sometimes all consuming.

On the other hand, the consumption of ICP is also a function of the technological advances that have provided for its increased availability. ICP cannot be approached simply as a problem of individual sexual deviancy. The growth of the child pornography problem in the Internet age is a classic example of supply-led demand. What has changed since 1982 is the easy access to images with which latent sexual interest in children can be satisfied, and it is this that has fueled the rapid escalation of the problem. Therefore, we need to understand how the structure and functioning of the Internet have increased the availability of child pornography.

Most importantly, we also need to understand the reciprocal relationship between the Internet and its user—how individuals use the Internet and how the Internet affects the individuals using it. People behave differently in the virtual Internet environment than they do in other areas of their lives. The Internet has not just made it easier for dedicated offenders to access the images that they crave, but interacting on the Internet can have disinhibitory effects that allow individuals to access images that they might otherwise never have considered seeking out.

Just as we need to understand the causes of ICP in terms of a person-situation interaction, we also need to develop strategies to tackle the problem of ICP to address individual and technological factors (and the interaction between the two). Strategies that focus on the characteristics of offenders seek to reduce the demand for child pornography. These approaches include deterring individuals who may be contemplating accessing child pornography images, arresting and punishing those who do access images, and providing treatment and risk management programs to known offenders to help reduce reoffending. Strategies that focus on the Internet itself seek to reduce the supply of child pornography images. These approaches include reducing the amount of child pornography available on the Internet or making it more difficult for offenders to access the child pornography that does exist. At the intersection of dispositional and technological approaches are approaches that seek to change the individual's relationship with the Internet. This involves challenging the disinhibiting perception by offenders of the Internet as an anonymous and safe environment in which they can act with impunity.

This introductory chapter defines child pornography and traces the history of its production and consumption up to the advent of the Internet. In doing that, this chapter also examines the changes in social attitudes and customs with respect to child sexuality and the development of laws specifically designed to govern child sexual behavior. It will be argued that the idea that children need special protection from the sexual attention of adults is relatively recent. The enduring sexual interest in children across time suggests that the emergence in the past 25 years of ICP as a serious social problem needs to be interpreted in the context of a historical continuum.

WHAT IS CHILD PORNOGRAPHY?

Before we embark on an analysis of child pornography, we need to be sure of what we mean by the term. In fact, child pornography is difficult to define, and there is even debate about whether the term is the appropriate one to describe sexual material involving children. There are two approaches to defining child pornography—as a legal term and as a working research construct.

Legal Definitions

Legal definitions of *child* and *pornography* vary considerably among jurisdictions. In the case of the definition of child, there is variation around the world regarding the age at which people are legally permitted to engage in sex (see Table 1.1). As we shall see in later chapters, this makes the international control of child pornography all the more difficult. Furthermore, in some countries, the definition of *child* for the purposes of child pornography is different from the age of consent. For example, in the United States, child pornography covers the depiction of anyone under age 18, whereas the age of consent is as low as 14 in some jurisdictions. The higher age requirement for child pornography clearly reflects concerns about the exploitative nature of pornography in comparison to the consensual nature of sexual relations among peers. However, one perverse side effect of this discrepancy in the age criteria is that couples under the age of 18 years who engage in legal sex are breaking the law if they take naked photographs of one another. Indeed, there have been numerous arrests in the United States for so-called *sexting*, where teenagers send naked or seminaked pictures of themselves to their boyfriend or girlfriend via their cell phones (Ahmed 2009; Seate 2009).

Another legal gray area surrounding the definition of child involves the issue of "virtual child" pornography. A virtual child may be created in two ways. The most common method is to show pornographic images involving people over the

Table 1.1 Age of Consent for Selected Countries

Country	Male/Female	Same Sex
Australia*	16–17	16–18
Canada*	16–18	16–18
Chile	14	18
China	14	14
France	15	15
Germany	14	14
India*	14–16	18
Japan*	13–18	13–18
Mexico*	12–18	12–18
Netherlands	16	16
New Zealand	16	16
Philippines	18	18
Russia	16	16
Saudi Arabia	Married	Illegal
Spain	13	13
Sweden	15	15
United Kingdom	16	16
United States*	14–18	14–18

*varies depending on domestic jurisdiction
Source: Avert (http://www.avert.org/age-of-consent.htm)

legal age of consent but who appear to be minors (often tagged as "barely legal" pornography). In the United States, an attempt was made to shift the definition of child from chronological age to apparent age (Child Pornography Protection Act 1996). However, this was overturned on appeal on the basis that the proposed definition of child was too broad (Ashcroft v. Free Speech Coalition 2002). Because of the difficulties involved in assessing apparent age, most jurisdictions around the world use chronological age as the criterion.

The other method of creating a virtual child involves computer-generated or composite (morphed) images. This typically involves digitally attaching the head of a child to the body of an adult engaged in sexual activity. The same legislation in the United States that attempted to change the basis on which the age of the child was determined (Child Pornography Protection Act 1996) also outlawed the use of computer-generated images and this was similarly overturned on appeal (Ashcroft v. Free Speech Coalition 2002). However, in some jurisdictions (e.g., the European Union, Australia), the portrayal of computer-generated pornographic images of children is illegal.

The definition of pornography, or obscenity, is similarly variable. Portrayal of sexual acts that are illegal in one country may be lawful in another. Legal definitions typically strive to distinguish obscene material from artistic portrayals of nudity and eroticism and may refer to community standards as the benchmark against which acceptability is judged. For example, the U.S. Supreme Court defined obscene material as that "utterly without redeeming social value" and "patently offensive because it affronts contemporary community standards relating to the description of sexual matters" (*A Book Named "John Cleland's Memoirs of a Woman of Pleasure" v. Attorney General* 1966). Generally speaking, a different and more stringent standard is applied to images involving children than to images involving adults. Pornography involving a child typically does not have to involve obscene behavior but may include sexually explicit conduct that is lascivious or suggestive. For example, in *United States v. Knox* (1993), a man was convicted for possessing videos in which the camera focused on the clothed genital region of young girls.

A summary of U.S. legislation and court judgments with respect to pornography is provided in Table 1.2.

Nonlegal Definitions

Because legal definitions of child pornography differ among jurisdictions, nonlegal definitions of child pornography are often used for research, prevention, and advocacy purposes. According to the Office of the United Nations High Commissioner for Human Rights (2002) "Child pornography means any representation, by whatever means, of a child engaged in real or simulated explicit sexual activities or any representation of the sexual parts of a child for primarily sexual purposes." Similarly, according to Fournier de Saint Maur (1999) of the Interpol Specialized Crime Unit, "Child pornography is the consequence of the exploitation or sexual abuse perpetrated against a child. It can be defined as any means of depicting or promoting sexual abuse of a child, including print and/or audio, centered on sex acts or the genital organs of children" (1).

For the purpose of this book, child pornography is defined as any record of sexual activity involving a prepubescent child or a young adolescent. Pornographic records include still photographs, videos, audio recordings, and written material. It is also recognized that child pornography varies in severity. Taylor, Quayle, and Holland (2001) identified 10 levels of child pornography severity—known as the COPINE scale—ranging from nonsexualized pictures of children collected from legitimate sources (such as magazines) to graphic depictions of children engaging in sexual acts with other children, adults, and even animals (Table 1.3). In the UK, a modification of this scale, involving five levels of severity, is currently used as a guideline for sentencing those convicted of child pornography offenses (Sentencing Guidelines Council 2007).

Table 1.2 Development of Child Pornography Law in the United States

Date	Legislation/Ruling	Comment
1966	*A Book Named "John Cleland's Memoirs of a Woman of Pleasure" v. Attorney General*	Definition of obscene material in terms of social value and community standards. No specific mention of child pornography.
1978	Sexual Exploitation of Children Act	First federal law specifically dealing with child pornography. Prohibited manufacture and commercial distribution of obscene material involving minors under 16 years old.
1982	*New York vs. Ferber*	Child pornography not protected by the First Amendment. Child pornography separated from obscenity laws—to be judged on a different standard.
1984	Child Protection Act	Age of minor covered by child pornography legislation was raised to 18 years and distinction between child pornography and obscenity codified.
1986	*United States v. Dost*	Expanded the definition of child pornography to include sexually suggestive depictions of a "lascivious" nature.
1988	Child Protection and Obscenity Enforcement Act	Illegal to use a computer to depict or advertise child pornography.
1990	*Osborne vs. Ohio*	Private possession of child pornography ruled to be illegal.
1996	Child Pornography Protection Act	Definition of child pornography expanded to include virtual images of children and images that "appear to be" of a minor.
1998	Child Protector and Sexual Predator Punishment Act	Required Internet Service Providers to report known incidents of child pornography to authorities. They are not required to actively monitor customers or sites.
2002	*Ashcroft v. Free Speech Coalition*	"Virtual" images ruled not to be pornography; "appear to be" of a minor ruled to be too broad.

Source: Wortley and Smallbone (2006a)

A Note on Terminology

There is much debate in the literature and among advocacy groups and law enforcement agencies about the proper term for sexual material involving children. Some have objected to the term *child pornography* on the grounds that it

Table 1.3 The COPINE Scale

Content	Description
1. Indicative	Nonsexualized pictures collected from legitimate sources (e.g., magazines)
2. Nudist	Naked or seminaked pictures of children in appropriate settings collected from legitimate sources
3. Erotica	Photographs taken secretly of children in which they reveal varying degrees of nakedness
4. Posing	Posed pictures of children in varying degrees of nakedness
5. Erotic posing	Pictures of children in sexualized poses and in varying degrees of nakedness
6. Explicit erotic posing	Pictures emphasizing the genitals
7. Explicit sexual activity	Record of sexual activity involving a child but not involving an adult
8. Assault	Record of children subjected to sexual abuse involving digital touching with an adult
9. Gross assault	Record of children subjected to sexual abuse involving penetrative sex, masturbation, or oral sex with an adult
10. Sadistic/bestiality	Record of a child subjected to pain or engaging in sexual activity with an animal

Source: Taylor, Quayle, and Holland (2001)

trivializes the severity of the offense by linking the problem too closely with the legal production and consumption of adult pornography and erotica. Typical of this sentiment is the following explanation by the Cospol Internet Related Child Abusive Material Project (CIRCAMP n.d.):

> CIRCAMP and other Law enforcement agencies believe it is time to stop the use of the misleading term "Child Pornography" when describing images of the sexual abuse of children, and use a term or title that gives a better understanding of the crime and more respect to the child victims. A sexual image of a child is "abuse" or "exploitation" and should never be described as "pornography." Pornography is a term used for adults engaging in consensual sexual acts distributed legally to the general public for their sexual pleasure. Child abuse images are not. They involve children who cannot and would not consent and who are victims of a crime. Adults that are sexually aroused by these abuse images of children do not care or believe that the child is being abused so to underpin their belief by calling the images "porn" or "kiddy porn" allows them to think that it is somehow acceptable.

Alternative terms in use include *child abuse images, child sexual abuse material, indecent images of children, documented child sexual abuse,* and *child exploitation material.* We understand that views about terminology are held very strongly. However, we have retained the use of the term *child pornography* in this book. We have done this because we believe that *child pornography* is the term that is most readily recognized by the public. It also remains as the most widely used term in legislation and by law enforcement agencies around the world (Akdeniz 2008). In using the term, there is no intention on our part to minimize the seriousness of offenders' behavior nor the harm suffered by victims.

THE HISTORY OF CHILDREN AS SEXUAL OBJECTS

For most of us, the idea that adults could derive sexual pleasure from children is disturbing and repellent. We typically regard child sex offenders as members of a small and deviant subculture, and we interpret their attraction to children as a sign of psychopathology—literally, as a psychological illness or mental disorder. Such offenders are the particular target of moral outrage from the public, and they are singled out by the criminal justice system for special treatment. There may be laws that allow them to be kept in prison after the expiry of their sentence, and they may be placed on a sex offender register for the rest of their lives. Even in prison, child sex offenders are regarded as the lowest of the low, requiring protection from other prisoners to prevent them being beaten or even murdered.

However, we need to reconcile this view of child sex offenders as a small band of sexual deviants on the one hand with the history of children as sexual objects on the other. The current legal protection from sexual exploitation we now give children is a relatively modern phenomenon, and even today, the age of consent varies significantly across societies (as shown in Table 1.1). The fact is, history reveals that throughout the millennia, the sexual exploitation of children has been commonplace. Indeed, some historians have argued that the notion of childhood as a separate stage of development, characterized by innocence and the need for special care, is a modern invention (Ariès 1962).

The Sexual Status of Children

There is a long documented history of children being treated by adults as sexual beings (Bullough 2004; deMause 1991, 1988, 1997; Linz and Imrich 2001; Tyler and Stone 1985). According to Bullough (2004), in ancient Greece, it was common practice for boys of 12 years or so to enter into sexual relationships with older males around the age of 20 until they themselves were 20. At this point, the older male usually married a young girl of 12 to 14, while the younger male repeated the cycle by finding a young boy. A few centuries later, during the Roman Empire, sex with children was common and the average age of marriage for a girl was 14. deMause (1991) also reports institutionalized sexual abuse of children in traditional Indian and Chinese societies, a practice that he claims still exists in some regions.

In medieval and early modern European societies, the age of marriage remained low, with documented cases of brides as young as seven years, although marriages were typically not consummated until the girl reached puberty (Bullough 2004). Shakespeare's Juliet was just 13, and there is no hint in the play that this was considered to be exceptional. The situation was similar on the other side of the Atlantic; Bullough reports the case in 1689 of a nine-year-old bride in Virginia. Bullough also makes the point that domestic circumstances during this period enforced high levels of sexual intimacy between children and adults. Privacy was almost unknown, and people were much more open about bodily functions. It was usual to belch and fart in public, and there was no private area designated for urination and defecation. Most families slept in the same room and often in the same bed. From an early age, children would frequently observe their parents having sex, and they imitated these sexual behaviors in their play.

At the start of the nineteenth century in England, it was still legal to have sex with a 10-year-old girl. Contemporary accounts indicate that prostitution involving young girls was common and avidly pursued. In his *Memoirs of a Georgian Rake*, written between 1808 and 1810, William Hickey (1995) describes numerous accounts of child prostitution, including one involving the recruitment and tutoring of a 12-year-old beggar girl by a brothel keeper. Customers included rich gentlemen, and children who could be passed off as virgins (often on multiple occasions) were especially valued. Widespread child prostitution continued well into the nineteenth century, although the legal age of consent rose steadily during the Victorian era: to 12 in 1861, 13 in 1875, and 16 in 1885. Over the same period in the United States, the age of consent remained as low as seven years in one state (Delaware), with 10 years common in the other states (Robertson n.d.). However, by the 1920s, most states had raised the age of consent to 16 years as a result of vigorous campaigning by social reformers. Nevertheless, a preference for youth persisted; in the 1950s, the modal age for brides across the United States was just 17 (Bullough 2004).

The Production of Pornography

The view of children as sexual beings was reflected in contemporaneous depictions of children in art and literature. Written and pictorial child pornography existed in ancient Greece and Rome (Bullough 2004). Renaissance paintings are full of naked images of children, albeit populating religious and allegorical scenes. In England, the seventeenth to nineteenth centuries seemed to be a period of particular literary interest in children as sex objects. One popular book was *Aristotle's Masterpiece*, anonymously published in 1684. This was a sex manual that talked about the "ripe age" of female virgins as 14 or 15. Another well-known publication (reputedly selling 8,000 copies annually) was *Harris's List of Covent Garden Ladies*, which circulated in London between 1757 and 1795.

This purported to be a guidebook describing the physical attributes and sexual specialties of prostitutes who worked in the Covent Garden area and included many entries referring to young girls. It is widely believed that the intention of the publication was to satisfy the prurient interests of readers rather than to be a practical guide. One entry (cited in Bullough 2004) described one prostitute, Eleanor, as:

> A plump little girl, with good eyes, and indifferent teeth, firm breasts, and fit for those who love a tight piece, having passed several times for a maidenhead, by the help of a little art of sex and acquainted with, such as alum water etc. She had sold this commodity a dozen times, within these five months, and has been well paid for the same. An old matron is her conductor and introduced her where she thinks the man can easily be duped. A practice very common in London, and as surprising that men are such fools.

However, it was the invention in 1826 of a true camera (i.e., one capable of making a permanent image) that heralded the production of pornography as we typically know it. The most notorious producer of naked and seminaked images of young girls in the nineteenth century was Charles Lutwidge Dodgson, better known as Lewis Carroll (Bullough 2004; Tyler and Stone 1985). Carroll recorded in his diary that he had photographed naked girls as young as six years old. He is thought to have taken over 3,000 photographs, although by no means were all of children. Before his death in 1898, he destroyed most of his photographs of nude children, and only a handful survive. These are available freely and legally online and are highly mannered by today's standards and not explicit; they would probably be assessed as 4 ("posing") on the COPINE scale (see Table 1.3). The children's parents were apparently present during the photographic sessions. There is ongoing academic debate about whether Carroll had an unhealthy sexual interest in young girls or was merely interested in creating photographic art. In the light of the revelations of Carroll's photographs, his famous books *Alice's Adventures in Wonderland* and *Through the Looking-Glass* have been subjected to revisionist analyses by researchers looking for hidden sexual meanings. There are indications that there were suspicions about Carroll at the time; the mother of Alice Liddell, upon whom the character Alice was based, eventually denied him access to her daughter. In any event, Carroll's notoriety has become such that one of the largest ICP rings of the 1990s was called the Wonderland Club, an explicit reference to *Alice's Adventures in Wonderland*.

The first half of the twentieth century was a period of increasing sexual conservatism and censorship. The trade in child pornography remained a hidden and secretive activity, barely registering as a social issue. However, the 1960s saw a marked increase in the availability of child pornography coinciding with the general social liberalization of the era and the relaxation in sexual mores and censorship laws (Jenkins 2001). The importation of child pornography from Denmark, Sweden, and the Netherlands became particularly problematic. Content varied from films of nudist camps to the portrayal of explicit sexual acts. The problem peaked between the years 1969 and 1979, during which many "classic" child pornography films were produced (Tate 1990). By 1977, some 250 child pornography magazines were circulating in the United States, with such titles as *Lolita*, *Children-Love*, and *Nudist Moppets* (Crewdson 1988; Tate 1990). The relaxation of social attitudes is reflected in mainstream cinema, with the release in this period of well-known films dealing with child prostitution, such as *Taxi Driver* (in 1976) and *Pretty Baby* (in 1978).

Even so, despite this relative surge in the availability of child pornography, it was still expensive, of generally poor technical quality, and had limited distribution. Burgess (1984) reported that in 1976–1977, imported child pornography magazines in the United States sold for between $6 to $12, while domestically produced magazines sold for $25 and videos for $50. We can multiply those prices by at least five to get the present-day equivalence. And according to Burgess, in some cases, the production quality was such that it was not possible to determine if the victim was male or female. Furthermore, material was still hard to come by, and the number of individuals accessing child pornography was relatively small. Jenkins (2001) has argued that many of the claims made at the time about the extent of the child pornography problem—often linked to the existence of extensive pedophile rings and the abduction of children for use as victims—were grossly exaggerated and the product of a moral panic. He cites a report to the Illinois state legislature in 1980 that claimed that "[t]he longest lasting, biggest-selling underground child porn magazine of the 1970s, the *Broad Street Magazine*, ... never sold to more than 800 individuals, nor grossed more than $30,000 per year."

Whatever the reality concerning the extent of the child pornography problem, for the first time, child pornography was taken up as a serious social issue. Perceptions that the problem was out of control sparked an inevitable public backlash and prompted political action. In 1978, the Sexual Exploitation of Children Act became the first piece of legislation in the United States to explicitly define and outlaw child pornography, distinguishing it from general obscenity (see Table 1.2). In 1980, Sweden and Denmark legislated against child pornography, cutting off an important source of supply into the United States and other countries. Importation into the United States was further restricted by increased vigilance by Postal Inspection and Customs Services, while other law enforcement agencies, such as the FBI, policed domestic distribution with greater vigor. By 1982, it was believed that these measures had proven successful in controlling the child pornography problem, a conclusion reflected in the quote from the U.S. General Accounting Office that appears near the beginning of this chapter.

Clinical Conceptualizations of Offenders

The first formal conceptualization of the sexual attraction to children as a psychological disorder did not occur until 1886, with Krafft-Ebing's coining of the term *pedophilia*. Prior to Krafft-Ebing, to the extent that sexual exploitation of children was considered to be inappropriate, it was judged in moral rather than psychological terms. Those exhibiting a sexual interest in children were considered to be rakish, decadent, or weak willed. Krafft-Ebing was a psychiatrist and was writing at a time when psychology was in the process of being established as a scientific discipline separate from philosophy. Developments in psychology were part of an increasing dominance in the late nineteenth century of positivistic approaches to understanding human affairs. Borrowed from the physical sciences, positivism is the idea that truth can only be uncovered through the scientific method and empirical research. Thus, Krafft-Ebing sought to put the explanation of child sexual abuse on a sound scientific footing.

In fact, Krafft-Ebing did not view all child sexual abusers as pedophiles, distinguishing between nonpsychopathological and psychopathological cases. Nonpsychopathological child sexual abuse was a vice, or "perversity," the result of moral weakness; psychopathological child sexual abuse was a disease, or "perversion," the result of mental weakness and caused by head injury, alcoholism, syphilis, epilepsy, or some other physical or psychological infirmity. Psychopathological pedophiles were consumed by a morbid and preferential attraction to children that infected their whole personality. However, Krafft-Ebing thought that such individuals were relatively uncommon, and he claimed to have personally only ever known four cases.

Despite Krafft-Ebing's qualifications concerning the prevalence of true pedophilia, the portrayal of sexual attraction to children as psychopathology has dominated clinical models to the present day (Angelides 2005). While the description of the underlying mechanisms have changed over time as different theoretical perspectives have gone in and out of fashion, explanations of the sexual exploitation of children are variations on a disease model, underpinned by the assumed psychological distinctiveness of offenders. Reflecting Krafft-Ebing's original nosological system, pedophilia is listed as a mental disorder in the American Psychiatric Association's (2000) *Diagnostic and Statistical Manual of Mental Disorders* (DSM-IV-TR), alongside other "paraphilias," such as fetishism and transvestism. Amid a great deal of controversy, DSM-V proposes to include for the first time the new categorization *hebephilia*, thus also defining sexual interest in young adolescents (under 15 years of age) as a mental disorder. The problem of the sexual exploitation of children has been medicalized and the solution to the problem is seen to require the psychotherapeutic treatment of offenders designed to cure their psychopathological dispositions.

Why Is the Historical Context Important?

The history of the sexual exploitation of children provides more than just an interesting background to the development of ICP. We argue that the consideration of this history is crucial to understanding why the Internet has had such a dramatic impact on the child pornography problem, and this in turn provides the basis for the formulation of effective prevention strategies. What history tells us is that the potential to become sexually attracted to children is not a rare phenomenon confined to a small deviant subsection of the community. The human sexual response is extraordinarily flexible. Within the range of sexual behaviors available to the human species, the most powerful determinant of what responses are acceptable and not acceptable is the prevailing community standard. In societies in which the sexual exploitation of children has been considered to be acceptable, there have been plenty of members of that society willing to take advantage of this social acceptance.

Some researchers see the potential to become attracted to children in evolutionary terms. According to this argument, men in particular have been evolutionarily designed to prefer youthful partners (Thornhill and Thornhill 1987, 1992). The behavior of any species is driven by the inherent drive to pass on genes to the next generation. This is not a conscious motivation; humans do not go about their daily lives strategizing about the best way to ensure their genes are passed on. But this drive has determined the way that humans have been constructed and the types of behavioral preferences that comprise human nature. From this perspective, males prefer young female sex partners because youthfulness is associated with fertility. This preference is reflected in sexual offenses against females. For example, Simon and Zgoba (2006) found that 69 percent of all female sex-crime victims were under age 17, compared with the 31 percent of victims who were over age 17.

We need to make something very clear. Our historical analysis of children as sexual objects is in no way intended to provide a justification for their sexual exploitation today. We are *not* making the point that attraction to children is natural and should therefore be allowed or that offenders are helpless victims of their impulses and should not be held accountable for their actions. On the contrary, we suggest that it is the medicalization of child sexual exploitation that has the greater potential to obscure the culpability of offenders. Whether or not men are designed to prefer youthful sexual partners has no bearing on the moral or legal status of the sexual exploitation of children. If one accepted the logic of a link, then it could be equally argued that assault and murder should be legalized because human beings are naturally aggressive or that theft should be legalized because everyone desires to own nice things. We make certain behaviors illegal precisely *because* people want to perform them (otherwise, there would be no point). Laws are an expression of society's moral sentiments. In the case of the sexual exploitation of children, it is illegal because we have chosen to make it illegal; as a society, we have declared that we find such behavior abhorrent and we want to stamp it out.

We should also emphasize that we are not arguing that all men are at equal risk of performing sexually exploitive behavior toward children. Sexual attraction to children is best conceptualized as falling along a continuum rather than as a condition that is either present or not present. Human nature provides the potential for sexual attraction to children, but the extent to which that potential is realized—if at all—depends on a range of biological, developmental, social, and situational factors. Particular childhood experiences, individual moral standards, personality differences, and so on, all account for variations among individuals in offending risk. Most men will not develop a preferential sexual attraction to children and will happily fulfill their sexual desires with appropriately aged partners. Their risk of sexually abusing children is low, although some may be tempted to engage in sexually exploitative behavior in a moment of weakness and given the "right" situational conditions. However, a relatively small core of men will become strongly predisposed to sexually exploit children. They need little in the way of encouragement to offend and will actively and determinedly seek out opportunities to satisfy their sexual urges.

Our purpose, then, is not to excuse or normalize the behavior of those who sexually offend against children but to try and understand it. We realize that with a topic such as this that arouses such passionate responses this is a fine line to walk. Moreover, few people are comfortable contemplating the possibility that they may have dark thoughts buried deep in the private recesses of their mind. It is much more comforting to portray the offender as the alien "other." However, it is the widespread latent potential to become sexually aroused by children that explains why the Internet has caused such a surge in child pornography over the past few decades. The Internet has allowed many individuals who otherwise would not have used child pornography to now do so. These individuals have been provided with the opportunity to explore their perhaps casual and vaguely formed sexual attraction to children. Had they lived in the pre-Internet era, most would not have sought out hard copy child pornography images. If they had sought them out, the task would have been much more difficult, the choice would have been much more restricted, and the collection of images they would have managed to accumulate would have been much smaller.

CONCLUSION

The proliferation of child pornography requires two preconditions. First, there must be potential offenders who have an interest in viewing images of the sexual exploitation of children. Second, there must be the opportunity for these potential offenders to gratify their sexual interests. We have contended that the sexual exploitation of children has a long history and that the potential to develop a sexual interest in children is more widespread than most people would like to acknowledge. Against this background, the Internet has provided unparalleled opportunity for this latent sexual interest to be acted on. There are undoubtedly many more child pornography images available now and many more individuals accessing those images than would have been the case had the Internet not existed. ICP was a problem waiting to happen.

The Internet, then, is not just a passive platform on which dedicated pedophiles access child pornography that they would have obtained in any case; the Internet is an active cause of child pornography. Just how the Internet has exacerbated the problem of child pornography is the topic of the following chapter.

Enter the Internet

THE INTERNET AND associated digital technologies have provided new and very efficient means by which child pornography can be produced, distributed, and accessed. Digital cameras and webcams have made possible the production of technically high-quality—often homemade—child pornography. Images may then be uploaded onto Internet websites from anywhere in the world or exchanged directly among individuals via e-mail, newsgroups, bulletin boards, chat rooms, and peer-to-peer networks. Consumers of child pornography can obtain images cheaply and (apparently) anonymously at any time or place and in a form that is convenient to catalogue and store, does not deteriorate, and can be digitally modified if desired.

This chapter examines the impact the Internet has had on the child pornography problem. It begins with an overview of the Internet, tracing its development from the late 1960s to the present day and providing a basic tutorial on how the Internet works. It then outlines the role the Internet has played in exacerbating the problem of child pornography, examining the strategies employed by offenders and the size of the ICP problem.

WHAT IS THE INTERNET?[1]

The Internet is a network of cables, telephone lines, and satellite links that connects computers from around the world. The Internet is actually made up of millions of smaller networks and for this reason is often described as a network of networks. It is estimated that about 90 percent of Internet usage occurs on the World Wide Web (WWW) (Arnaldo 2001). The WWW refers to the worldwide collection of documents and other files stored on webpages and in websites. Via

---

[1]This section has largely defied our efforts to provide individual in-text references in the usual academic way. It goes without saying that authors should cite all their sources and not take credit for others' work. However, the information covered in this section is essentially descriptive rather than the product of individual research. The information we present comes from cross-checking facts from numerous sources. The main sources consulted in the writing of this section include: Chapman 2009; Horton 2001; Leiner et al. 2011; Shuler 2005; and Tyson 2004.

the WWW, individuals can access text, graphics, and audio and video files on almost any topic and can upload files for others to access. In addition to the WWW, the Internet provides a range of other applications that permit individuals to communicate directly with one another and to exchange files. These tools include e-mail, newsgroups, bulletin boards, chat rooms, and person-to-person (P2P) networks.

A Brief History of the Internet

The idea of connecting computers to a network was raised as a theoretical possibility as early as 1960 (Licklider 1960), and the first connection between two computers occurred in 1969 (see Table 2.1). The original network—known as Arpanet—was confined primarily to universities and research institutes and was soon joined by a number of other research-focused networks. However, different networks used different methods of transferring data, meaning they could not communicate with one another. In 1983, common communication protocols were agreed on that allowed for the development of a unified network now called the Internet.

Growth of the Internet was rapid—in terms of technological development and the number of users. As the Internet moved from academia and research institutes to the general community, opportunities for commercialization saw a dramatic improvement in functionality. By the early 1990s, the key features of the Internet we rely on today to source information—the World Wide Web, web browsers, search engines—were in place. The development and growing popularity of social networking applications, such as e-mail, Internet chat, Facebook, and Twitter, have revolutionized the way people interact with each other.

The uptake of the Internet is staggering. In 1981, the Arpanet had just 231 hosts (Hafner 1998). By 1987, the Internet was estimated to have 30,000 users, growing to 16 million by 1995 and 2.11 billion by June 2011 (Internet World Stats 2011; see Figure 2.1). With a current (2011) worldwide population of 6.78 billion, this means approximately one person in three is an Internet user.

How Does the Internet Work?

For most of us who use the Internet even on a daily basis, the mechanics of the process remain largely a mystery. Typically, we have learned the necessary skills of how to log on, search for information, and send each other e-mails, but beyond that, we have little idea of what happens when we click "Download" or "Send." However, if we are to understand how ICP offenders commit their crimes and how they might be thwarted in these endeavors, then we need to understand at least the rudiments of how the Internet works. We examine four key components of the Internet: communication protocols, domain names, Internet servers, and networks.

Figure 2.1 Internet Users (Millions) Since 1995

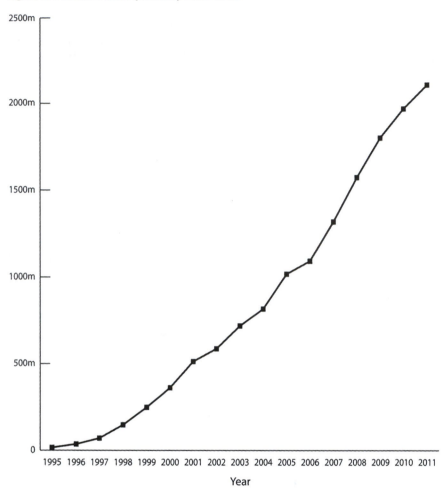

Year

Communication Protocols

In order for computers on a network to communicate with one another, they need a common language. A communication protocol is an agreed-upon language or format for transmitting data. The Internet has numerous communication protocols—known collectively as the Internet Protocol Suite—that work together, each dealing with a different communication task. The protocols are built into each computer's operating system (e.g., Windows). The suite is "stacked"; that is, protocols are arranged in hierarchical layers based on their level of abstraction—from high-level interaction with the relevant application program (e.g., e-mail) to low-level interaction with the computer hardware. A message sent from computer A moves down the stack (from application to hardware); when the message is received by

Table 2.1 The History of the Internet

Year	Innovation
1969	First digital link between computers at UCLA and Stanford. The network was known as Arpanet and was followed by other networks, mostly focused around universities and research institutes. These networks were the forerunner of the Internet.
1971	First e-mail, establishing the protocol of using "@" to separate the user name from the domain name.
1974	Beginning of the Internet Protocol Suite known as TCP/IP (Transmission Control Protocol/Internet Protocol). TCP/IP are common communication protocols (i.e., agreed-upon formats for transmitting data) that allow hosts to connect with one another. The introduction of TCP/IP permitted the merging of the various separate networks that had developed. An important feature of TCP/IP is that each host is responsible for application functions, meaning there is no central control of the network. This is known as the end-to-end principle. The term *Internet* was first used to denote any network that employed TCP/IP.
1977	The PC modem introduced. Modems are devices for connecting a host to the Internet. They include dial-up and ADSL modems that use standard telephone lines and dedicated cable modems.
1978	The Bulletin Board System (BBS) introduced. BBS is an application that permits the posting of messages on a network. Participants can also share and exchange images and files. A bulletin board is usually devoted to a specific topic or area of interest and may involve its own jargon and culture that helps build a sense of community. Bulletin board communication may occur in real time to allow contributors to engage in online chat. Bulletin boards are hosted by an owner and may be accessed directly via a modem without going through the Internet.
1979	Usenet introduced. Usenet is a network of newsgroups, which are devoted to specific topics or categories. A newsgroup allows contributors to have discussions about a particular subject by posting messages, documents, pictures, etc., and responding to previous posts. In some cases a password may be required, and some newsgroups filter posts through a moderator. Usenet is similar to BBS. However, Usenet is an Internet-based system distributed among an ever-changing collection of servers; in most cases, no one owns a newsgroup and there is no central authority.
1983	Arpanet adopts TCP/IP, paving the way for standardized communication protocols and the unified Internet as we know it.
1988	Internet Relay Chat (IRC) introduced. IRC provided the first widely available Internet-based chat room service. A chat room is a location on a server that permits multiple users to engage in real-time conversations as well as exchange electronic files. Chat rooms are usually organized around discussion forums or themes. Anyone can set up a chat room. Many chat rooms are open to anyone to log in to, while some are closed. They may employ a moderator, but users can nominate a pseudonym. In addition to IRC, there are now many different providers of chat room services.

(continued)

Table 2.1 (Continued)

Year	Innovation
1990	First commercial dial-up Internet Service Provider (ISP) called The World. An ISP is a company that connects customers to the Internet. ISP services typically include e-mail, uploading and downloading (File Transfer Protocol or FTP), and web hosting (creation of personal websites).
1991	World Wide Web (WWW, W3, or the web) created. WWW is the collection of electronic documents and other files stored throughout the Internet. WWW provides an interface to the Internet that locates and organizes files, documents, images, and other information distributed across the network. WWW employs hypertext—links provided within a webpage to connect it with other related webpages. The protocol managing the web is called the Hypertext Transfer Protocol (HTTP).
1991	First webcam. A webcam is a video camera that permits live images to be displayed via a webpage.
1993	First commercial graphical web browser called Mosaic. A web browser is a software program that enables users to navigate the WWW to access, retrieve, and view webpages and other information. Users can locate information by entering the relevant Uniform Resource Locator (URL), and move between webpages by using hyperlinks. Major web browsers now include Internet Explorer, Firefox, Google Chrome, Opera, and Safari.
1993	First web search engine called W3Catalog. A search engine is a tool for finding information on the web. Search engines collect, analyze, and index information about webpages, and relevant pages are retrieved when a user types in an appropriate search term. Google is currently the dominant search engine, with more that 80 percent of the market share; other search engines include Yahoo!, Lycos, and Bing.
1999	First Internet-based peer-to-peer (P2P) file-sharing program called Napster. Napster permitted hosts to download music by searching the hard drives of other hosts on the network (and was subsequently closed down for copyright infringement). While Napster operated through a centralized server, later P2P networks (e.g., Kazaa, Morpheus) connect hosts remotely without going through a central server. Each computer is an equal partner, and all work co-operatively together. All computers in the network have a common file-sharing program, allowing users to connect directly to each other's hard drive to search for and exchange files, images, etc.
2003	Introduction of Skype, a peer-to-peer application (hence the name sky + pe) that permits audio and video calls over the Internet.
2003	MySpace introduced, signaling a boom in the popularity of Internet social networking. Social networking had long been a feature of the Internet (e.g., e-mail, newsgroups, chat rooms), but MySpace incorporated a number of popular features, such as bulletin boards, groups, user profiles, and friends' lists. By 2008, Facebook, launched in 2004, overtook MySpace in popularity.

computer B, it moves up the stack (from hardware back to application). The suite is usually referred to by two core protocols—abbreviated to TCP/IP.

TCP is short for Transmission Control Protocol and sits above IP in the stack. TCP is responsible for dividing a file generated by an application into "packets" of data that can be transmitted across the Internet, ensuring that data does not get lost in the process. At the receiving computer, TCP reassembles these packets into a single file.

IP is short for Internet Protocol. The IP directs the packets of data from the source host to the destination host. Every computer on the Internet must have a unique IP address. An IP address is generated in binary code (32 bit, yielding more than four billion permutations, for the mathematically minded), although you can read it off your computer as a series of digits and periods (e.g., 191.158.1.64). IP addresses come in static and dynamic forms. Static IP addresses do not change and are manually assigned by a system administrator. Major computers (e.g., servers) and computers within a local area network (LAN) will typically have static IP addresses. However, static IPs are an inefficient way to manage an increasingly scarce resource. (We are running out of IP addresses!) For home computers, most Internet Service Providers (ISPs) automatically assign a new dynamic IP address each time a host connects to the network. This means that the IP address you had during your last Internet session has probably had many previous owners, although during your session, you were the only person on the Internet using that address. By allocating and reusing IP addresses as required, ISPs are able to manage with fewer addresses than they have subscribers. However, in some cases, dynamic IP addresses are changed relatively infrequently, in which case they are referred to as being "sticky." One important implication for us is that static and sticky IP addresses are much easier to trace than are dynamic IP addresses.

Domain Names

In order to connect with another computer, you need to tell your computer the other computer's IP address. However, having to remember and specify IP addresses would seriously limit the functionality of the Internet. A domain name is a human-readable version of an IP address. Not all IP addresses have domain names; domain names are mainly for servers that store information and services that are made available to others (and have static IPs). The domain name is the information that appears after the "www." in a web address or after the "@" in an e-mail address. For example, let us suppose that the IP address 191.158.1.64 corresponds to the Internet address griffith.edu.au (it does not).

Domain names are constructed in a nested fashion, like a Russian doll. The final suffix refers to top-level domains (TLDs). In the United States, the TLD code is usually a generic category or organization type (e.g., .com, .org, .edu, .gov, .net). For other countries, the TLD is usually their country code (ccTLD) (e.g., .uk, .au, .ca, .jp). As we move left through to second-level domains (2LDs), locations get more specific. Working back from left to right, the Internet address griffith.edu.au is for Griffith University (griffith), which is part of the education domain (edu) in the country of Australia (au).

In 2010, the number of registered domain names worldwide passed 200 million (Verisign 2011). Domain names are registered by an organization or commercial enterprise accredited to be a domain name registrar. There are thousands of domain registrars around the world. The accreditation process for registrars is coordinated internationally by the Internet Corporation for Assigned Names and Numbers (ICANN), headquartered in the United States. ICANN is a self-regulatory, industry-based organization, but its role is recognized by government. Different countries may have their own government-recognized bodies that are affiliated with ICANN and can accredit local domain registrars. For example, au Domain Administration (auDA) is an industry organization endorsed by the Australian government to license domain registrars allocating 2LD names with an "au" TLD.

The domain name specifies the computer on which the information or application you require sits, but it is just part of the Uniform Resource Locator (URL) or the e-mail address required to locate a specific website, file, or person. For example, if we were to post this book chapter as a webpage at Griffith University, the URL might be http://www.griffith.edu.au/publications/ICPchapter2. The "http://www" part of the URL is an instruction to locate the domain on the World Wide Web by using the Hypertext Transfer Protocol (HTTP); the "publications/ICPchapter2" part of the URL indicates that the chapter is located at Griffith University in a file called "publications." In the case of e-mails, a specific username is required to the left of the "@" to direct the message to the correct person at the domain in question.

The protocol that manages the conversion between the IP addresses and domain names is the Domain Name Service (DNS). To understand how this and other essential Internet functions occur, we need to examine the role of Internet servers.

Internet Servers

Computers on the Internet can be divided into two basic sorts: clients (such as your home computer) and servers. A server is a computer that has been configured to provide a service to other computers in a network, including access to hardware, software, and centralized data storage. Servers are essential for the operation of the Internet, and different servers perform specialized functions. However, a specific server is not necessarily a separate machine; different server functions may be carried out on the same computer by using different ports. Key servers on the Internet are DNS (or name) servers, web servers, FTP servers, e-mail servers, and authentication servers.

Name servers match IP addresses with their respective domain names. DNS does not sit on any one name server, but it is a distributed database hosted by many name servers across the Internet. Each name server holds only a small portion of the database; if a name server is unable to match the IP address and domain name, it redirects the request to another name server. Like the domain name, the distribution of the DNS is also hierarchical. Returning to our example domain name griffith.edu.au, a name server for the TLD "au" will know the IP addresses for the "edu" name servers but not for the specific university servers, such as "griffith"; these are held by "edu" name servers. Hence, a DNS query will necessarily pass through more than one name server.

Web servers and FTP servers contain most of the information accessed over the Internet. These servers are distributed around the world. The main function of a web server is to host websites and to deliver webpages to clients on request. Many companies provide web-hosting services that allow individuals or organizations to lease space on a web server and to create their own websites. An FTP server permits file sharing over the Internet. FTP stands for File Transfer Protocol and manages the downloading and uploading of electronic files. Downloading is the process by which a computer receives an electronic file from the Internet via a FTP server; uploading is the process of transferring electronic files from a computer to a FTP server on the Internet. Files stored on a FTP server may be made freely available or they may be password protected. Clients typically connect to web and FTP servers by using a web browser (e.g., Internet Explorer, Safari). The specific information held on the server is identified and accessed through its URL, as described earlier. Clients may use search engines (e.g., Google) to interrogate the servers in order to locate information related to specified key terms.

An e-mail server, as the name suggests, is responsible for the transfer of mail between computers. The transfer of mail is managed by the Simple Mail Transfer Protocol (SMTP). Mail servers send and receive e-mails using SMTP. However, the e-mail application on your computer typically only uses SMTP to send e-mails to your e-mail server, which then relays the message to the e-mail server used by the addressee. To read mail from your home computer, you must log into your e-mail server and download messages from your mailbox by using the Internet Message Access Protocol (IMAP). E-mail servers keep records of the e-mails they process, so e-mail traffic is relatively easy to trace. However, servers called *anonymous remailers* can be used to strip e-mails of their identifying information before forwarding them on to their destination. There can be legitimate reasons for using an anonymous remailer—e.g., to enable an employee to blow the whistle without the fear of repercussions—but remailers can also be used by individuals to facilitate illegal activities, including the dissemination of child pornography.

Finally, authentication servers manage access to the Internet by verifying the identity of the user. Your ISP will require you to provide a username and password before allowing you to access services. Authentication servers also keep records of Internet use matched against allocated IP addresses. Even in the case of dynamic IP addresses, there is a record kept of which username was assigned a particular IP at a given time. This makes it theoretically possible to trace individuals who access illegal sites on the Internet, although as we shall see, there may be legal and practical problems to overcome.

Most online traffic—but not all—relies on Internet servers. ICP offenders may access or share images via web servers, FTP servers, and e-mail servers, while authentication servers record Internet usage against specified IP addresses. There-fore, servers have a critical role to play in the investigation and prevention of ICP.

Networks

How then do messages travel the often vast distances between one computer and another? The client and server computers that comprise the Internet hardware are inter-connected by a mixture of telephone wires, fiber optic cables, and, increasingly, wire-less signals and satellite links. The Internet has often been called a network of networks. In keeping with the logic of other Internet architecture, these networks are hierarchical. The exact nature of these hierarchies varies among countries, but the sit-uation in the United States serves as an example. In the first instance, your home com-puter is connected to your local ISP, along with all the other local customers; if you are using a work computer, you are probably part of a LAN. Your ISP will be part of a regional ISP network that in turn will be part of a larger Network Service Provider (NSP). Different NSPs connect at Network Access Point (NAPs), thus allowing their respective customers to communicate with one another across the networks. The prin-cipal data routes between the networks are referred to as the Internet backbone.

Messages navigate the complex pathways to their destination via routers. Data packets contain "control information" that provides the network with details needed to deliver the message. Routers are machines that read this control informa-tion and guide the transfer of data packets from one network to another. Routers have partial Internet maps in their memories—sufficient at least to get the packet to the next router. The structure of the Internet means there is no single route between any two points on the network. Routers determine optimal pathways and can change those pathways if links become slow or drop out. A message will typ-ically pass through numerous routers. It is remarkable that despite the complexity of the network, packets of data can cross the world in a fraction of second.

The flexible, distributed nature of these networks means the Internet is extremely resilient, capable of withstanding concerted cyberattacks and signifi-cant infrastructure damage. Equally, this flexibility makes the Internet essentially ungovernable. The end-to-end principle that underpins the Internet means that most of the necessary software (such as TCP/IP) is located on computers that join the network. The Internet has no centralized hub nor is it managed by any single authority. Unless you are in a country where the government exercises tight con-trol over Internet infrastructure (such as China), it is simply not possible to close off all access to information. There is an obvious positive side to this ungovern-ability. The Internet has often been called the ultimate democracy—a forum for open access and free speech. However, it is because of this ungovernability that the control of illegal activity on the Internet is so challenging.

Summary

In this section, we have presented what we believe is essential background knowledge about the virtual environment in which ICP offenders commit their crimes. We have tried to strike a balance between presenting a readable account of how the Internet works and providing necessary technical detail. No doubt, some readers will have sophisticated computing knowledge and will regard our coverage as simplistic. It may also be that there are other readers who will find it unnecessarily detailed. Stripping away all jargon, the following are the key points we would like you to take from this section:

- The Internet is very new, officially dating from 1983, but the technological advancement has been rapid.
- The growth of Internet usage is staggering, with no sign of it plateauing.
- The Internet exists because computers use a common computer language that allows them to communicate with each other.
- Every computer on the Internet has a unique address that allows messages to be delivered, but this also means that all Internet traffic can potentially be traced.
- The instructions you type on your computer to find a website or to e-mail a friend is another form of the address of the destination computer. All these addresses (or domain names) must be registered.
- The Internet depends on a number of different types of computers that perform essential tasks, such as locating computer addresses, storing files and websites, managing e-mails, and granting access to the Internet. These computers retain traces of the Internet traffic passing through them.
- Internet connections involve a complex network of networks that span the globe. There are many routes between any two computers, making the control of Internet traffic very difficult.

Let us turn now to the role that the Internet plays in ICP.

THE INTERNET AND CHILD PORNOGRAPHY

In 1980, the biggest-selling child pornography magazine in the United States was estimated to sell about 800 copies (Jenkins 2001); 20 years later, one ICP company was found to have more than a quarter of a million subscribers from around the world (Krone 2005). There is no doubt that the Internet has been instrumental in the exponential growth of the child pornography problem. The very features of the Internet that have made it so useful in modern times for performing legitimate activities have also made it an ideal platform for those carrying out illegitimate activities. In this section, we examine three questions: how has the Internet exacerbated the child pornography problem; where do offenders locate child pornography on the Internet; and what is the size of the ICP problem?

How Has the Internet Exacerbated the Child Pornography Problem?

Child pornography offenses involve three elements: the production, distribution, and viewing of abuse images. The Internet and associated technologies have revolutionized the way each of these elements is carried out. The Internet has exacerbated the problem of child pornography by increasing the volume of child pornography that is available, the efficiency with which it is disseminated, and the ease by which it can be accessed and managed.

Production

Production involves the creation of pornographic images. In the pre-Internet era, child pornography images were typically grainy and blurred, with many of those in circulation decades old—copied and recopied from earlier magazines and films. The digital technologies associated with the Internet permit the production of technically sophisticated images. Digital technologies provide for a variety of formats (pictures, videos, sound) as well as the potential for real-time and inter-active experiences via webcams. Producers can digitally manipulate images to create composite or virtual images ("morphing").

The production of child pornography may be done professionally, involving sophisticated pedophile rings or organized crime groups that operate for profit (Internet Watch Foundation 2010). However, the widespread access to digital technologies also permits the active involvement of amateur producers of child pornography who seek no financial reward (Wolak et al. 2005a). Using inexpensive electronic recording devices (digital cameras and video recorders), individuals can create high-quality, homemade child pornography, often involving records of their own sexual abuse exploits. With the advent of cell phone cameras, clandestine photographing of children in public areas is also becoming an increasing problem. A premium by collectors is placed on new child pornography images, and offenders can use new images as currency to gain access to child pornography networks and to trade with other offenders.

Distribution

Distribution involves the dissemination of pornographic images, moving them along a supply chain from producers to users. Pre-Internet child pornography images were distributed, sold, and traded in hard copy form. Child pornography coming in from overseas had to pass through border controls, and the U.S. Customs Service and the U.S. Postal Service claimed considerable success in stemming the flow of imported material (Ahart 1982). Domestic distribution was equally problematic. The supply chain was restricted, unreliable, and surrounded by secrecy. Child pornography was available only in certain locations, and even there, customers had to know where to find it.

The Internet provides an unsurpassed distribution network, reaching from all corners of the Earth into almost every Western home. Child pornography images accessed in the United States are likely to have been uploaded to a server sitting in Russia, Eastern Europe, or Southeast Asia. As with the production phase, the distribution of child pornography may involve organized crime rings operating for profit. However, the Internet also allows offenders to interact directly with one another, exchanging files without needing to go through a third person.

Viewing

Before the Internet, viewing child pornography required the possession of hard copies. In the Internet era, viewing means downloading child pornography from another computer or server on the Internet. In some cases, a pop-up link may appear for child pornography on an unrelated site or child pornography may be embedded in a legal pornography site. However, in most cases, users must actively seek out pornographic websites or subscribe to a group dedicated to child pornography. Note that images do not need to be saved to the computer's hard drive or to a removable disk in order to constitute downloading; they simply need to be accessed.

For users, child pornography accessed from the Internet provides many advantages over hard copy alternatives. ICP is instantly available at any time or place. It can be accessed in private, from the comfort of one's home, and with apparent anonymity. While some sites charge for images, other images may be free or provided on an image-exchange basis. The images themselves do not deteriorate and can be conveniently catalogued and stored on the computer's hard drive or on a removable disk. Files can be encrypted for added security. The social networking facility of the Internet allows offenders to build a virtual community of offenders, providing mutual support for each other's belief systems, and a forum in which to exchange information and tips about offending.

Where Is Child Pornography Found on the Internet?

In this section, we examine the main methods by which child pornography is distributed and accessed on the Internet: websites, webcams, e-mail, newsgroups, bulletin boards, chat rooms, and peer-to-peer networks. These forums vary considerably in the amount of security they afford offenders, and efforts by law enforcement agencies and ISPs to stop the dissemination of child pornography on the Internet have led to changes for how offenders distribute and obtain images. Open areas of the Internet are becoming increasingly risky places to search for child pornography because of the possibility of becoming ensnared in a police sting operation. Those distributing child pornography are employing more sophisticated security measures to elude detection and are being driven to hidden levels of the Internet. It is possible that an individual may stumble across child pornography during legal Internet surfing, but usually, child pornography needs to be actively searched for. Those seeking to find images in a secure environment increasingly need good computer skills and inside knowledge of where to look.

Websites

Specific child pornography websites may be created or child pornography images may be embedded in general pornography sites. However, there is debate about how much child pornography is freely available on the web. Some argue that it is relatively easy to find images (Financial Coalition Against Child Pornography 2008, 2011; Internet Watch Foundation 2010). Others argue that because of the vigilance of ISPs and police in tracking down and closing child pornography websites, it is unlikely that a normal web search would reveal much genuine child pornography (Jenkins 2001). Instead, the searcher is likely to find legal sites with adults purporting to be minors, sting operations, or vigilante sites.[2]

In order to thwart detection efforts of authorities, web-based ICP tends to involve temporary hosting arrangements in which images are automatically rotated through numerous sites (Internet Watch Foundation 2010). Large collections are typically split into smaller subsets and hosted across numerous sites rather than on a single webpage. The route to sites is also typically convoluted, requiring the visitor to pass through a number of redirects (Financial Coalition Against Child Pornography 2008). One specific strategy of distributors is to post temporary sites that are then advertised on pedophile bulletin boards (Jenkins 2001). To prolong their existence, these sites may be given innocuous names (e.g., "volleyball") or other codes (e.g., "ch*ldp*rn") in order to pass screening software employed by ISPs. The websites may be immediately flooded with hits before they are closed down. Often, the websites will contain zip archives, the password for which will then be posted on a bulletin board at a later date. Closing down ICP websites has been likened to playing a game of whack-a-mole; as soon as a website is closed down, it reappears at another location (Financial Coalition Against Child Pornography 2008).

All information available on the web, even illegal sites such as those containing child pornography, must have a registered domain name. The Internet Watch Foundation (2010) identified nearly 17,000 potentially illegal child pornography websites in 2010. The sites were hosted in 41 different countries. The six top-level domains were .com, .ru (Russia), .jp (Japan), .net, .es (Spain), and .org, and these accounted for 86.4 percent of all URLs. By continent, 42 percent of websites were hosted in North America, 41 percent in Europe and Russia, 17 percent in Asia, and less than 1 percent each in Australia and South America. In an earlier analysis (Internet Watch Foundation 2008), 74 percent of websites were found to originate from commercial enterprises, with 26 percent being amateur productions.

Webcams

A webcam is a camera attached to your computer (either as a built-in feature or connected via a USB port) to transmit images to another computer. In the original set-ups, images were uploaded from the source computer to a FTP server before being downloaded by the destination computer and refreshed every few seconds. More

---

[2]As researchers in this field, the authors routinely need to search the Internet for information by using search terms such as "child pornography." All we have ever been offered are scholarly papers on the subject or the websites of agencies and organizations involved in combating the problem.

recently, Skype software permits peer-to-peer (P2P) connections in which images are streamed directly from the source computer to the destination computer.

Webcams have been implicated in child pornography in two main ways. First, a webcam may be used to broadcast real-time sexual abuse of children. In one documented case of a live broadcast, viewers were given the opportunity to make online requests for particular sexual activities to be carried out on the victim (Burke et al. 2002). Second, offenders may develop online relationships directly with victims—typically young teens—and convince them to perform sex acts on camera (ABC News 2006).

E-Mail

Professional distributors may sometimes send child pornography via e-mail attachments. However, this is considered a risky strategy because e-mail affords a low level of security. More frequently, inexperienced offenders may use e-mail to share images with other offenders or to send images to potential victims as part of their efforts to groom them. Using e-mail in this way carries the additional risk of unwittingly engaging with undercover police officers who have been encountered in chat rooms—either posing as children who may be potential victims or as adults seeking child pornography.

Bulletin Boards and Newsgroups

Specific child pornography bulletin boards and newsgroups may be used to host discussions that provide advice to seekers of child pornography, including the URLs for child pornography websites and ratings of those sites, and to post and exchange child pornography. These forums are one of the major methods of distributing child pornography. There are a number of notorious newsgroups—for example, the abpep-t or "alternative binaries pictures erotica pre-teen" group—familiar to offenders and police. Carr (2002) reports that most child pornography is concentrated in 28 newsgroups and just three account for nearly half of all activity. Nearly two-thirds of newsgroups originate in the United States.

Forums may be monitored by system administrators in order to exclude bogus or irrelevant postings, such as from vigilantes. Entry to the forum may require a password, and prospective members may need to prove their credentials by providing new child pornography images for trade. Access to these sites is blocked by most reputable ISPs. If offenders do access these sites, they run the risk of having the IP address or credit card details captured and used in any subsequent investigation. However, there are techniques that computer-savvy offenders may utilize to conceal their IP address and thus anonymize their identity.

Chat Rooms

Chat rooms may be used to exchange child pornography with other offenders as well as to locate potential child victims. Chat rooms dedicated to sex with children provide forums in which offenders can network with other offenders in a manner similar to that of bulletin boards and newsgroups. Notoriously, offenders may also enter youth-oriented chat rooms in order to groom children in an attempt to convince them to send naked photographs of themselves and in some cases to arrange a face-to-face meeting (Mitchell et al. 2007). While the popular image of groomers is of a much older man pretending to be a peer of the victim, it seems that in most cases, offenders do not lie about their age—or if they do, they may shave off a few years—nor do they disguise their sexual interest in the victim (Wolak et al. 2008). Victims are typically young girls 14 to 15 years old who are seeking a relationship with an older man. Open chat rooms are avoided by seasoned child pornographers because they are commonly infiltrated by undercover police.

Peer-to-Peer Networks

P2P networks facilitate file sharing among hosts and are a major method for disseminating child pornography (GAO 2004; Mehta et al. 2002). These networks permit closed groups to trade images. There are two models for P2P networks (GAO 2004). In the first model, all hosts are connected to a central server, which maintains a directory of shared files stored on host computers (e.g., Napster). Requests for a particular file are made through the server, which then seeks out the location of that file among the other hosts. The file sharing then occurs directly between the relevant hosts. The server then performs a brokering role. In the second model, there is no server; requests for a file are made directly to the other hosts (e.g., Kazaa, Morpheus). Because these peer-to-peer connections pass through no central server, there is no centralized record of the transaction. The decentralized model is now most common and is among the most difficult Internet platforms to police.

The Size of the Problem

There are a number of different ways that the size of the ICP problem might be measured. We could look at the number of people who access child pornography on the web, the number of children who are victims of ICP, the percentage of Internet activity devoted to child pornography, the number of child pornography sites, the number of hits child pornography sites receive, the number of images available online, the growth in the number of images uploaded, the number of images in offenders' collections, and the amount of money generated by the ICP industry. Figures have been produced for each of these measures. However, in most cases, estimates are just that—often amounting to little more than someone's informed (or not so informed) best guess. Figures are often recycled from one publication to the next so they take on an air of authority and authenticity through their repetition. Leaving aside questions of reliability, estimates are therefore often also dated—a particular problem for such a dynamic and fast-growing medium as the Internet. At the risk of perpetuating this cycle, here are some oft-quoted figures:

- The number of individuals accessing ICP is in the millions (National Center for Missing and Exploited Children 2005).
- The number of offenders connected to the Internet at any one time is esti-mated to be 750,000 (Maalla 2009).
- It has been estimated that there are between 50,000 and 100,000 pedophiles actively involved in organized pornography rings around the world (Jenkins 2001).
- The number of children estimated to be victims of ICP is between 10,000 and 100,000 (Maalla 2009).
- It has been estimated that 12 percent of the Internet is devoted to pornography and 20 percent of pornography involves depictions of minors (Jayachandran 2003).
- There are estimated to be between 100,000 (Ropelato 2011) and 480,000 (Maalla 2009) child pornography websites.
- It has been reported that a single child pornography site received a million hits in a month (Jenkins 2001).
- At any one time, there are estimated to be more than one million porno-graphic images of children on the Internet, with 200 new images posted daily (Wellard 2001).
- Offenders have been arrested with as many as a million downloaded child pornography images (NewsFlavor 2011).
- ICP is estimated to turn over between $3 billion (Ropelato 2003) to $20 bil-lion (Hoover 2006) per year.

Despite questions about the accuracy of many of these figures, there can be no doubt that ICP is a serious problem. Not only has the Internet increased the amount of child pornography that is available, but it has been argued it has also increased the severity of the images (Internet Watch Foundation 2007). In the pre-Internet era, when images were scarce, collections included many photo-graphs taken from legitimate magazines, artworks, and naturist films (Jenkins 2001). The Internet has encouraged the production of many new, purpose-made, graphic images. There have been a number of content analyses of seized ICP images. In images examined by the Internet Watch Foundation (2010), 73 percent of victims were assessed as being under 10 years old. Around two-thirds of the images involved penetrative sexual activity between the victim and an adult, equivalent to levels 9 to 10 on the COPINE Scale (Table 1.3). In another set of studies, Wolak et al. (2005a, 2005b) examined the images that were in the possession of offenders arrested for producing or possessing child pornography (Table 2.2). Note that the figures in Table 2.2 refer to the percent-ages of offenders possessing different types of image, not the percentage of images themselves. Thus, 19 percent of offenders arrested for possession of child pornography had images of children under the age of three, while 80 percent possessed images of the sexual penetration of children.

At the same time, it is important to retain perspective. As serious as the ICP problem is and as devastating as the consequences for victims are, we need to avoid being swept along in a moral panic (Cassell and Cramer 2008; Jewkes 2010; Potter and Potter 2001; Schottenfield 2007). A moral panic occurs when people perceive that an issue becomes so serious that it is out of control and threatens the social order (Cohen 1972). It is perhaps too easy for us to imagine that the Internet is awash with child pornography that will appear unsolicited on our screens or that at any moment our children will be groomed by an online predatory pedophile.

There have been a number of careful research studies that permit us to better assess the magnitude of the ICP risk. Steel (2009) examined search terms used on Google and Dogpile. He found that between 1 in 200 and 1 in 500 related to child

Table 2.2 Arrested Child Pornography Offenders by the Type of Image They Produced or Possessed

Age of Victim	Producers	Possessors
Younger than 3 years	N/A	19%
3–5 years	N/A	39%
Younger than 5 years	10%	N/A
6–12 years	43%	83%
13–17 years	47%	75%
Gender of Victim		
Mostly girls	80%	62%
Mostly boys	20%	14%
Girls and boys	N/A	15%
Severity		
Genitals or sexual activity	71%	92%
Sexual contact between adults and minors	43%	71%
Penetration of a child	N/A	80%
Penetration of child by adult	30%	N/A
Penetration of child not by an adult	15%	N/A
Violence	6%	21%
Nude or seminude, not graphic	73%	79%
Suggestive poses, clothed	40%	N/A
Morphed images	N/A	3%

Source: Wolak et al. (2005a, 2005b)

pornography. Similarly, Latapy et al. (2009) analyzed the traffic on a major P2P network: eDonkey. They found that 2 in 1,000 queries related to child pornography and that this was also the same ratio of individuals on the network making the queries. While these levels of enquiry clearly reinforce that ICP is serious problem, the web and P2P connections were overwhelmingly being used for legitimate purposes.

Mitchell et al. (2007) looked at online victimization of youth—an area of particular societal concern. They conducted telephone interviews with 1,500 youth (10 to 17 years old) Internet users. They found that 4 percent of respondents reported receiving distressing sexual solicitations in the previous year. Overall, the rate of online solicitations had declined over the previous five years. Of those receiving solicitations, 90 percent were 13- to 17-year-olds; 39 percent said the solicitor was an adult (over 18 years); 56 percent said the solicitor requested naked photographs of them; one sent photographs as requested; most removed themselves from the situation (66%), warned the solicitor (16%), or ignored them (11%); and 28 percent said they were upset by the experience. Mitchell et al. do not seek to diminish the risks to youth on the Internet; indeed, their findings give rise to genuine concerns. However, they argue that effective prevention and treatment initiatives must be built on a solid research foundation, not on myths (see also Wolak et al. 2008).

CONCLUSION

The Internet has become an indispensible part of modern life and has changed human activity in profound ways. Not all these changes are positive. The same features that make the Internet a useful communication tool have been exploited by offenders to facilitate their criminal activities. The Internet has revolutionized all stages of child pornography offending. It has increased the volume of child pornography that is available, the efficiency of its dissemination, and the convenience with which it might be accessed.

There is no doubt that the Internet is responsible for a dramatic increase in child pornography offending. However, exactly how big the ICP problem is is difficult to quantify. Without diminishing the seriousness of the problem, we need to be wary of slipping into a moral panic in which we exaggerate the size of the problem and the detrimental effects it has on society.

A feature of a moral panic is the identification of a group of "folk devils" who we see as responsible for the breakdown of the social order and toward whom our moral rage can be directed (Cohen 1972). As we have previously argued, it is particularly unhelpful if we conceptualize the ICP problem simply in terms of an "us" and "them" distinction between offenders and nonoffenders. The Internet has democratized child pornography offending by giving many individuals unparalleled opportunities to satisfy their sexual curiosities. The characteristics, motivations, and behaviors of the users of child pornography are the focus of the following chapter.

Who Are the Offenders?

IN THIS CHAPTER, we turn our attention to the producers, distributors, and users of Internet child pornography (ICP). There seems to be wide agreement that the Internet has brought with it an unprecedented volume and variety of child pornography. There is less agreement about why this has occurred and in particular why so many people appear to have taken advantage of these new opportunities to access child pornography. Addressing these questions involves, in part, understanding the characteristics and motivations of ICP offenders themselves. We begin the present chapter by reviewing available research on the demographic and psychological characteristics of these offenders. Next, we examine the extent to which ICP offenders also engage in contact sexual abuse offenses and vice versa. We then outline various schemes for distinguishing different types of ICP offenders. Finally, we consider the motivations for ICP offending.

OFFENDER CHARACTERISTICS

We should note at the outset that knowledge about ICP offenders is based almost wholly on studies of persons arrested, convicted, or treated for ICP offending. Findings may therefore not be representative because by all accounts, only a very small proportion of ICP users are ever arrested, much less included in research studies. Correctional and especially clinical samples, which make up the bulk of the research, are likely to be particularly selective. Furthermore, it is difficult to know in what ways such samples might be biased. Studies of arrestees may disproportionately include novice or unsophisticated users on the one hand (e.g., those who lacked the forethought or expertise to conceal their ICP activity) or experienced and highly organized producers and distributors on the other (e.g., members of particular networks targeted proactively by specialist police units). Police may find ICP during investigations of other offenses (e.g., Internet fraud or contact sexual abuse), potentially inflating the observed coincidence of ICP and other criminal activity, especially contact sexual offenses. On the other hand, researchers concerned particularly with the overlap of ICP and contact sexual abuse offending may disregard the potential significance of other (nonsexual) offending among ICP offenders.

A key strength of clinical studies is that they afford an opportunity to obtain rich self-report data, but clinical samples are likely to be selected because of pre-existing concerns about psychological and behavioral problems. Another important limitation of treatment studies is that depending on the circumstances, offenders may obtain secondary gains by either underreporting or overreporting personal and behavioral problems, including previous offending. These potential biases are also likely to be present in samples of other kinds of sexual offenders, with whom ICP offenders are often compared. The main difference is that research into ICP offending is much less advanced and sample sizes are often smaller than with sexual offending more broadly. We therefore know a lot less about ICP offenders than we do about other types of offenders, including other sexual offenders.

Demographic Characteristics

The largest and most representative study of ICP arrestees conducted to date is a longitudinal survey of U.S. law enforcement agencies conducted by the Crimes Against Children Research Center (CACRC). Findings have so far been reported on two national probability samples involving persons arrested during 2000 and 2001 (Wolak, Finkelhor, and Mitchell 2005) and 2006 (Wolak, Finkelhor, and Mitchell 2011). The first thing to note is the surprisingly small number of arrests for ICP offenses. For the most recent CACRC survey (2006), there were an esti-mated 3,672 arrests nationally for ICP offenses. To put this in perspective, in the same year, there were some 14.4 million arrests for all offenses (excluding traffic violations) across the United States, including more than 600,000 arrests for vio-lent offenses (U.S. Department of Justice 2007). There were more than 92,000 reports to police of forcible rape in that year (U.S. Department of Justice 2007). The number of arrests for ICP offenses also represents a very small proportion of the estimated "tens of thousands" of individuals in the United States who download ICP via peer-to-peer networks alone (Wolak et al. 2011).

A second noteworthy feature is that while estimated arrests for ICP more than doubled from 2000 (1,713) to 2006 (3,672), violent crime (including sexual crime) in the United States declined by 13 percent from 1997 to 2006 (U.S. Department of Justice 2007), and the incidence of child sexual abuse appears to have declined by as much as 53 percent from 1992 to 2007 (Jones and Finkelhor 2009). While still very small, the number of detected ICP offenders has thus been rising at the same time the incidence of other sexual offenses has been declining. The dramatic increase in the availability of ICP generated by the Internet does not appear to have resulted in an increase in the incidence of contact sexual abuse.

The single most commonly observed characteristic of ICP offenders, as with other sexual offenders, is male gender. Proportions of males in the CACRC sur-veys were 100 percent in 2000 and 99 percent in 2006. Most were adults (older than 18 years old) (97% in 2000; 95% in 2006), although there were significantly more young adults (younger than 26 years old) in 2006 than in 2000 (18% versus 11%). The majority in both surveys were "white, non-Hispanic" (91% and 89%, respectively). Offenders' place of residence was fairly evenly distributed across urban, suburban, large town, small town, and rural locations. Most were in full-time employment (73% and 61%, respectively), about one-third were married or living with a partner, and a substantial minority were living with children under age 18 (31% and 21%) (Wolak, Finkelhor, and Mitchell 2011).

We are not aware of any similar probability studies having been conducted in other countries; however, these U.S. findings are broadly consistent with studies of more selective clinical samples in other countries. For example, a study of outpatient forensic psychiatry patients in the Netherlands found that ICP offenders were on average 37 years old. All were male. ICP offenders were younger ($M = 37$ years versus 47 years), less likely to have a partner (40% versus 64%), and less likely to have children (18% versus 60%) than contact sexual abuse offenders attending the same clinic (Reijnen, Bulten, and Nijman 2009). A British clinical study similarly found that ICP offenders (all male) were younger ($M = 38$ years versus 45 years) and less likely to have been living with a partner in the past year (57% versus 75%) than contact offenders (Webb, Craisatti, and Keen 2007).

Babchishin, Hanson, and Hermann (2011) recently reported a meta-analysis of 27 published and unpublished studies reporting characteristics of online sexual offenders ($N = 4,844$), including nine studies that had compared online and offline offenders. All the individual online offender samples included ICP offenders, but about half also included Internet grooming offenders (who may or may not have used ICP). The number of online offenders included in this meta-analysis who had also committed contact sexual offenses was unknown. Results are therefore unlikely to be representative of ICP-only offenders. The only demographic variables examined in the meta-analysis were age and race. Consistent with the findings from the individual studies noted earlier, online offenders were on average younger (39 versus 44 years) and less likely to be of minority race (8% versus 35%).

All in all, the demographic profile of detected ICP offenders comprises few notable features: ICP offenders are usually white, educated, employed adults—many of whom are married or living with a partner (Baron 2010; Blundell, Sherry, Burke, and Sowerbutts 2002; Schwartz and Southern 2000; Wolak et al. 2011). Observers have noted that those arrested for ICP offenses come from all walks of life and include judges, soldiers, dentists, teachers, academics, and police officers (Calder 2004). The most commonly observed characteristic is male gender. Males are overrepresented in most forms of crime and are especially overrepresented in sexual crime. In all other respects, though, the demographic profile of ICP offenders is quite different from general offenders (who tend to be younger, less educated, less likely to be employed, and more likely to be of minority race) and contact sexual abusers (who are generally older, more likely to be in a relationship, more likely to have children, and more likely to be of minority race).

Psychological Characteristics

Very few ICP arrestees in the CACRC cohorts were found to be mentally ill (5 to 6%) or sexually disordered (3 to 5%). These data were obtained from police records and thus are unlikely to have been based on formal testing or diagnosis. Clinical studies using standardized tests show somewhat higher proportions of ICP offenders with psychological problems. Where differences are observed, ICP offenders are generally reported to have fewer or less severe psychological problems than other offenders, although findings are mixed and sometimes conflicting.

Laulik, Allam, and Sheridan (2007) examined Personality Assessment Inventory (PAI) profiles of 30 ICP offenders undergoing community-based treatment. Compared to PAI population norms, the offenders scored significantly higher on depression, schizophrenia, borderline features, and antisocial features and significantly lower on mania. However, apart from depression (30%), borderline features (17%) and schizophrenia (13%), fewer than 10 percent of offenders scored in the clinically significant range for any of the clinical scales. Reijnen et al. (2009) compared Minnesota Multiphasic Personality Inventory (MMPI) profiles of 22 ICP offenders, 47 other sexual offenders, and 65 nonsexual offenders attending an outpatient forensic psychiatry clinic. All three groups had a clinically significant elevation on the "psychopathic deviation" scale, which indicates general problems with aggression, deceptiveness, and manipulation of others. Offenders did not score in the clinically significant range on any of the other clinical scales, and there were no differences between the three groups on any of the 10 scales. Tomak et al. (2009) compared MMPI profiles of 48 ICP offenders attending an outpatient sexual offender treatment facility and 104 incarcerated sexual offenders. Mean scores fell below clinically significant levels for all scales for both groups. ICP offenders scored significantly lower than the other offenders on the "psychopathic deviation" and "schizophrenia" scales. Webb, Craisatti, and Keen (2007) compared 90 ICP and 120 contact sexual offenders on the Millon Multiaxial Clinical Inventory (MCMI-III) and found no differences on any of the clinical or other MCM-III scales.

Studies of undetected ICP offenders paint a somewhat similar picture. Seigfried, Lovely, and Rogers (2008) surveyed 307 Internet users, of whom 30 anonymously admitted to having used ICP (defined as pornography depicting persons under 18 years old). A surprising finding, given the generally low prevalence of female sexual offending, including detected ICP offending, was that 10 of the 30 self-identified ICP users were female. As a proportion of all respondents, 15.9 percent of males and 5.5 percent of females admitted to using ICP. No differences were found between ICP and non-ICP users on the "big five" personality dimensions (extraversion, neuroticism, openness to experience, conscientiousness, and agreeableness); however, the groups did differ on two other psychological dimensions. ICP users scored significantly lower on moral choice internal values, suggesting that even though they understand that ICP use is not socially acceptable, they may personally construe it as morally acceptable. ICP offenders also scored significantly higher on a measure of exploitation, manipulation, and dishonesty. The authors noted that this exploitive-manipulative trait has also been found in individuals involved in other (nonsexual) computer crimes, including hacking (Rogers et al. 2006).

Neutze, Seto, Schaefer, Mundt, and Beier (2011) examined 155 adult males who had sought help for sexual behavior problems but who were not presently involved in the justice system, including 42 self-identified ICP offenders and 50 mixed (ICP + contact) offenders. Only those who met diagnostic criteria for pedophilia (70%) or hebephilia (30%) were included in the study, presumably indicating that this was a particularly disturbed sample. Average scores for depression were elevated, but scores for emotional loneliness, neuroticism, and conscientiousness were all close to general population norms. No differences were found between ICP-only offenders, contact sexual abuse offenders, and mixed (ICP + contact) offenders.

These personality studies have generally not set out to test specific expectations concerning the psychological characteristics of ICP offenders; the interpretation of findings, such as they are, has therefore been speculative and atheoretical. It is not clear whether depressive symptoms, for example, might be somehow causally related to ICP offending or whether for some they are a consequence of offending or being caught. The presence of antisocial or exploitative features in some ICP offenders is intuitively more relevant—ICP use is, after all, a crime—but findings indicate that serious antisocial features are present in only a minority of detected and undetected ICP offenders. Other studies have investigated so-called criminogenic factors thought to be relevant to contact sexual offending, such as loneliness, low victim empathy, and cognitive distortions, but findings for ICP offenders have again been weak and mixed (e.g., Bates and Metcalf 2007; Elliot, Beech, Mandeville-Norden, and Hayes 2009; Howitt and Sheldon 2007).

Babchishin et al.'s (2011) meta-analysis examined a wide range of psychological variables, including many of those considered earlier. Average findings indicated that compared to contact sexual offenders, online sexual offenders had fewer problems with victim empathy, cognitive distortions, and emotional identification with children. No differences were found between the two offender groups in loneliness or self-esteem. However, online offenders were found to be more sexually deviant. This latter finding is perhaps counterintuitive because one might expect direct sexual abuse of a child to involve a higher level of sexual deviance than viewing images of unknown children. This finding is important and deserves some additional attention here.

A consensus has emerged among clinical researchers that sexual offending involves antisocial and "sexual deviance" dimensions. Sexual deviance—variously defined and measured—has been identified as a statistically reliable predictor of sexual recidivism (Hanson and Bussiere 1998). But defining and measuring sexual deviance can be theoretically and methodologically problematic. Using aspects of sexual offending or its effects to define sexual deviance leaves us with an unhelpful tautology—an individual is sexually deviant because he has committed sexual offenses (or particular kinds of sexual offenses) and he has committed these sexual offenses because he is sexually deviant. Babchishin et al.'s (2011) meta-analytic conclusions were based on only three studies, each employing a different measure of sexual deviance. The most influential of these studies employed phallometric assessment (a laboratory-controlled measure of penile erection in response to various visual and auditory stimuli), finding that ICP offenders on average showed greater sexual arousal to images of children than did contact sexual abusers (Seto, Cantor, and Blanchard 2006). The authors came to the conclusion that ICP offenders were therefore more likely than contact sexual abusers to be pedophiles, even though they were less likely to sexually abuse an actual child. An alternative interpretation is that Seto et al.'s findings reflect the effects of viewing ICP. Phallometric assessment more closely resembles the context of ICP offending than of contact sexual abuse, which by contrast typically occurs in the context of a relationship with a specific child (a context that is obviously not reproducible in a laboratory setting). The shaping of sexual arousal through viewing ICP is important in itself: it may be that for some offenders, prolonged exposure to ICP leads to the acquisition or strengthening of sexual preferences for children. However, this leaves open the question of how and why offenders become involved with ICP in the first place. We will return to these questions later in this chapter.

OVERLAP BETWEEN ICP AND CONTACT SEXUAL ABUSE OFFENDING

There are several ways in which the incidence or prevalence of ICP offending and contact sexual abuse may overlap. First, the production of ICP is likely to simultaneously involve sexual abuse because an actual child must generally be present when an ICP image is first produced. Exceptions include virtual-child pornography and perhaps some cases in which the child is unaware that he or she is the subject of such images (e.g., the use of hidden cameras). Notwithstanding these exceptions, we would naturally expect a high coincidence of ICP production and contact sexual abuse offending. Second, active or former contact sexual abuse offenders may use or distribute ICP as an extension of their already-established sexual interests in or abuse of children. We would expect a considerable degree of overlap in these circumstances. Third, exposure to ICP may generate or reinforce sexual interests in children, thus leading to contact sexual abuse in circumstances where contact offenses may otherwise not have occurred. This is one of the most worrying and contentious aspects of ICP use. Research studies generally do not distinguish between these three types of overlap; thus, unfortunately, little is known about the specific ways in which ICP and other sexual offending coincide.

The most comprehensive study to date of the overlaps between ICP and contact sexual abuse offending is two meta-analytic reviews by Seto, Hanson, and Babchishin (2011). Seto et al. did not examine the proportion of ICP offenders who had produced ICP (and who are, by definition, also likely to have committed contact offenses). In fact, such data are difficult to find; ICP producers, if this status is known at all, are apparently simply grouped with other ICP users in most studies. Seto et al.'s meta-analyses examined the extent to which ICP offenders have official or self-reported histories of contact sexual offending (21 studies, $N = 4,464$) and recidivism rates among ICP offenders (9 studies, $N = 2,630$).

The average prevalence of officially recorded contact sexual offending histories was found to be 12 percent, with findings from individual studies ranging from as low as 0 percent to as high as 43 percent. This wide variation no doubt partly reflects sampling differences. For example, one of the lowest prevalence rates for prior contact sexual offending (less than 1%) was found in a study that included all persons arrested for ICP possession in Switzerland as a result of an international police operation (Endrass et al. 2009). The highest prevalence (43%) was found in a highly selective study of ICP offenders referred by correctional, legal, and medical practitioners to a Canadian sexual behavior laboratory for specialized assessment (Seto, Cantor, and Blanchard 2006). Known or suspected contact sexual offending by this group may have been one of the concerns that led to these referrals.

The average prevalence of self-reported contact offense histories in the Seto et al. meta-analysis was 55 percent—much higher than official data indicated—with five individual studies reporting rates ranging from 32 percent to 85 percent.The highest by some margin was reported by Bourke and Hernandez (2009), who examined self-reported contact sexual offending among 155 ICP offenders attending an intensive prison-based treatment program. Prior to treatment, 26 percent of these ICP offenders were already known to have a history of contact sexual offending. Following treatment, which included routine polygraph testing, 85 percent disclosed past contact offending. Obtaining such disclosures seems to have been a specific expectation and goal of this treatment program. Bourke and Hernandez go so far as to argue that virtually all ICP offenders will have also committed contact offenses and that there is no useful distinction to be made between ICP and contact sexual offenders. Considering their aggregated findings from multiple studies, Seto et al. were more circumspect, concluding that while there is considerable overlap, there is nevertheless a distinct group of online offenders whose only sexual offenses involve ICP or, less frequently, online solicitation.

Seto et al. (2011) did not examine previous nonsexual offending in their meta-analysis, presumably because the researchers involved in the original studies did not themselves report these data. Returning to the CACRC U.S. law enforcement surveys, ICP arrestees in the combined 2000 and 2006 surveys were about twice as likely to have previous convictions for nonsexual offenses (22 to 27%) than for sexual offenses (10 to 12%). More generally, contact sexual abuse offenders are about twice as likely as the ICP arrestees in the CACRC studies to have previous convictions for sexual (20 to 25%) and nonsexual offenses (40 to 50%), suggesting that ICP offenders may be less criminally involved than contact sexual offenders.

The second meta-analysis reported by Seto et al. (2011) examined sexual recidivism among ICP offenders. For the nine studies included in these analyses, the average recidivism for any sexual offense was 4.8 percent after follow-up periods ranging from 1.5 to 6 years. For the seven studies that had reported different kinds of sexual recidivism, 2 percent committed contact sexual offenses and 3.4 percent committed further ICP offenses. For five studies that had reported nonsexual violent recidivism, an average recidivism rate of 4.2 percent was found. Again, general (nonviolent, nonsexual) offending was not considered. These figures are much lower than those usually found for contact sexual offenders, for whom a sexual recidivism rate of about 14 percent (and a general recidivism rate of about 37%) would be expected over a similar average follow-up period (Hanson and Bussiere 1998). Again, this suggests that ICP offenders tend to be less criminally involved—in terms of contact sexual offending and nonsexual offending—than other sexual offenders.

TYPES OF ICP OFFENDERS

Psychological Typologies

As we have seen, studies of the psychological characteristics of ICP offenders indicate that, on average, these offenders present with few discernable psychological problems. However, these data sometimes show considerable within-group variations, and average findings may mask the existence of meaningful subgroups of ICP offenders. Unfortunately, research is not yet sufficiently advanced or organized to be able to confirm the existence of specific types of ICP offenders. Several typological schemes have been proposed, and some of these have good face validity, but none have been adequately empirically validated.

Persons who engage in legal online sexual activity (e.g., general pornography use, adult virtual sex) have been categorized into three broad types: recreational users who use sexual content on the Internet for entertainment or to satisfy sexual curiosities and who suffer few personal problems as a result of doing so; at-risk users who may have few pre-existing problems but whose Internet sexual behavior may lead to offline personal and relationship problems; and sexually compulsive users who have pre-existing sexual problems that may be exacerbated by their Internet use (Cooper, Putnam, Planchon, and Boies 1999). To the extent that parallels may exist among ICP users (see Wortley and Smallbone 2006), it is likely that psychological problems are concentrated in the latter two groups.

Calder (2004) noted that for some ICP users, the desire to engage sexually with children follows rather than precedes their ICP use, rather like Cooper et al.'s at-risk group. Sullivan and Beech (2004) proposed three primary types of ICP offenders: situational offenders whose ICP use may best be understood as curious and impulsive (similar to Cooper et al.'s recreational users but also likely to include at-risk users); preferential offenders who may be drawn to ICP because of pre-existing sexual interests in children (like Cooper et al.'s sexually compulsive group); and miscellaneous offenders, including those who access ICP as a prank or to pursue an ostensibly legitimate interest, such as personal research.

Middleton, Elliot, Mandeville-Norden, and Beech (2006) used a range of psychometric measures to examine whether any of Ward and Siegert's (2002) sexual offending pathways (intimacy deficits, distorted sexual scripts, emotional dysregulation, antisocial cognitions, and multiple dysfunctional) fit a sample of 72 ICP offenders. Results suggested a weak fit, with about 40 percent of the ICP offenders unable to be assigned to any of the five pathways. The most common assigned pathway, accounting for 21 percent of the offenders ($n = 15$), was intimacy deficits, operationalized as higher than normal levels of emotional loneliness.

The most substantial typological study to date involved a cluster analysis of extensive psychometric data obtained on 422 ICP offenders (Henry, Mandeville-Norden, Hayes, and Egan 2010). Three groups were identified: a normal group ($n = 166$; 40% of the sample), who were near or within the normal range for all measures; an inadequate group ($n = 108$; 26%), who presented with socioaffective problems (e.g., emotional loneliness) but who were low on criminogenic features; and a deviant group ($n = 148$; 35%), who were high on emotional loneliness but also high on criminogenic features (emotional congruence with children; low victim empathy; high cognitive distortions).

A Behavioral Typology

Psychological variations among offenders may be reflected in different patterns of ICP-related behavior. Krone (2004) proposed nine types of ICP offending, varying in the level of involvement with ICP, the degree of networking with other offenders, the degree to which security strategies are employed to avoid detection, and the extent to which the offender is involved in contact sexual abuse.

"Browsers" do not seek out ICP but may knowingly download or save images they have encountered. They are not involved in networking with other offenders and do not employ security strategies to avoid detection. "Private fantasizers" obtain or create images (e.g., through morphing) for private use to satisfy personal sexual desires. These offenders also do not network with other offenders and do not employ sophisticated security strategies. "Trawlers" seek ICP on the web through open browsers. They may engage in minimal networking, but they employ few security strategies. These three offender types are likely to vary in the extent of their sexual interests in ICP material, but none involve contact offending. For all three types, it seems that a certain boundary is maintained between the offender's personal fantasy world and the real world, where real children are abused. Maintaining this boundary presumably requires ignoring or minimizing the impact on the children who are the subjects of the ICP material they consume as well as their personal contribution to the wider demand for new material to be produced. Alternatively, the boundary between ICP and contact offending may be maintained because the offender has limited access to potential victims or may not be prepared to take the additional risks associated with contact offending.

"Nonsecure collectors" seek ICP in nonsecure chat rooms and other open levels of the Internet. They are involved in relatively high levels of networking and, by definition, do not employ security strategies. Because of the nonsecured nature of their activities, there are limits to the number and nature of the images they can collect. "Secure collectors" are members of a closed newsgroup or another secret network. They engage in high levels of networking and employ sophisticated security measures to protect their activities from detection. Because they operate at hidden levels of the Internet, they have access to a larger volume and wider range of images. They may engage in obsessive levels of collecting, which not only involves amassing large numbers of images but also carefully cataloging and cross-referencing them. As with other types of (legitimate) collectors, they may expend considerable effort in obtaining rare and highly prized images. The large number of images collected by these offenders suggests a stronger appetite for or the desire for variation in ICP material, and for some, the collection may almost become an end in itself. Once again, a boundary seems to be maintained between the expression of their online and offline sexual interests in children.

"Groomers" develop online relationships with children and send pornography to children as part of the grooming process. They may or may not be involved in wider networking with other offenders, but their contact with children exposes them to a greater risk of detection. The child may tell someone about the relationship or the offender may be unwittingly communicating with an undercover police officer. "Physical abusers" sexually abuse children, and their involvement with ICP is just part of their problematic sexual behavior. They may record their own abuse behaviors for their personal use. They may or may not network. By definition, a physical abuser directly abuses victims and his security depends on the child's silence. Because of their interests in physical contact with children and because of the additional risks this entails, we might assume that groomers and physical abusers possess stronger deviant sexual motivations. Groomers and physical abusers seem to have blurred the boundary between fantasy and reality or may have stronger antisocial tendencies that allow them to exploit and abuse actual children.

"Producers" record the sexual abuse of children for the purpose of disseminating it to others. The extent of their networking varies depending on whether they are also distributors. Again, the producer's direct abuse of the victim compromises his security. "Distributors" are involved in disseminating abuse images. In some cases, they may have a purely financial interest in child pornography. More often, offenders at any of the aforementioned levels who share images may be classified as distributors. Thus, the extent of a distributor's networking, his level of security, and whether he engages in direct abuse of children depends on the level at which he is operating.

Krone's typology is a descriptive scheme with good face validity but, like other schemes, has not been empirically validated. It is a typology of ICP behavior rather than of offenders. Offenders themselves may desist without progressing to a more concerning level of behavior, they may persist but remain at the same level, or they may graduate from lower to higher (and possibly higher to lower) levels of behavior. This issue of how ICP offending begins, progresses, and desists is a critical one theoretically and practically, but little empirical or theoretical attention has yet been given to these basic dimensions of the problem.

Adolescent Offenders

In the wider field of sexual offending research, important distinctions have been drawn between adolescent and adult sexual offenders. While there is undoubtedly some overlap, low rates of adult sexual recidivism among adolescent sexual offenders and a low prevalence of adolescence onset among adult sexual offenders indicate that these are largely distinct populations. At the same time, many of the most serious and persistent adult sexual offenders begin their sexual offending "careers" in adolescence (Smallbone and Cale, in press). Youth under 18 years of age are the identified perpetrator in about 20 percent of all known sexual offenses (e.g., U.S. Department of Justice 2009). Particularly given that young people are naturally sexually curious and are avid and sophisticated users of the Internet, it would be unsurprising if a significant proportion of ICP users were adolescents.

Research on young people's exposure to general (legal) Internet pornography indicates a high level of exposure among youth aged 14 years and older but a low level of exposure among younger children (Ybarra and Mitchell 2005). The extent of adolescents' exposure to ICP is much less clear. Involvement of young people in sexting (youth sending sexually explicit images, usually of themselves or their peers, via cell phones or other social media) has emerged as a serious new concern, particularly because these images may legally be classified as child pornography. Some estimates indicate that as many as 20 percent of all adolescents in the United States have had some experience with sending or receiving such images (National Campaign to Prevent Teen and Unplanned Pregnancy 2008). A substantial volume of legal and social commentary on sexting has been published in recent years. Authors often point to a small number of publicized cases in which young people have been arrested, jailed, and even placed on sex offender registers for sending or receiving sexual images of themselves or their peers. Without dismissing these concerns, fears that large numbers of adolescents may be inadvertently swept up in heavy-handed legal responses designed to combat ICP seem to have been largely unrealized. The most recent figures from the CACRC surveys indicate that only 5 percent of ICP arrestees were under 18 years of age (Wolak et al. 2011). The small number of detected adolescent ICP offenders in any given jurisdiction presents even greater research limitations than is the case with their adult counterparts.

Moultrie (2006) described seven 13- to 16-year-old male youth referred over a three-year period to a specialized treatment service in the UK. Details of the ICP material itself was unclear, and there seems to have been considerable variation even within this small sample, but it appears that the offending was generally similar to that observed among adult offenders. Indeed, some of the youth had engaged with adults in chat rooms and through peer-to-peer networks, including for the purposes of obtaining and distributing ICP images. Two were known to have committed contact sexual offenses, but none had been in trouble for nonsexual offenses (except for one charged with fraudulent use of a credit card to access a child pornography site). The kinds of psychological, behavioral, and family problems commonly found in adolescent contact sexual offenders were uncommon in the ICP group. For example, none had learning problems, none were known to have been physically or sexually abused, and none were previously known to social services agencies. There were some indications that the young ICP offenders had difficulties with peer relationships, but it was not clear whether these were present prior to or developed as a consequence of their offending or their arrest. It would be unsafe to draw any firm conclusions from such a small study, but results suggest that like their adult counterparts, adolescent ICP offenders present with fewer psychological and behavioral problems than other adolescent sexual offenders.

OFFENDER MOTIVATIONS

In our interpretation, available evidence indicates that ICP offenders possess few, if any, defining demographic or psychological characteristics, except that they are almost always adult (and sometimes adolescent) males. Apart from this and apart from their offending behavior itself, it is the ordinary rather than the unusual characteristics of these offenders that is striking. Our concern in the remainder of this chapter is with the motivations of ICP offenders. These cannot be studied directly but must be inferred from the evidence. We are mindful of the limitations of this evidence but can also draw some inferences indirectly from the more extensive empirical literature on contact sexual abuse offenders. We will bring our own theoretical perspective to bear on the problem.

We have set out elsewhere a comprehensive theory of the onset and progression of sexual offending generally (Smallbone and Cale, in press) and of child sexual abuse offending in particular (Smallbone, Marshall, and Wortley 2008). In essence, the theory proposes that by virtue of our evolutionary history, humans—and adolescent and adult males in particular—possess a more or less universal potential for antisocial behavior, including sexual violence and abuse; positive socialization constrains but does not eliminate this potential; risk and protective factors for offending and victimization are located at various levels of offenders' and victims' natural social ecologies (family, peer, organizational, neighborhood, and sociocultural systems), with more proximal systems exerting the strongest effects; situational factors that comprise the immediate offense setting (opportunity structures and precipitating conditions) are the most proximal elements of the social ecology of sexual offending and therefore exert the most powerful effects on offense-related motivations and behavior (see also Wortley and Smallbone 2006); and repeated offending is more likely if the offending behavior is experienced by the offender as rewarding and if opportunity structures and precipitating conditions continue to be presented. We will draw on this theoretical framework to address three key questions concerning ICP: What are the origins of sexual interest in children; why do some people act on these interests by using child pornography; and why might the Internet have increased demand for child pornography?

Origins of Sexual Interest in Children

If media and public commentary are anything to go by, sexual offending against children, including ICP offending, seems to be popularly conceived of as a unique, inexplicable phenomenon. The public may be concerned, even outraged, by other sorts of crime, but this is not usually accompanied by the same kind of perplexity. Human desires for material goods, status, revenge, and so on, are seen as natural, essentially understandable motivations, and it is widely understood that behaviors that violate accepted social boundaries need to be circumscribed by laws and controlled by systems of punishment. It seems to be much more difficult to accept that sexual interest in children could be in any way similarly "natural."

Psychiatric conceptions of the problem align with this popular view, classifying sexual interest in prepubertal children as a mental disorder—pedophilia—and thus adding an authoritative stamp to the idea that experiencing such interests (not just the objectionable behavior itself) is pathological. Indeed, the forthcoming version of the American Psychiatric Association's *Diagnostic and Statistical Manual of Mental Disorders* (DSM) proposes to include the new category of hebephilia, so sexual attraction to older (pubescent) children may soon also be officially classified as a mental disorder. The implication of this psychiatric perspective is that there exists a limited number of mentally disordered individuals who experience sexual attraction to children and young adolescents and, on the other side of the diagnostic rule, a "normal" population who does not. DSM does not deal with the causes of mental disorders; indeed, there is no consensus about the causes of pedophilia or hebephilia.

Even if we accept the idea that sexual attraction to prepubescent (generally younger than 12 years old) and pubescent children (12 to 14 years) is the result of a mental disorder, we are still left with the fact that legal definitions of child pornography extend to depictions of persons up to 18 years of age. Evolutionary theories suggest that humans are in fact biologically organized to prefer youthful sexual partners because of the evolutionary advantage this conferred on our ancestors (Buss 1994; Thornhill and Thornhill 1987). Of course, there can be no evolutionary advantage in sexual attraction to prepubescent children. But nor is there such an advantage for males to be sexually attracted to postmenopausal women, for example, even though such behavior is commonplace and socially unproblematic. The point is that humans (including persistent sexual abusers) are not biologically organized with a fixed preference for youthful (pubescent and postpubescent) sexual partners. Rather, according to evolutionary theory, the opposite is the case: Humans possess an evolved *flexibility* in their social and sexual behavior that allows individual survival and reproductive fitness in a very wide range of circumstances.

Furthermore, it is patently the case that virtually everyone does, in fact, experience sexual interest in children and young adolescents—when they themselves were children and young adolescents (DeLamater and Friedrich 2002). The vast majority presumably shifts their sexual attentions to older partners as they themselves mature. The problem is therefore not that sexual attraction to young people is inherently abnormal but that as they mature, some individuals fail to observe social and legal rules prohibiting sexual involvement with young people, including the use of child pornography.

Why Do Some People Use Child Pornography?

Sexually mature males are much more likely than females to sexually abuse children and to use child pornography, and we think that biologically based gender differences are part of the reason for this. Neurobiological evidence shows that aggression plays a more prominent role in male social and sexual behavior and that the attachment-nurturing systems that normally serve to protect children and vulnerable others are less developed in males (Panksepp 1998). Nurturing motivations are more instrumental for males and are thus more susceptible to competing (including sexual) motivations. This may manifest in a wide range of behaviors involving the exploitation of vulnerable others, including the pursuit of sexual gratification through using child pornography.

Despite this significant biologically based potential for males in particular to use child pornography, apparently very few actually do so. One reason, we think, is that socialization is generally very successful in constraining this potential. For our present purposes, positive socialization essentially involves the acquisition of the capacity for and commitment to exercising self-restraint in order to conform to social rules concerning irresponsible and unlawful sexual behavior. While secure personal attachments establish the psychological and behavioral foundations for individual self-restraint, secure personal attachments and strong (pro) social attachments provide individuals with strong incentives to refrain from irresponsible social and sexual conduct and therefore act as important informal social controls. In sum, most people do not use child pornography because they have been socialized not to, just as they have been socialized not to engage in other socially irresponsible and unlawful behavior.

This formulation suggests that poorly socialized adolescents and adults are more likely to succumb to temptations and to recognize and seize opportunities to use child pornography. Certainly, evidence concerning contact sexual abuse offenders indicates that these offenders, like other (nonsexual) offenders, are often exposed to developmental circumstances that compromise the process of successful socialization (Smallbone 2006). But evidence concerning ICP offenders suggests that this is less often the case for these offenders. This in turn suggests that the circumstances of ICP offending are different from contact sexual abuse offending.

Why Might the Internet Have Increased Demand for Child Pornography?

In Chapter 1, we argued that child pornography offending, like any other behavior, is best understood as a person-situation interaction. In short, the offending behavior is the result of an interaction between the offender's vulnerabilities or dispositions on one hand and the circumstances of the immediate situation on the other. Poorly socialized offenders (those with strong vulnerabilities or dispositions) may require little in the way of suitable opportunities and may actively seek out opportunities to access ICP. Some of these offenders may have become involved with child pornography even without the convenience of the Internet. However, as we have seen, the majority of ICP offenders apparently do not possess the kinds of characteristics (e.g., childhood abuse, general criminality) that would suggest serious personal vulnerabilities.

All other things being equal, a crime is more likely to be committed when the offender estimates that he has a low risk of detection, the crime requires little effort, and the offender anticipates a valued reward (Cornish and Clarke 1986). These are quintessential elements of the behavioral setting in which ICP offending typically occurs, and all three (low risk; low effort; high reward) distinguish the circumstances of ICP offending from contact sexual abuse offending and from child pornography offending in the pre-Internet era. In terms of the person-situation interaction, the convenience (low effort) and apparent anonymity (low perceived risk) afforded by the Internet has profoundly changed the interactional balance. Where before only the most committed offenders were prepared to expend the effort required to obtain child pornography and to negotiate the associated risks, the material can now be obtained literally with a click of a button in the privacy of one's own home. The material so obtained is often of high technical quality, and from the user's viewpoint, there is no actual victim to resist or reject him (high reward).

CONCLUSION

Understanding ICP in large part requires understanding the characteristics and motivations of ICP offenders. It is only in the last decade that ICP has become a prominent concern, and it is only in the last few years that empirical research on ICP offenders themselves has begun to emerge. This is partly because it is only in the last few years that large enough numbers of ICP offenders have been arrested to make it feasible to engage them in quantitative research studies. Still, by all accounts, only a very small proportion of ICP users are ever arrested, much less included in research studies. The picture that emerges from available research is therefore patchy and incomplete.

Available evidence suggests that detected ICP offenders are less criminally involved and possess fewer social and psychological problems than other offenders, including other sexual offenders. What is most striking about ICP offenders is their ordinariness, not their psychopathology. This apparently ordinary profile of ICP offenders suggests that the increased availability and ease of access afforded by the Internet has pushed the problem of child pornography further into the normal population. Whereas in the pre-Internet era only the most committed offenders were prepared to invest the effort and take the risks required to obtain child pornography, ICP can now be obtained with apparent anonymity and in the apparent security of the offender's home.

However, it may be the variations that have been found among ICP offenders rather than these average findings that tell the most interesting story. For example, while most ICP offenders do not present with serious psychological problems, some do. After their arrest, most apparently do not go on to commit further ICP offenses—at least in the short to medium term—but some do. Most do not go on to commit contact sexual abuse offenses, but some do. Understanding these exceptions is important to inform the wider prevention agenda and to prioritize prevention efforts.

Researchers may not have taken full advantage of even these limited opportunities to study ICP offenders. Virtually absent are much-needed studies that examine how and why offenders first encounter ICP, how these initial encounters are experienced and how this affects their subsequent motivations, whether patterns of individuals' involvement with ICP change over time or remain stable, why some persist even after being arrested, and why some proceed to contact sexual abuse.

4

Investigating Child Pornography

THIS CHAPTER EXAMINES local, national, and international efforts to enforce ICP laws. Law enforcement agencies involved in investigating ICP perform two main roles. The first role is a reactive one, involving the detection and arrest of offenders who have produced, distributed, and/or possessed child pornography. The second role is a proactive one, involving the prevention of new crimes by reducing the availability of child pornography on the Internet and deterring new offenders. These two roles are clearly interrelated. Arresting a major distributor will prevent that distributor from committing further crimes—at least while he is incarcerated. Also, as we shall argue in more detail later, the arrest of offenders for Internet pornography crimes plays an important role in countering perceptions that the Internet is a safe environment in which to offend. Nevertheless—and somewhat arbitrarily, we admit—we will split the reactive and proactive roles of investigation. We will deal largely with the arrest element of police investigations in this chapter and include the prevention outcomes of investigations in our examination of Internet-focused prevention efforts, to be covered in Chapter 7. The current chapter will examine the challenges facing law enforcement agencies investigating child pornography on the Internet, the techniques used by investigators, and the outcome of investigations, including some of the notable instances of major international investigations of ICP rings.

CHALLENGES IN INVESTIGATING ICP

ICP presents unique challenges for law enforcement agencies. These challenges include the decentralized structure of the Internet; the cross jurisdictional nature of Internet crime; inadequate and inconsistent legislation and the failure to enforce legislation that does exist; the increasing technological expertise of offenders and their adoption of new Internet technology; and the sheer amount of Internet traffic.

The Structure of the Internet

The structure of the Internet makes control of child pornography difficult. It has been argued that the Internet is the ultimate democratic entity and is essentially ungovernable. The Internet is a decentralized system with no single controlling agency or storage facility, making it difficult to screen content, enforce legislation, and track offenders. Much of the software required to make Internet connections is located on host computers, while other applications are distributed on servers across the network. Because it is a network of networks, even if one pathway is blocked, there are many alternative pathways that can be taken to reach the same destination. Similarly, if one website or newsgroup is closed down, there are many others that can instantaneously take their place. Some Internet connections, such as P2P, require no servers at all and allow direct communication among hosts.

Working Across Jurisdictions

The Internet is an international communication tool that crosses jurisdictional boundaries. Child pornography may be produced in one country, uploaded to a server located in another country, and accessed by people living in yet another country. Police investigations of child pornography will almost always involve multiple law enforcement agencies. If an Internet child exploitation unit in the United States discovers child pornography on a server in Russia, it can block access to that server by U.S. residents, but it must rely on Russian colleagues to ensure that the offending material is taken down and that appropriate legal actions are taken against the Russian citizens involved. Unless the material is taken down, any blocked pathways can be quickly re-established by moving the material to another server. Therefore, most of the major investigations of child pornography on the Internet have involved cooperation among jurisdictions—often at an international level.

Not only is cooperation among law enforcement agencies necessary to track offenders and victims across jurisdictions, but it is also required to coordinate resources and avoid the duplication of efforts (Jewkes and Andrews 2005). Parallel operations run from different jurisdictions may unknowingly target the same organization or offender. Equally problematic is the issue of who is responsible for investigating child pornography on the Internet when there is no clue as to the location of where the images originate. There is a potential for pornography crimes to go uninvestigated because they do not fall within a particular law enforcement jurisdiction. There are numerous law enforcement agencies within the United States and internationally designed to help coordinate enforcement activities among individual police forces and other investigative bodies. We will examine these agencies in more detail a little later in this chapter.

Inadequate Legislation

While it is true that the Internet by its nature is difficult to regulate, it is also true that there is a reluctance in many jurisdictions to introduce laws that might help control Internet use. The International Centre for Missing and Exploited Children (2008) lists five criteria for model child pornography legislation: There is specific reference to child pornography; child pornography is defined; computer-facilitated offenses are criminalized; possession, irrespective of the intention to distribute, is criminalized; and ISPs are required to report suspected child pornography. Of the 187 member countries of Interpol, only five (Australia, Belgium, France, South Africa, and the United States) were found to meet all criteria, while another 24 meet all criteria except mandatory reporting by ISPs. Thirty-six countries do not criminalize possession, and a further 95 countries have no child pornography legislation at all.

Within countries that have some level of ICP legislation, there is often debate about how far that legislation should go. The debate may be framed as a contest between the appropriate weight to give to protection of the community on the one hand and to freedom of speech and commercial interests on the other (Graham 2000; Stanley 2001; Thomas 1997). For example, it may be recalled from Chapter 1 that attempts in the United States to legislate against virtual child pornography images was overturned on appeal. That appeal was launched by the Free Speech Coalition, an association representing the adult entertainment industry.

Alternatively, the debate may contrast governmental legislation and industry self-regulation as opposing models of control. This debate pertains particularly to the perceived role that the Internet industry should play in the regulation of child pornography. Only six countries require ISPs and other web-hosting companies to report child pornography discovered on their servers, and even in those countries, those offering web-hosting services are typically not obliged to actively search for such material. To the extent that the issue is addressed in other countries, regulation of ISPs relies largely on codes of practice drafted by the respective ISP associations that may explicitly bind members to not knowingly accept illegal content on their sites and to remove such sites when they become aware of their existence. However, other web-hosting companies are less regulated and have no industry-based organization that parallels the various ISP associations (Financial Coalition Against Child Pornography 2008).

Inconsistent Legislation

Even for countries that meet all five criteria specified by the International Centre for Missing and Exploited Children, there are variations in the exact content of the legislation. For example, while in the United States a child is defined as someone under 18 years old, in some Australian jurisdictions, the age is 16 years (Griffith and Simon 2008). On the other hand, while the United States permits virtual images of children, Australia does not. In one Australian case, a pornographic cartoon depicting Bart and Lisa from *The Simpsons* was found to be illegal (McEwen v. Simmons and Anor 2008)—a judgment that would be inconceivable in the United States. In an attempt to achieve some level of international uniformity, the International Centre for Missing and Exploited Children (2008) has set out explicit recommendations on the content of model child pornography law. For example, they recommend that for the purposes of child pornography, "child" should be defined as anyone under age 18 in every jurisdiction.

Lack of Enforcement

Countries vary in their capacity and commitment to enforce child pornography laws and to act against offenders—either because of cultural reasons, through a lack of resources and know-how, or because of corruption (UNICEF 2009). In his United Nations report on the sale of children, child prostitution, and child pornography, the Special Rapporteur found that in many countries

> . . . a culture of social and legal impunity for exploiters encouraged the demand for sexually exploitative services such as child prostitution. The problem generally does not seem to result from a lack of legal provisions criminalizing sexual exploitation, but rather from an implementation gap. Respondents pointed to a lack of effective law enforcement measures, difficulties in reporting crimes to the authorities and ensuring their effective investigation. Some respondents also stressed that not enough technical and human resources were dedicated to combating sexual exploitation. Non-governmental organizations operating in a range of countries also explained that corruption and the complicity of police and officials in cases of trafficking exacerbated the problem of impunity. In addition, a number of respondents noted a failure to adequately protect and assist victims in the criminal process, causing victims to refuse to testify. (Petit 2006, 9)

Because of the international nature of ICP, what happens in one country has knock-on effects in others. Countries that fail to adequately police child pornography may become production and distribution centers. However, to play this role, countries also need the necessary technological infrastructure to support Internet-hosting services. For this reason, ICP is not considered to be a serious problem in most poor and developing countries. However, the combination of inadequate law enforcement and increasing access to communication technologies has led to the identification of Russia, Eastern Europe, and parts of Asia as emerging sources of ICP (Carr 2004; ECPAT 2008).

The Expertise of Offenders

As the typology of Internet offending behavior described in Chapter 3 suggests, offenders vary to the degree to which they employ elaborate security measures to avoid detection. Many offenders, especially those with a casual interest in child pornography, may not be especially skilled. However, there is a core of veteran offenders—some of whom have been active in pedophile newsgroups for more than 20 years—who possess very high levels of technological expertise (Jenkins 2001). Pedophile bulletin boards often contain technical advice from old hands to newcomers to the subculture. It has been argued that many of the sting operations used on the Internet succeed only in catching inexperienced, low-level offenders.

Wolak et al. (2005b) examined the technical expertise of convicted child pornography possessors. They found that 3 percent of offenders were described by investigators as "not at all" knowledgeable about the Internet; 40 percent were described as "somewhat" knowledgeable; 44 percent were described as "very" knowledgeable; and 10 percent of offenders were described as "extremely knowledgeable." Of course, these figures are based on convicted offenders. It is likely that the more sophisticated the skills of the offender, the less likely it is that he will be arrested.

The Sophistication of Internet Technology

For those offenders with good computing skills, their ability to avoid detection is enhanced by the rapid advances in Internet technology. Recent developments include P2P networks that enable direct communication between offenders; anonymous remailers that strip the sender's identity from e-mail; and file encryption that permits offenders to hide or scramble images.

Wolak et al. (2005b) found that the take-up of these technologies was in fact modest. Twelve percent of convicted offenders used password protection; 6 percent encrypted their files; 3 percent used evidence-eliminating software; 2 percent used remote data storage; 2 percent partitioned their hard drive; less than 1 percent used anonymous remailers; and less than 1 percent used P2P networks. Again, these findings are from convicted offenders, so they may not be representative of offenders as a whole. In addition, the data are based on arrests in 2000–2001, when some of these technologies were relatively new. Nevertheless, these findings—and the findings for offender expertise—reinforce the view that there is wide disparity in the sophistication and commitment of offenders. While some offenders will take elaborate precautions to avoid detection, many will not.

The Volume of Internet Activity

The sheer amount of traffic in child pornography makes the task of tracking down every person who visits a child pornography site impossible (Jewkes and Andrews 2005). Police become aware of many more offenders than they could possibly arrest. Capturing IP addresses, linking those addresses to individuals, and launching a prosecution against those individuals is time consuming and resource intensive. Many offenders realize that their chances of being caught are realistically quite remote. Similarly, while perhaps worthwhile activities in themselves, catching peripheral offenders or disrupting individual networks may have little overall impact on the scale of the problem.

Because of the volume of ICP crime, police forces need to prioritize their efforts and concentrate on the most serious offenders and, in particular, those actually involved in abusing children and producing pornographic images. It has been noted that success in combating child pornography is too often judged in terms of the number of images recovered rather than by the more significant criterion of whether the ongoing sexual abuse of children has been stopped (Taylor and Quayle 2003). There are a number of triage methods. One strategy is to cross-reference lists of ICP offenders with sex offender registries to increase the chance of targeting hands-on offenders. The allocation of the investigative resources may also be based on the nature of the image. Greater attention might be given to offenders who possess new or "first generation" images because it is likely that these offenders have produced the images themselves and are therefore also responsible for perpetrating child sexual abuse. The severity of the image (e.g., as assessed against the COPINE scale) can also be used as a basis for further investigation. While the link between ICP and child sexual abuse is complex (as we discussed in Chapter 3), there is evidence that among dual offenders (i.e., offenders convicted of ICP offenses and contact child sexual abuse), the severity of contact abuse correlates with the severity (but not volume) of the ICP images possessed (Deane 2011). Moreover, as we will argue in Chapter 7, investigation strategies need to be seen within a broader picture of preventing ICP offending before it occurs, not just arresting offenders once they have committed a crime. The general deterrence effect of policing the Internet may have more impact on offending rates than the incarceration of individual offenders.

THE INVESTIGATIVE PROCESS

ICP is unlike most other crimes with which police departments have to deal. It requires the acquisition of new knowledge about a different kind offender and his modus operandi, the utilization of specialized technical expertise, and the forging of new links with other police agencies, the Internet industry, and nongovernment organizations. In this section, we examine how law enforcement agencies go about the task of investigating ICP. We look at who is involved in the investigations, the sorts of investigative strategies employed, the tools employed to aid investigations, the sorts of digital evidence that can be collected, and examples of major coordinated law enforcement operations.

Who Is Involved in Investigating ICP?

Like the Internet itself, investigations of ICP involve networks of law enforcement agencies distributed in hierarchical layers. Investigations can be carried out at local, state/provincial, national, and international levels. Generally speaking, the higher up in the hierarchy, the greater the coordinating and service-provision roles that are played.

While the investigation of ICP often involves specialist personnel, it would be a mistake to underestimate the importance of local police in detecting and investigating offenses. As a rule, local police will not carry out major operations. However, because of the increasing use of computers in society, all police departments are likely to encounter ICP crimes at some time, and the responsibility for day-to-day investigations will often fall to general duties officers (Jewkes and Andrews 2005; Williams 2003). One study found that 56 percent of arrests for ICP crimes originated from nonspecialized law enforcement agencies (Wolak et al. 2003). By concentrating on problems that occur within their jurisdictions, local police may uncover evidence that initiates a wider investigation. Alternatively, they may receive information from other jurisdictions about offenders in their districts.

Many larger police departments have their own dedicated Internet child exploitation teams. These units are often supported by various national agencies that maintain centralized databases, help coordinate investigations, track offenders and victims across jurisdictions, provide specialized expertise and training, and establish international links with agencies in other countries (Table 4.1). In the United States, a number of national law enforcement agencies have a stake in preventing and investigating ICP and have established specific programs or sections to focus resources and coordinate ongoing responses. These include the Child Exploitation and Obscenity Section (CEOS) of the U.S. Department of Justice; the Cyber Crimes Center (CCC)—Child Exploitation Section of the U.S. Immigration and Customs Enforcement Service; the Innocent Images task force of the FBI; and the Internet Crimes Against Children (ICAC) task force of the Office of Juvenile Justice and Delinquency Prevention.

National agencies in turn may be interconnected via various international agencies and programs (Table 4.1). For example, the Virtual Global Taskforce (VGT) is an international partnership comprising nine members—national agencies from seven counties (Australia, Canada, Italy, New Zealand, the United Arab Emirates, the UK, and the United States) and two international agencies (Europol and Interpol). The United States is represented on VGT by the Immigration and Customs Enforcement Service. The VGT conducts coordinated international law enforcement operations and helps track down victims and offenders across borders.

There are also a number of nongovernment organizations that play a role in the investigation of ICP (Table 4.1). These organizations variously manage ICP hotline reporting services (e.g., CyberTipline, INHOPE), monitor ISPs (e.g., IWF), provide training and technical advice (e.g., NCMEC), and advocate for improvements in Internet regulation and legislation (ECPAT, ICMET). While these organizations are independent of government, they support and are supported by government agencies. For example, ECPAT, ICMEC, INHOPE, and NCMEC are industry partners in the VGT.

Table 4.1 Major National and International Agencies and Organizations Involved in the Investigation of ICP

US Agencies	
Agencies	*Function*
Child Exploitation and Obscenity Section (CEOS)	A division of the U.S. Department of Justice, the section specializes in prosecutions and runs training sessions for federal prosecutors and federal law enforcement agents on technical aspects of Internet investigations and law.
Cyber Crimes Center (C3)	A division of the U.S. Immigration and Customs Enforcement Service, containing the Child Exploitation & Obscenity Section. The section focuses on undercover operations into international production and distribution of child pornography on the Internet.
Innocent Images	The central operation and case management task force coordinating FBI investigations into child exploitation via the Internet.
Internet Crimes Against Children (ICAC)	A task force program initiated by the Office of Juvenile Justice and Delinquency Prevention, U.S. Department of Justice. It provides regional clusters of forensic and investigative expertise to assist state and local law enforcement agencies in dealing with Internet child exploitation.

Other National Agencies	
Agencies	*Function*
Child Exploitation & Online Protection Centre (CEOP)	UK-based cross-agency policing unit affiliated with the Serious Organized Crime Agency (SOCA) charged with eradicating child sexual abuse—either through direct action or in partnership with other agencies.
Child Protection Operations (CPO)	A division of the Australian Federal Police (AFP), the CPO investigates online child sexual exploitation and plays a coordinating role nationally and internationally.
National Child Exploitation Coordination Centre (NCECC)	A division of the Royal Canadian Mounted Police that coordinates efforts by municipal, territorial, provincial, federal, and international police agencies to eradicate online exploitation of children by providing training and investigative support.

International Agencies	
Agencies	*Function*
Cospol Internet Related Child	CIRCAMP is a European-based initiative driven by Norway and involving 13 other countries (UK, Ireland, France, Sweden, Italy, Finland, Belgium, Spain, Malta, Denmark, the

(*continued*)

Table 4.1 (Continued)

International Agencies	
Agencies	*Function*
Abusive Material Project (CIRCAMP)	Netherlands, Poland, and Germany) as well as Europol and Interpol. CIRCAMP focuses particularly on disrupting the distribution of child abuse images on the web and promotes the use of ISP-based web filtering by using the Child Sexual Abuse Anti-Distribution Filter (CSAADF).
Europol	The European law enforcement agency designed to coordinate the fight by European member states against serious international crime, including child sexual exploitation. Europol works with member states to identify perpetrators, identify cross-border modus operandi, and identify victims.
Interpol	An international policing organization with 188 member countries, focusing on transnational crimes, including child sexual exploitation. Interpol programs include working with ISPs to block access to child pornography, identifying victims portrayed in child pornography, locating missing children moved across borders, and providing training and expertise to other police forces.
Virtual Global Taskforce (VGT)	An association of law enforcement agencies from seven countries (Australia, Canada, Italy, New Zealand, UAE, UK and USA) as well as Europol and Interpol designed to co-ordinate international investigations into Internet crime and especially child sexual exploitation.

Nongovernment Organizations	
Organization	*Function*
End Child Prostitution, Child Pornography and Trafficking of Children for Sexual Purposes (ECPAT)	A global network of more than 80 organizations from more than 70 countries headquartered in Bangkok. ECPAT works with governments, law enforcement agencies, and Internet industries to encourage the development of reporting hotlines, to advocate for comprehensive child pornography laws, and to raise awareness about child exploitation.
CyberTipline	U.S.-based online clearinghouse for tips and leads on Internet child exploitation. The program is jointly sponsored by the NCMEC, the U.S. Postal Inspection Service, the U.S. Customs and Border Protection, and the FBI.
INHOPE	INHOPE is the International Association of Internet Hotlines, representing more than 40 hotlines around the world. INHOPE members provide an anonymous reporting service for members

Table 4.1 (Continued)

Nongovernment Organizations	
Organization	*Function*
	of the public to report illegal materials on the Internet, especially child pornography. Reports are passed to relevant law enforcement agencies and ISPs.
International Centre for Missing and Exploited Children (ICMEC)	Established in Belgium and based on NCMEC, the ICMEC now has an international network of partners in 17 countries. ICMEC disseminates images about missing and exploited children, provides training, and advocates for changes in laws and treaties pertaining to child exploitation.
Internet Watch Foundation (IWF)	UK-based nongovernmental organization funded by the Internet industry but backed by police and government. The IWF promotes self-regulation and can issue notice and takedown (NTD) orders to UK ISPs.
National Center for Missing & Exploited Children (NCMEC)	U.S.-based private, nonprofit organization whose mission includes following up tips from the CyberTipline and providing technical assistance and training to other agencies.

How Are Investigations Carried Out?

The activities of Internet child exploitation (ICE) investigators fall into three main categories: searching the Internet for child pornography images, engaging in undercover operations on the Internet, and tracking offenders caught in honeypot traps. In addition, investigations may be carried out as part of routine policing.

Searching the Internet

Police agencies may undertake the scanning of the Internet to locate and remove illegal child pornography sites, to track offenders who visit those sites, and to identify perpetrators and victims portrayed in the images. Many areas of the Internet are not accessible via the usual commercial search engines and investigators need to be skilled at conducting sophisticated searches of the "hidden net." Police may search for sites directly or they may act on information received about illegal sites from one of the various hotlines or from ISPs (either voluntarily or because of their legal obligation). In many jurisdictions, police can issue a "notice and takedown" (NTD) order, requiring an ISP to remove illegal sites from their servers or to disable access by their customers to illegal sites on other servers outside of their control. Police can only intervene directly with ISPs within their jurisdiction; where they become aware of offenses in other jurisdictions, police need to pass that information on to local police for action.

In most cases, police do not have the time or resources to track down the individuals who are seeking to access the child pornography sites, and they limit their actions to the NTD order. However, in some cases, police may apply for a court order to examine ISP accounts in order to identify and prosecute those who have downloaded the images (Ferraro and Casey 2005).

Apart from taking down images and prosecuting users, police may use images to identify the perpetrators and victims who are portrayed. Every child pornography image is a record of child sexual abuse. The images are therefore graphic evidence of criminal activity that may be used by police agencies to prosecute offenders and rescue victims. The National Child Victim Identification Program (NCVIP), jointly hosted by CEOS and NCMEC (see Table 4.1), has the largest child pornography database in the world and is dedicated to identifying victims of child sexual abuse.

Undercover Investigations

The most serious cases of ICP occur in chat rooms, newsgroups, and P2P networks, and investigating these forums is a priority of law enforcement agencies. These investigations typically involve police entering these forums in undercover mode. There are two strategies. Law enforcement agents may enter forums posing as pedophiles and request child pornography images from others in the group (U.S. Department of Justice 2004). Alternatively, they may enter child or teen groups posing as children and engage predatory pedophiles lurking in the group. Offenders may send or request pornography and in some cases suggest a meeting with the "child."

Because of the prevalence of undercover police on the Internet, offenders are becoming increasingly suspicious of these tactics. Undercover investigators need to learn how to adopt a convincing persona of an offender or vulnerable child, and they may receive training to help them perfect their role-playing. Many of the forums are closed or monitored, and the undercover investigator must establish credibility in order to gain access. For example, to join a network, an undercover investigator may have to provide child pornography images in order to earn the right to trade with other members, and police forces may have a collection of stock images to be used for this purpose.

Honeypot Traps

Honeypot traps are sites that purport to contain child pornography but in fact are set up by police and are designed to capture the IP address or credit card details of visitors trying to download images. For example, the FBI began employing this tactic in 2008, posting fake hyperlinks to child pornography sites and raiding homes of those clicking on the link (McCullagh 2008). Honeypot traps are a type of sting operation and are controversial. While legal in most jurisdictions, they are considered by some to be a form of entrapment and to be a violation of civil liberties. From a policing perspective, the number of arrests may be less important than the deterrent effect that such sites might have. Their existence on the Internet is designed primarily to create uncertainty in the minds of those seeking child pornography on the Internet and thus to reduce to the sense of freedom and anonymity they feel.

Traditional Police Investigations

While most media attention is often given to technological aspects of investigating ICP, in fact, many arrests in this area arise from traditional investigative police work. Investigations may begin with information received from variety of sources: The public may contact police directly or information may be received from one of the various child pornography hotlines; downloaded child pornography may be reported by computer repairers/technicians; child pornography might be discovered during the investigation of "hands on" child sexual abuse cases; the arrest of one offender may lead to the arrest of other offenders with whom he has had dealings, producing a cascading effect; and police may find evidence of ICP while investigating unrelated crimes, such as drug offenses.

Investigative Tools

Internet technologies not only aid offenders in carrying out their offenses, but they also aid police in their investigations of these offenses. A technological race has developed between offenders and law enforcement agencies. The investigative tools employed by police may be grouped into four categories: filtering software, image recognition software, surveillance software, and data-linking software.

Filtering

A filter is blocking software that denies access to nominated sites or types of sites. Filters may be applied at the home computer level, on local area networks (e.g., within a particular workplace), or by ISPs. Police are concerned mainly with ISP filtering. There are a number of different filtering systems, and depending on jurisdiction, they may be used voluntarily by ISPs or mandated by legislation. Perhaps the most widely used filter in law enforcement is the Child Sexual Abuse Anti-Distribution Filter (CSAADF), promoted in Europe by CIRCAMP (see Table 4.1). In countries where CSAADF operates, police are responsible for drawing up a "blacklist" of banned URLs. The blacklist is compiled on the basis of the outcome of investigations, information from other participating agencies, and tips from hotlines. Suspect sites are inspected and checked against national legislation, and if they are found to be illegal, they are added to the list. When a customer tries to access the blacklisted site, the ISP redirects the request to a proxy server, which sends the customer a message that the connection has been blocked. CSAADF operates at the domain level rather than site level. That is, if a domain is found to contain child pornography sites, the whole domain is blocked. It is then up to the domain administrator to take down the offending sites in order to have access to the domain unblocked.

Under current models of ISP filtering, no information about the person making the request to view child pornography is collected. Thus, filtering serves largely as a prevention function, and we pick up on this issue again in Chapter 7. However, it is technically possible using filtering software to automatically capture the IP address of individuals seeking to access illegal sites and to use that information to initiate criminal investigations (Dedman and Sullivan 2008). This is essentially the same technology that is used to identify offenders caught in honeypot taps. However, the general use of this technology would be controversial and probably require specific enabling legislation in most jurisdictions in order to gain the necessary participation of ISPs.

Image Recognition

Given that some offenders have been arrested in possession of over one million child pornography images, we can conclude that there must be at least that many images in circulation at one time or another on the Internet. Identifying, assessing, linking, and cataloguing these images is a time-consuming and potentially traumatic task for law enforcement officers. Considerable effort is going into developing image recognition software to aid in these tasks.

Assigning images a digital signature is a reasonably straightforward task. Using a hash function, an algorithm converts the digital image to a hash value. In this way, known child pornography images can be assigned a unique identifier (a series of digits and letters). When an offender is arrested with a collection of images, those images can be hashed and checked against existing databases, meaning that investigators do not need to personally inspect each image to identify illegal content.

However, simple hashes have serious limitations. If an image is modified in any way—cropped, enlarged, compressed, or morphed—the hash value changes, nullifying the ability to match it against the database. Furthermore, an image has to be physically inspected and identified as child pornography prior to hashing.

More sophisticated image recognition software is attempting to overcome these limitations. A perceptual image hash—sometimes also referred to as a robust hash or a fingerprint—extracts certain features from an image and creates a similar hash value for similar images (Zauner 2010). Similar fingerprinting techniques are also being developed for video and audio files. Thus, within limits, even where offenders have modified images, a match can be made against the database. In addition, perceptual image hashes provide the potential to link different images that may involve the same victim, perpetrator, or location. A previously unknown image may be digitally identified as child pornography on the basis of its perceptual similarity with other known images in the same series. Important variations among images of the same series may also be revealed. For example, a series of images may be identified as involving the same perpetrator and location but different victims, thereby initiating a search for the new victims.

Remote Surveillance

While we have the perception of being anonymous online, unless we take specific precautions to hide our identities (e.g., using anonymous remailers), our activities are easily tracked. We can see this for ourselves in the form of corporate surveillance. When we search the Internet, we are likely to begin to receive advertisements related to the websites we have visited. In this case, "cookies" on our computers track our web-surfing behavior and relay this information back to the search engine company (e.g., Google). In a similar way, law enforcement personnel can use various software applications that allow them to analyze traffic and monitor illegal activity on such networks as P2P and Internet Relay Chat (IRC). A recent ruling in the United States decreed that police do not need a search warrant in order to remotely interrogate a suspect's computer (U.S. v. Borowy 2010). Generic, commercially available programs, such as NetDetector, NetIntercept, Wireshark, KaZAlyser, and Nmap, analyze network traffic, capturing and extracting IP addresses, server and IRC passwords, websites accessed, e-mail, and graphic and video file transfers (Casey 2004; Ferraro and Casey 2005). Other more powerful, purpose-built spyware applications—sometimes referred to as policeware—may also be available to investigators. Occasionally, police release the outcome of their infiltration of networks (Artur 2010; Lemos 2008; Leyden 2008). Understandably, however, they are usually reluctant to discuss operational details, and there is little in the way of publicly available information on what software they use or how their surveillance is carried out.

Data Linking

As previously discussed, a central challenge for law enforcement agencies is the need to coordinate investigations across jurisdictions. With jurisdictions carrying out independent investigations, the danger is the proliferation of silos of unconnected data. One response to this problem has been the Child Exploitation Tacking System (CETS). CETS comprises a set of applications designed specifically to aid the investigation of Internet child sexual exploitation. It was jointly developed by Microsoft and Canadian law enforcement agencies (the Royal Canadian Mounted Police and the Toronto Police Service) and was launched in 2005. CETS is a centralized repository that links such information as credit card purchases, Internet chat room messages, and conviction histories. It enables different police forces to share and interrogate huge volumes of data in order to cross-reference evidence, identify offending patterns that link offenders to different offenses, track offenders across jurisdictions, match up investigations, and examine social networks of offenders. CETS permits agencies to coordinate resources and expertise and avoid the duplication of efforts.

The Evidence Trail

Once offenders have been located, it is necessary to collect evidence of their Internet pornography offending. Internet child exploitation teams will typically include forensic investigators, whose job it is to examine seized equipment or other Internet records. Despite the difficulties involved in policing the Internet, computers and their associated technologies retain a considerable amount of evidence of the uses to which they have been put (Ferraro and Casey 2005). While determined, computer-savvy offenders may take precautions to cover their tracks, many offenders will have neither the foresight nor the necessary expertise to do so and will leave a trail of incriminating evidence. Evidence of criminal activity may be found on the computer on which child pornography is viewed or stored, the peripherals used to record or manage images, and the servers through which Internet connections were made.

The Offender's Computer

The most obvious evidence of pornography use is actual downloaded images saved to the computer's hard drive. There are numerous documented cases in which computer repairers have found child pornography on an offender's hard drive and notified police, the most notorious case involving pop singer Gary Glitter (BBC 1999). Some jurisdictions have mandatory reporting of child pornography by repairers (DeMarco 2005).

Even if images have been deleted from the hard drive, they may still be retrieved through forensic examination (Jewkes and Andrews 2005; Wardwell and Smith 2008). There are also more subtle records that technicians can locate during an examination of a suspect's computer. For example, log files can show who was logged on to the computer and when; modem logs record when a computer was connected to the Internet; web browser history entries can help trace an offender's online activity; and e-mail and chat logs can reveal online communication with cohorts and/or potential victims. The seizure of a suspect's computer requires specialized expertise, and if handled incorrectly, it may result in the loss of critical evidence (Ferraro and Casey 2005).

Peripherals

Computer peripherals are devices attached to a computer to extend its functionality. They include input peripherals (e.g., keyboards), output peripherals (e.g., printers, scanners), communication peripherals (e.g., digital cameras, smartphones, iPods), and data storage peripherals (e.g., external hard drives, flash drives). Many of these devices have embedded computer systems that control the functions they perform and that retain records of their use in their memory cards. Some of these devices are also implicated in the production, distribution, and storage of child pornography. Digital cameras can be used to record abuse that can then be easily uploaded to the Internet; smartphones permit the taking, storing, and transmitting of digital images as well as being used for voice conversations and text messaging between perpetrators; and printers and scanners can be used to print downloaded images or digitize hard copy images.

Servers

Different servers may provide information with which to track pornography use (Ferraro and Casey 2005). ISP authentication servers record customer account details against IP addresses (authentication logs) that can then be used to identify users. FTP and web servers used to upload and download electronic files will have logs that record the IP address of users and what files were accessed and when. Similarly, e-mail servers retain logs of customer usage. LAN servers may be used to store collections of pornography for personal use. Individuals may utilize local servers connected to their work computers so searching a suspect's work server may reveal hidden collections of pornography. In order to assist in the prosecution of offenders, ISPs and systems administrators need to maintain good records of IP logging, caller ID, web hostings, and so forth.

Major Coordinated Operations

In addition to the ongoing day-to-day investigations of ICP, there have been a number of major interagency and international operations. Krone (2005) categorized these coordinated operations into three types based on the nature of the offenders targeted and the investigative strategies employed. The first type of operation targets offenders who are members of covert groups. These groups typically operate in closed chat rooms, newsgroups, and P2P networks. Once the group has been infiltrated by police, the arrest of one offender and the interrogation of his Internet records can quickly lead to the arrest of other members of the group. Three such operations—Operation Cathedral, Operation Candyman, and Operation Rescue—are described in Table 4.2.

The second type of operation targets website subscribers. These are offenders who purchase access to child pornography sites, typically by using their credit cards. The sites themselves are run as organized businesses. Once accounts of the business are seized, offenders are usually tracked through their credit card details. Operation Avalanche/Ore and Operation Basket are the best-known examples of this investigative approach (Table 4.3).

Table 4.2 Coordinated Operations Targeting Covert Groups

Operation Cathedral

The Problem	The Response	The Outcome
The Wonderland Club was an exclusive online pedophile ring in which members reportedly had to produce 10,000 child pornography images for membership. At least 180 individuals from at least 33 countries had met this criterion, and seven members had contributed 750,000 images combined.	In 1996, two U.S. offenders charged with online child pornography offenses (the Orchid Club) cooperated with police and provided information about a British offender. Evidence from that offender's computer hard drive led to the discovery of the Wonderland Club. The operation was conducted between 1998–2001, involving U.S. and British police coordinate through Interpol. While agents were unable to gain undercover entry into the club, they were able to monitor transactions and gather evidence from the outside. Eventually, the names of 35 members were identified. Police forces in 12 countries carried out more than 100 simultaneous raids on suspects.	The Wonderland Club was smashed and there were 107 arrests around the world, 14 of which were in the United States.

Operation Candyman

The Problem	The Response	The Outcome
Candyman was the name of an open e-group, maintained by Yahoo!, that was involved in exchanging child pornog-raphy. It had 7,000 members, of which 4,600 were in the United States and the remain-ing 2,400 from around the world.	Undercover FBI agents identified and infiltrated the e-group in a yearlong undercover operation ending in 2002. The task force comprised 56 FBI field officers. A court order was obtained to compel Yahoo! to provide the unique e-mail addresses of all members and subpoenas issued to all ISPs to provide the addresses of U.S. users.	The FBI was able to obtain 1,400 addresses, from which 707 suspects were identified, 266 searches carried out, and 89 arrests made to date. Those arrested include a school bus driver, law enforcement personnel, clergy, and a teacher's aide.

Operation Rescue

The Problem	The Response	The Outcome
A legal discussion forum boylover.net was the gateway	The operation began in 2007 when the Australian Federal	The group was closed down in 2009. The Dutch

Table 4.2 (Continued)

	Operation Rescue	
The Problem	*The Response*	*The Outcome*
to a covert group of offenders. Once contact was made in the legal forum, members moved to private channels, where they exchanged e-mail and child pornography images. There were over 70,000 members across the UK, the United States, New Zealand, Australia, and Thailand. The founder of the group lived in the Netherlands.	Police and CEOP independently found boylover.net, and the investigation was expanded to involve the other members of the VGT. Officers first infiltrated the group and then took over the account of the UK administrator. This gave them access to details of members, including occupation, country of residence, and date of birth. Officers went through all posts to prioritize their efforts, concentrating on offenders who were sexually abusing children.	founder of the group was jailed. 670 other suspects were identified and 184 arrests made internationally (121 from Britain). 230 child victims were identified and safeguarded.

Source: Wortley & Smallbone, 2006a

Table 4.3 Coordinated Operations Targeting Website Subscribers

	Operation Avalanche (United States)/Ore (UK)	
The Problem	*The Response*	*The Outcome*
Landslide Productions was a child pornography company run out of Fort Worth, Texas. Landslide involved a complex network of some 5,700 computer websites around the world, especially in Russia and Indonesia, that stored the child pornography images. The operation at Fort Worth acted as a gateway into the network. Online customers provided credit card details to obtain network	The investigation began in 1999 when the U.S. Postal Inspection Service discovered that Landslide's customers were paying monthly subscription fees into a post office box or via the Internet. A joint investigation between the Postal Inspection Service and the Internet Crimes Against Children Task Force (ICAC), comprising more than 45 officers, was conducted over two years	To date, there have been 120 arrests in the United States, including the two principal operators, who were given a life sentence and a 14-year sentence, respectively, in 2001. In the UK, some 7,000 customers were identified, 1,300 people arrested, and 40 children taken into protective custody. Despite the closing down of

(continued)

Table 4.3 (Continued)

Operation Avalanche (United States)/Ore (UK)		
The Problem	*The Response*	*The Outcome*
access. These credit card numbers were scrambled by Landslide to protect customers' identity. There were more that 250,000 subscribers from 60 countries, generating a monthly turnover of up to $1.4 million.	(Operation Avalanche). Officers cracked the code that scrambled the credit card numbers and then tracked down the owners of cards. Landslide's bank accounts were seized, and 160 search warrants were executed that recovered large quantities of child pornography. The investigation was expanded to include the UK police (Operation Ore).	Landslide Productions, there has been criticism that relatively few offenders have been successfully prosecuted.
Operation Basket		
The Problem	*The Response*	*The Outcome*
The operation targeted 230 pay-per-view child pornography websites located in the Ukraine. 30,000 customers were identified in 132 countries.	The operation began in 2006 from information obtained by the U.S. Immigration and Customs Enforcement Service and was taken up by the VGT. Agents made test purchases from the sites in order to gain evidence of illegality. Ukraine was encouraged by VGT to act against the websites hosted in that country.	The operation ended in 2010, when the sites were closed down. Hundreds of arrests of customers in the United States were reported. Five members of Ukrainian criminal organization were arrested.

Source: Wortley and Smallbone 2006a

The third type of operation involves "stings," such as the classic honeypot trap described earlier. The best-known ongoing example of a coordinated honeypot trap is Operation Pin (Table 4.4).

CONCLUSION

The Internet is a challenging environment to police. Local citizens may access child pornography images that were produced and/or are stored on another continent. Different countries have different laws and levels of permissiveness

Table 4.4 Coordinated Operations Involving "Stings"

Operation Pin		
The Problem	*The Response*	*The Outcome*
The operation is directed at the general proliferation of child pornography websites and the number of people accessing these sites. In particular, it is aimed at casual or first-time offenders.	The operation was begun in 2003 by West Midlands (UK) police and expanded to include other VGT members (the FBI, the Australian Federal Police, the Royal Canadian Mounties, and Interpol). Far from being a covert operation, it was officially launched with media releases by the relevant police forces. It is a classic honeypot trap operation. A website purporting to contain child pornography was set up. Visitors to the site were required to go through a series of webpages, which appeared to be identical to real porn sites, searching for the image they wanted. At each point, it was reinforced that they were in a child pornography site, and they were given the option of exiting. When they did try to access an image, they were told they had committed a crime. They were tracked down via their credit card details, which they were required to provide in order to log on.	The operation has resulted in numerous arrests, although precise numbers are not available. The main purpose of the operation was as a crime prevention initiative designed to shake the confidence of searchers for child pornography on the Internet that they can do so anonymously. Details of the "sting" operation were widely publicized on child pornography sites, contributing to the deterrent effect.

Source: Wortley and Smallbone 2006a

pertaining to child pornography. Moreover, the Internet is a decentralized system with no single controlling agency or storage facility, making it difficult to enforce legislation or to electronically screen content even when there is agreement between jurisdictions. Because it is a network of networks, even if one pathway is blocked, there are many alternative pathways that can be taken to reach the same destination. In addition, rapid technological developments, such as P2P networks, remailers, and file encryption, exacerbate the control problem.

Considerable law enforcement resources are now dedicated to tackling the child pornography problem on an ongoing basis, with many police forces establishing dedicated Internet child exploitation teams. Police are fighting technology with technology in an ongoing arms race with offenders. Moreover, the ICP problem has stimulated unprecedented international cooperation among law enforcement agencies, resulting in coordinated efforts to catch offenders and close off the supply of images.

There is evidence that these efforts are paying dividends. The everyday investigation of ICP has been complemented by a steady rollout of coordinated police operations that have smashed major ICP organizations and have accumulatively resulted in thousands of arrests. Perhaps more importantly, there is an increasing emphasis on and success in identifying and rescuing children who are sexually abused to produce the pornographic images.

At the same time, our satisfaction with the evidence of success must be tempered by our recognition of the size of the problem. As we noted in Chapter 2, if we assume the number of individuals accessing child pornography runs in the millions, the proportion of those actually arrested for their offenses is tiny. No more than a few thousand people are arrested annually for child pornography offenses in the United States and fewer still in other countries. Even highly successful coordinated international operations typically result in fewer than a couple hundred arrests worldwide. We note these figures not to denigrate the efforts of law enforcement agencies and certainly not to argue that such efforts are not worthwhile. There is no doubt that the ICP problem would be many times worse without the efforts of law enforcement. Rather, we think these figures highlight the need for prevention strategies to be added to our armory in the fight against ICP. We will turn to the issue of prevention in Chapters 6 and 7. Before doing so, in the following chapter, we consider the impacts of ICP.

5

Impacts of Internet Child Pornography

CONCERNS ABOUT ICP are focused primarily on its harmful effects. At the center of these concerns are the presumed harmful effects on the children and youth who are the subject of such images. We say "presumed" effects not because we doubt that involvement in ICP can be harmful but because, as we will see, there has been surprisingly little research examining the actual impacts on these young people. There are also serious concerns about the harmful psychological and behavioral effects on the users of ICP. In contrast to the dearth of research on victims, there is now a substantial and rapidly growing body of research on ICP offenders (see Chapter 3). However, research focused specifically on the *effects* of their exposure to ICP is sparse. We nevertheless draw on available evidence and established theory to examine the disinhibiting effects of the Internet as well as the potential effects of offenders' exposure to ICP. There are additional concerns that also need to be considered, particularly the impact on investigators and others who deal with ICP in the course of their day-to-day work. Our focus in the present chapter, then, is on the impacts of ICP—on victims, offenders, and others whose work involves a legitimate but high level of exposure to ICP.

IMPACTS ON VICTIMS

The production of ICP often occurs in the context of contact sexual abuse. Abusers may produce still-picture or video images of the abuse for their own purposes (e.g., for later private viewing) and in some cases may also distribute or exchange the images with others. It may be very difficult in these circumstances to distinguish the effects of producing the abuse images from the effects of the abuse itself. However, the production of sexual images of children and youth does not always involve sexual abuse—or at least the person who is the subject of such images may not experience the original situation as abusive or harmful. For one thing, in many jurisdictions, there are different legal age thresholds for involvement in sex and being the subject of sexual images; for example, it may be legally permitted to have sex with but illegal to produce, possess, or view sexual images of 16- and 17-year-old youth. Of course, these older youth may still be tricked, pressured, or forced into pornography production, in which case, the production of the sexual images is clearly abusive. But in other cases, sexual images may be produced in a private, consensual, adolescent peer relationship setting. These may later be distributed without (or perhaps sometimes even with) the knowledge and consent of the person(s) concerned. Possession of these images by third parties and even by the original participants will be illegal in many jurisdictions. Self-produced sexual images may also be sent to another person (e.g., boyfriend or girlfriend) but then distributed more widely—either by the original receivers or by the self-producers themselves. In these circumstances, the production of the images may not cause harm, although their distribution may. For older and younger children, in some cases, victims may be unaware that they have become the subject of sexual images at all (e.g., through secret filming).

These various scenarios illustrate something of the complexity of the problem of defining ICP and of understanding its effects on victims. Because the production of ICP may or may not involve sexual abuse, for our present purposes, we will consider separately the effects of its production and the effects of its dissemination and use. In this section, we first briefly summarize empirical research on child sexual victimization. Next, we examine what is known about the effects of ICP victimization. Finally, we consider the potential victimization or, in many cases, revictimization effects of ICP distribution.

Effects of Child Sexual Victimization

A great deal has been written about the effects of child sexual abuse victimization, and we will not provide an exhaustive review here. However, because the production of child pornography often involves contact sexual abuse, a brief summary is necessary to establish the context of our present problem.

Sexual abuse victimization has been empirically associated with many serious negative short- and long-term outcomes. Compared to children who have not been sexually abused, victims have been found to suffer more anxiety and depression, somatic complaints, social withdrawal, anger, and aggressive and sexual behavior problems (Briere and Elliot 2001; Kendall-Tackett, Williams, and Finkelhor 1993). Negative outcomes are apparently not universal though. Some studies have shown that as many as 25 percent of maltreated children, including victims of sexual abuse, experience no discernable long-term symptoms (McGloin and Widom 2001). It is not always clear whether this is due to a greater resilience of some victims, to the lesser duration or severity of the abuse to which they were exposed, or to the insensitivity of the outcome measures used to detect harm.

More frequent and more severe negative outcomes are generally found in clinical samples, presumably because such samples are more likely to include children referred by child protection agencies and adults referred because of already-identified psychological and behavioral problems. Reviews of nonclinical studies suggest that negative effects of childhood sexual contact with older youth and adults are less pervasive and, on average, less severe than are typically reported in studies of clinical samples (Rind, Tromovitch, and Bauserman 1998). Nonetheless, these nonclinical studies point to the same aspects of sexual abuse that are associated with the greatest harm. In general, more adverse outcomes have been associated with a longer duration of abuse, the use of force or violence, and being abused by a father or father figure (Hebert et al. 2006). Key protective factors seem to be support from nonoffending parents (Spaccarelli 1994) and, more generally, a supportive family or school environment (Chandy, Blum, and Resnick 1997; Elliot and Carnes 2001), particularly following detection or disclosure.

Among the more troubling long-term outcomes of sexual abuse, particularly for female victims, is an increased risk of further sexual victimization later in life—often in apparently unrelated circumstances. Estimates of sexual revictimization rates range from 15 percent to an alarming 72 percent (Van Bruggen, Runtz, and Kadlec 2006). In one study, women who had experienced sexual abuse as a child were twice as likely as previously nonvictimized women to be raped, even when controlling for the presence of childhood physical and emotional abuse (Messman-Moore and Brown 2004). Risk factors for sexual revictimization seem to be much the same as for other negative outcomes of sexual abuse, with duration, severity, and a familial context of the original abuse experience all being empirically associated with revictimization (Van Bruggen et al. 2006). One explanation is that women who have been sexually abused as children are more likely to engage in risky sexual behavior, such as engaging early in consensual sexual relationships, being less discriminating in their choice of sexual partners, and having more casual sex partners (Van Bruggen et al. 2006).

Effects of Child Pornography Victimization

We noted in our introduction to this chapter that there has been very little research that has examined the actual impacts on victims of ICP. Our analysis here is based on four primary sources. First, we have drawn on the work of Silbert (1989), who gave detailed descriptions of several cases of child pornography victimization among 100 such cases that came to light during a large-scale 1980s study of juvenile prostitution. Note that because this study predated the widespread use of the Internet, it was not specifically concerned with victims of *Internet* child pornography. The most systematic study of ICP victims to date is a report of 30 cases identified during several operations by Swedish police between 1992 and 2003, and who were subsequently assessed at a university hospital psychiatric clinic (Svedin and Back 2003). The largest study is a report of a national survey of victim services agencies in Germany (von Weiler, Haardt-Becker, and Schulte 2010). This study did not involve direct observation or questioning of victims. Instead, the report is based on the responses of victim services agencies to an open-ended questionnaire (N = 84) and semistructured face-to-face interviews with professionals (N = 28) who had dealt directly with ICP victims. This study identified 245 cases of ICP victimization and an additional 280 suspected cases. Finally, we have drawn from a commentary on two clinical case studies by Leonard (2010). This is methodologically the weakest study but does provide some useful insights.

There is very little in these studies that indicates distinctive harmful effects of child pornography production. With some notable exceptions, which we will discuss shortly, the incidents reported in these studies involved the production of sexual images as part of a more extensive experience of sexual victimization—often at the hands of known adults, including family members, upon whom the victims were dependent in a variety of ways. Many of the documented cases involved very severe abuse, including being abused from a young age and over a long period of time, the insertion of objects, and being pressured or forced to have intercourse with multiple abusers who were either friends of the original (often familial) abuser or prostitution "customers." In many of these cases, the specific effects of involvement in child pornography production are likely to have been obscured or overshadowed by the devastating effects of the abuse situations themselves.

The finding that in most instances sexual images are originally produced by family members or others already close to the child is consistent with analyses of ICP arrests reported elsewhere (Wolak et al. 2011; Wolak 2011). All the cases described by Svedin and Back (2003) involved contact sexual abuse, and in most cases, the sexual abuse images were produced by an abuser who was already well known to the child. Indeed, in 25 of the 30 cases, the offender was connected to the child's family in some way (e.g., stepfather or relative), although in only four cases was the offender a "biological or adoptive father." In only three cases was the offender a stranger. The severity of incidents ranged widely but included very severe abuse—often beginning at a young age (in one case, as young as six months) and proceeding over a long period (in one case, as long as eight years). In this study, nonoffending parents, perhaps surprisingly, tended to report few observed problems in the child's behavior; indeed, even in the early stages of disclosure (following the detection and arrest of the offender), the children themselves indicated they had suffered few harmful effects. More severe psychological and behavioral problems tended to emerge after the child began to disclose aspects of the abuse to professionals, and many remained very reluctant to discuss the abuse in any detail—if at all. Standardized assessments, using the well-known Child Behavior Checklist (CBCL) and Youth Self Report (YSR)— administered on average 17 months (range = 1–42 months) after the initial disclosure—revealed significant although not universal problems. Nearly two-thirds of the children who received this assessment were found to have above-average psychological or behavioral problems, including one in three who were found to have serious problems. The most prevalent behavioral problems were obstinacy, sulkiness, or irritability (88%); opinionated, contrariness (82%); preferring to be alone (76%); demanding lots of attention (65%); and swearing or using dirty words (65%). None of the parents indicated that the child had developed an increased interest in sex, although 6 of 10 children indicated they were troubled by thinking too much about sex. Here again, it is not possible to disentangle the effects of involvement in ICP from the effects of the abusive situations in which the ICP was originally produced.

Even when ICP is produced in a nonfamilial setting, there may be links to familial abuse. Silbert (1989) describes a case of a young woman who was sexually abused at home from the age of 12 by an older stepbrother and who eventually ran away. After spending some time on the streets, she took up with a man in his 30s who seemed to offer her protection but who later began using her as a subject of pornographic films. This young woman was drawn into increasingly degrading activities, including "performing" for the camera with multiple male partners and with a variety of objects. Her involvement with the older man exposed her to illicit drug use, and she became drug dependent. She escaped shortly before turning 18 but was pursued and persuaded to return to her involvement in pornography production. She was eventually able to leave—only to turn to prostitution as a means to earn a living and to support her drug dependence. This is a shocking although not entirely unique case, but again, it is difficult to distinguish the effects of this young woman's child pornography victimization from those of the many other abusive situations she had been subjected to.

While it would be unsafe to draw any general conclusions from the two case studies described by Leonard (2010), they do illustrate some of the potential differences between those who become the subject of ICP in the context of abusive and nonabusive situations. In one case, a young woman had been subjected to filming by her father from the age of seven to the age of nine. She reported that her father had never touched her sexually but instead directed her to undress and touch herself sexually while being filmed. Although she was never directly aware of it, police evidence indicated that on other occasions, her father had also filmed her while she was sleeping or bathing. The father was arrested and convicted for producing the images and selling them on the Internet. While later undergoing counseling, the young woman spoke about her sense of being complicit in the abuse mainly because she had "agreed" to her father's requests for her to perform for the camera. Apparently, a particular source of distress for her was that she complied when directed to smile while being filmed, presumably to convey an image of fun and enjoyment to those who would later view the images on the Internet. While this situation was clearly abusive in itself, the effects of posing for the camera may be a distinct aspect of child pornography. On the other hand, similar points of confusion are likely to arise in many sexual abuse situations that are not filmed or otherwise recorded—for example, when the abuser requests or directs the child to do or say certain things for his (the abuser's) own purposes.

The other case described by Leonard involved the production of sexual images in a very different set of circumstances. Indeed, in this case, the term *sexual images* may be more accurate for describing the context in which they may have later been viewed than the context in which they were originally produced. This case involved a 14-year-old girl who was photographed in her bedroom by a female friend while the two were trying on new clothes. Some of the images, captured on the friend's cell phone, were of the girl in her underwear. The clinical account suggests that the girl freely consented to the pictures being taken and had posed playfully in a "sexy manner." The girl who took the photographs transmitted them to a third friend, apparently still in the spirit of playfulness, and they were soon posted on YouTube. The victim herself estimated that as many as 600 other young people, including many fellow students at her school, viewed the pictures. We will return to the possible effects of the distribution of these images in the next subsection, but for now can only assume that unlike in the other cases described earlier, the production of these images was probably not in itself harmful. On the contrary, the clinical report indicates that the subjective experience of being photographed in this case was enjoyable.

In the larger German study (von Weiler 2010), most victim services agencies (85%) reported that they had had no or rare involvement with cases of child pornography victimization. Of those that had seen such cases, 80 percent of the victims had been girls and 62 percent had been under age 14. The proportion of boys was much higher (60%) in suspected (unconfirmed) cases, suggesting that pornography production involving boys may be much less likely to be disclosed. While all confirmed cases by definition involved the production of sexual images, in most cases (75%), these images were not known to have been distributed. Concerns nevertheless often focused on the possibility that they may be distributed at some point in the future.

Most (90%) of the identified abusers were males between 22 and 40 years old. Of 68 cases where detail concerning the offender was available, 21 (31%) were fathers or father figures, 21 were male relatives or family acquaintances, 10 (15%) were adolescent acquaintances (9 boys and 1 girl), 8 (12%) were male staff members of youth welfare institutions, and 2 (3%) were mothers. As with sexual abuse more generally, these child pornography incidents thus involved people, particularly older males, who were already close to the victim. In the remaining six cases (9%), the child was contacted online by the offender and requested to send sexual images, and in these cases, the offender also seemed to have been a person already well known to the victim. In fact, the report indicates that in all cases seen by these agencies, the sexual images had been produced as part of ongoing sexual abuse that occurred "within the close surroundings of the child" (216). Once again, then, we assume that it would be difficult to distinguish the effects of the pornography production from the effects of the other abuse.

Half of the professionals interviewed by von Weiler et al. thought that ICP cases were more complex and challenging than contact sexual abuse cases that did not involve child pornography, although most of the reasons given were concerned with the limitations of their own knowledge and expertise. Apart from the abusive context in which the sexual images were produced, concerns about the victims themselves were centered on the actual or potential distribution rather than on the production of the images.

Effects of Child Pornography Distribution

Whether or not sexual images are originally produced in the context of abusive situations, distribution of the images appears to be almost universally experienced by victims as abusive and harmful. However, even within the limited available literature on the topic, details are sketchy. Several interrelated themes can nevertheless be tentatively identified. For those whose images were produced in a nonabusive situation, experiences appear to include embarrassment and shame about how others who become aware of the images, including family and friends, may regard them; anxiety about who might view the images and what they might do with them; lack of control concerning the potentially permanent existence and availability of the images; and worries about the possibility of meeting someone who has seen the images. Similar experiences have been noted for those whose images were produced as part of a more extensive abuse situation, and for these victims, these problems are likely to be compounded by other aspects of their victimization. In addition, physically abused victims are said to experience problems with being able to define the end of the abuse. On the other hand, the existence of abuse images has been noted to reduce the ambiguity that often accompanies allegations of sexual abuse—for prosecutors and for families and others who may otherwise struggle to believe that abuse has occurred.

Von Weiler et al. (2010) describe how parents of child pornography victims are often angry and horrified and fear public humiliation because of the existence of the images of their child. While angry responses seem to be directed primarily at the offender (who were often family members or family friends), any guilt or responsibility felt by the victim may be extended to embarrassment and shame concerning the family's reactions. In many cases, a range of other problems exist within the family, and in some cases, the victim is blamed for his or her participation in the production of the images (and, by extension, for their distribution). Von Weiler et al. describe one case in which a mother excused the offending father for selling sexual images of their five-year-old son and eight-year-old daughter because the family was suffering financial problems and because the father had apparently not physically abused the children. Leonard (2010) describes how the girl whose friend distributed otherwise innocent images on YouTube was distressed by the knowledge that family and school friends may now have seen these images. Svedin and Back (2003) noted that for the children in their sample, "the mental stress was also greatly heightened by mass media pressure. The feelings that everybody knew who one was and what one had gone through were intense for both parents and children. Most parents had drawn up crisis plans to go into hiding or to move home" (29).

Another theme seems to be anxiety about who may view the images, and how they may be used. In both cases described by Leonard (2010), the victims were said to have developed a general sense of "unsafeness [sic], feeling sexualized, and feeling victimized" (252) because they did not know who may now be viewing their images and because they understood that some may use the images for sexual purposes. Particularly for older children and youth, who are more likely to form such concepts, imagining how a stranger may use their image for sexual gratification is likely to be deeply disturbing.

Anxieties about who may view images and how they may be used are greatly complicated by the potential provided by the Internet for the images to be in virtually permanent existence. Counselors interviewed in the von Weiler et al. (2010) study observed that concerns about the permanence of ICP images were more likely to be expressed by older victims, whom, they pointed out, were more likely than younger children to grasp the concept. Counselors expected that for younger victims, this would become a problem at some time in the future as the realization occurred to them and that this was likely to bring with it new experiences of loss of control, powerlessness, helplessness, shame, and fear. Counselors also reported that the permanence of the images was not always a primary concern for victims' nonoffending parents, who at first tend to be preoccupied with the immediate aftermath of disclosure or detection. But as they came to terms with the initial shock, the realization that the images might exist more or less permanently on the Internet became a new source of anxiety for many parents. Many counselors were at a loss as to how to help victims come to terms with this problem, although suggested strategies seemed to involve either taking steps to try to recover or remove the images from the Internet or accepting the loss of control over the ongoing existence of the images.

Because the Internet provides for such widespread availability of any given sexual images, victims can never be certain who has viewed them. For many victims, this leads to fears that the images may be recognized not only by someone who knows them but that they may also at some point encounter a stranger who has viewed the images and who will therefore recognize them. For example, in many jurisdictions, laws exist prohibiting the identification of sexual abuse victims through the media. Such laws are based on the recognition that people knowing that a child has been sexually abused can be harmful in itself. Thus, for individual victims, knowledge about their sexual abuse tends to be limited to close family and friends and others bound by their professional ethics to maintain confidentiality (although, see Svedin and Back 2003 for comments about the additional negative effects of media attention). By contrast, Leonard (2010) describes how both her clients feared that persons who had viewed their sexual images "could be people whom they meet every day in shops, offices, leisure centres, church, school and parks, as well as people whom they know" (252). Particularly for older youth victims, von Weiler et al. (2010) noted that the ongoing availability of sexual images "was a heavy extra burden in trying to cope and find some sort of closure for the child" (218).

Clinical accounts highlight the importance for sexual abuse victims to be able to identify a point in time when their abuse ended. From the psychotherapeutic perspective, this is understood to allow a line to be drawn between the actual harm experienced during the abuse from its psychological aftermath, to be able to define the abuse as a past experience, and to be able to focus on the present reality that the victim is now free from the threats of ongoing abuse. Leonard (2010) makes the point that it is much more difficult for ICP victims to progress beyond the point of "sickening anticipation" that often accompanies repeated sexual abuse.

On a more positive note, if that is an appropriate term in the present context, the distribution and ongoing existence of ICP images also makes it possible for police, child protection authorities, and victims' families to access what is often a clear record of the abuse that has taken place. As unsettling as it must be for many families, this nevertheless may remove any uncertainty they may otherwise have had about abuse allegations. Sexual abuse cases are notoriously difficult to prosecute because there is often no physical evidence and typically no witnesses other than the complainant and the accused, so for police and other officials, sexual images produced by the offender provide a source of evidence that would otherwise not be possible to obtain. Sexual abuse is also notoriously underreported, and police may occasionally be able to identify victims from images they have seized without having received a direct complaint. Because there are now larger numbers of persons viewing child pornography on the Internet, and although proportionally few are apparently involved in direct sexual abuse, arrests of users may lead police to intervene in abusive situations that are occurring or have in the past occurred elsewhere. In fact, while much is often made of police successes in this respect, proportionally very few victims are ever rescued from ongoing abuse in this way (Quayle, Loof, and Palmer 2008).

IMPACTS ON OFFENDERS

We saw in the previous section that whether or not the original production of child pornography images is abusive or harmful, victims are typically distressed by the distribution of their images on the Internet. Much of their concern is focused on how unknown persons might access the images and use them for their own sexual gratification. There are two additional ways in which the downloading and use of such images may be harmful.

The first is that the user is said to contribute to the demand for child pornography—that without this demand, there would be little point in producing child pornography and distributing it on the Internet, thus removing the incentive for its production in the first place. In this respect, the ICP user is therefore often held to be complicit in the hands-on sexual abuse of children. The second is that using child pornography may be harmful to the offender himself. Many of these potential harms (e.g., personal and social isolation; escalation to using more extreme images; intensification of sexual desires for children) are thought to present a more direct risk of sexual abuse.

In this section, we will examine both of these issues in turn. Note that we are concerned here mainly with the users and not the original producers of ICP. Returning to our central theme, we frame the first question—the extent to which users drive the demand for ICP—in terms of the person-situation interaction model—that is, in terms of the interaction between the characteristics of the user and the characteristics of the Internet environment at the point at which they access and download the ICP. Our argument is that the problem cannot be explained solely in terms of offenders' taking advantage of the new opportunities afforded by the Internet. Rather, the Internet itself drives much of the present demand for ICP. The primary mechanism, we propose, is the disinhibiting effects of the Internet environment.

Disinhibiting Effects of the Internet

Most observers agree that people are inclined to behave differently when interacting with the Internet environment than they do when interacting with others in the "real" world (e.g., Joinson 1998; Suler 2004). This phenomenon that has come to be known as the "online disinhibition effect." Online disinhibition may have positive aspects. For example, some people may express themselves more openly and more honestly than they otherwise would, they may seek out information concerning personal problems that they would be reluctant to ask anyone about in "real" life or they may even engage in unusual acts of kindness and generosity to others. Suler (2004) refers to this as "benign disinhibition." On the other hand, people are more likely to engage in blunt criticism or inquiry, unguarded self-disclosure, aggressive sexual solicitation, deceit, bullying, and so on, or to access areas of the Internet that they would regard as off limits in the "real" world. Suler has called this "toxic inhibition." It is this latter aspect of online disinhibition that concerns us here.

The tendency in certain circumstances for people to behave in negative ways contrary to personal and social norms has long been of interest to social and behavioral researchers. The psychological mechanism that is thought to cause such behavior is known as "deindividuation" (Diener 1980; Festinger, Pepitone, and Newcomb 1952; Zimbardo 1969). Essentially, deindividuation refers to "a psychological state of decreased self-evaluation and decreased evaluation apprehension causing antinormative and disinhibited behavior" (Postmes and Spears 1998, 238). In other words, deindividuation is a (usually temporary) state in which the usual restraints imposed by internal moral standards and by concerns about how one may be judged by others are reduced or absent. The environment in which ICP is typically viewed is a classic example of the kind of situation that would be expected to produce disinhibition because it involves two features thought to be closely associated with deindividuation: anonymity and heightened arousal.

We pointed out in Chapter 1 that in the pre-Internet era, obtaining child pornography required considerable effort and risk. It would have required some level of personal engagement with some kind of distribution network, even if, for example, only by providing a mailing address. The Internet has brought with it not just new opportunities to obtain child pornography but, importantly, new opportunities to do so with apparent anonymity. ICP can now be viewed and is probably now typically viewed in the privacy of the user's home and with the perception that no one else is ever likely to know that the viewing has occurred. Users may well underestimate the ability of police to detect and trace their unlawful online activities, but this is precisely the point—it is the user's *perception* of anonymity that is the relevant issue. In effect, anonymity frees viewers from concerns about the judgment and censure of others, thus reducing or removing their sense of accountability for their own behavior.

There are various ways in which the ICP-viewing environment may produce heightened arousal. The user's first encounter with ICP may occur following the viewing of legal pornography (e.g., by following a link from a legal pornography site to an ICP site), in which case the user is likely to already be in a heightened state of arousal. In other cases, the novice user may actively search for ICP, in which case the anticipation of viewing ICP for the first time may also produce heightened arousal. This anticipation is likely to be even greater for those who have already sexually abused a child. Even for those whose first encounter with ICP is unintentional, the initial viewing may be unexpectedly arousing. Heightened arousal contributes to deindividuation by reducing self-awareness and concentrating attention instead on external situational cues. We saw earlier in this chapter that ICP is often produced in ways intended to portray victims as active and willing participants (see also Taylor and Quayle 2003). In this immediate situational context, without the usual reference to social or personal norms (i.e., in the deindividuated state), the viewer may see ICP as permissible or even legitimate—if only momentarily.

Estimates of the number of ICP users can be alarming when presented in absolute terms (see Chapter 2). Nevertheless, it seems clear that only a small proportion of Internet users ever encounter ICP, much less actively seek it out. This leaves the question of why the disinhibiting effects of the Internet do not cause more people to view ICP. Deindividuation theory in fact does not propose a uniform or universal disinhibition effect. Rather, in accordance with the person-situation interaction principle, people's susceptibility to deindividuation in these circumstances will vary widely.

Part of this variation may be attributed to more or less stable individual differences. As Suler (2004) notes, "the online disinhibition effect will interact with . . . personality variables, in some cases resulting in a small deviation from the person's baseline [offline] behavior, while in other cases causing dramatic changes" (323). Little is known about the kinds of personality variables that may be associated with a greater or lesser susceptibility to online disinhibition as it relates to ICP, although it seems likely that variations in general self-control (Gottfredson and Hirschi 1990) or sexual self-regulation (Ward and Beech 2006) may be particularly relevant. Certainly, the potential to be sexually responsive to ICP is likely to vary widely. Nonetheless, our view is that the potential for experiencing sexual arousal to children extends far along a continuum of normal human sexual responsiveness and that under the "right" circumstances, many otherwise normal people may be susceptible to using ICP.

These latent sexual interests are normally kept in check by internal moral standards and deference to social norms and expectations and are therefore most likely to emerge in circumstances where these personal and social norms are weakened or absent. The disinhibiting effects of the ICP-viewing environment are thus likely to reach much further into the "normal" (especially adolescent and adult male) population than may often be assumed.

Susceptibility to online disinhibition may also vary according to transitory internal states and personal circumstances. Acute emotional problems, frustrations or failures concerning social or sexual engagement with others, loneliness, relationship and attachment problems, intoxication, depression, or simply heightened sexual desire may all increase susceptibility at particular times.

Effects of Viewing Internet Child Pornography

There are three main ways in which the viewing of ICP is considered to be harmful to the viewer: viewing ICP may precipitate new problems with personal relationships or exacerbate existing personal problems; the viewer may habituate to ICP images, leading to desires for more explicit or extreme images; and viewing ICP may create or reinforce sexual interests in children, leading to desires for sexual contact with actual children. Viewing ICP may also lead to arrest and prosecution, which from the offender's perspective is likely to bring with it additional harms.

Relationship Problems

About one-third of persons arrested for ICP offenses in the United States in 2001 and 2006 were living with a partner at the time of their arrest (Wolak, Finkelhor, and Mitchell 2011). Somewhat higher proportions (40%to 57%) are reported in clinical studies of convicted ICP offenders, although ICP offenders are generally found to be less likely than contact sexual abuse offenders to be in an adult intimate relationship (Reijnen, Bulten, and Nijman 2009; Webb, Craisatti, and Keen 2007). It is not known whether this indicates greater difficulties for ICP offenders in establishing or maintaining intimate relationships.

Relationship problems at the time of their initial sexual offending are quite common among contact sexual abuse offenders (e.g., McKillop, Smallbone, and Wortley, in press), but it is not known whether this is also the case for ICP offenders. One indicator of relationship problems may be emotional loneliness—a construct that has been examined in several studies of ICP offenders. Most studies have found that levels of emotional loneliness among ICP offenders are no greater than for either contact sexual abuse offenders or the general population (Babchishin et al. 2011; Elliot et al. 2009; Neutze et al. 2011). However, Middleton et al. (2006) identified a subgroup of ICP offenders whose predominant clinical feature was "intimacy deficits," defined as higher than usual levels of emotional loneliness. Similarly, Henry et al. (2009) identified two subgroups of ICP offenders with emotional loneliness problems: one with additional criminogenic features (35% of the sample) and one without these additional features (26% of the sample).

Elliot and Beech (2009) theorize that ICP offending may cause social isolation and withdrawal from personal relationships, and that offenders may become increasingly reliant on the sexual stimulation provided by ICP to cope with personal and emotional problems (see also Ward and Beech 2006). With respect to personal relationships, these authors do not distinguish between the effects of ICP offending and the effects of being arrested. Quayle and Taylor (2003) have proposed that ICP use can lead to decreased engagement with family and social relationships and that this withdrawal in turn distances the user from the usual "reality checks" on his inappropriate behavior. ICP use can also lead to encounters with online ICP communities that not only facilitate further access to ICP but also serve to permit or justify ICP use.

Evidence suggests that some—but by no means all—ICP offenders experience problems associated with relationship difficulties. Unfortunately, it is not yet possible to draw any conclusions about whether these personal problems precede ICP use, whether they are an effect of ICP use, or whether they are an effect of being detected or arrested. All three possibilities are plausible, but further empirical research is required to clarify and disentangle these potential effects.

Habituation

Habituation is a well-known psychological mechanism whereby repeated exposure to the same stimulus causes a reduction in the intensity of arousal to that stimulus. O'Donohue and Geer (1985) demonstrated a habituation effect for sexual stimuli presented to nonoffender males. Compared to participants who were exposed to varied sexual stimuli, subjective and physiological arousal was diminished for those who were repeatedly exposed to the same stimulus. Applied to ICP, it is therefore likely that offenders who repeatedly use an image for sexual gratification would require new images to maintain the same level of sexual stimulation. Zillmann and Bryant (1986) noted that some general (legal) pornography users graduate over time to increasingly more extreme and unusual sexual images, including bestiality and sadomasochism, and Elliot and Beech (2009) have suggested that habituation may similarly cause ICP users to search for more and more extreme and disturbing images.

At a population level, there are some indications that over time, the kinds of images depicted in ICP have become more extreme and more likely to involve children of younger ages (Beech et al. 2008), although this trend may have stabilized in recent years despite continuing advances in Internet access, connection speeds, and the availability and affordability of related technology (Quayle et al. 2008). Wolak et al. caution that because of the continuing limitations of research on this question, assertions about such trends remain untested hypotheses. In any case, escalation toward the use of more extreme images has not been demonstrated in individual cases. The habituation effect does not in fact predict such an escalation—the increased volume and variety of child pornography made possible by the Internet would presumably allow even the most dedicated user to obtain novel images of his preferred type without necessarily escalating in severity. Indeed, to the contrary, ICP offenders have been noted to be typically selective about the age, gender, physical characteristics, and sexual activities portrayed in the images they collect and use for sexual gratification (Quayle and Taylor 2002). Thus, viewing ICP may in many cases lead to the desire for new images but does not necessarily lead to an escalation in the severity of new images. We would expect the motivations of offenders who are drawn to violent or degrading ICP images to perhaps be driven by pre-existing antisocial, aggressive, or even sadistic dispositions rather than by the desire for sexual novelty.

Transition to Contact Abuse

In chapter three, we examined research evidence concerning the overlap between ICP and contact sexual abuse offending. We saw there that ICP and contact offending can overlap in various ways and that estimates of the degree of overlap vary widely. None of this research deals directly with the question of whether using ICP leads to contact sexual abuse. Certainly, very few ICP offenders appear to progress to contact sexual offending after they have been convicted of an ICP offense—at least in the short to medium term; a meta-analytic review of nine recidivism studies found that only 2 percent of ICP offenders were rearrested for a contact sexual offense after follow-up periods ranging from 1.5 to 6 years (Seto et al. 2011). However, it is well known that many child-victim sexual offenders offend repeatedly before being caught and then are statistically unlikely to be rearrested for a further sexual offense (Smallbone et al. 2008). One explanation for the very low recidivism rates among ICP offenders may therefore be that their arrest interrupts their ICP use and their transition to contact offending.

    The most compelling evidence that ICP use does not generally lead to contact sexual abuse is epidemiological data showing that the incidence of contact sexual abuse has apparently declined steadily since the early 1990s—over the same time period that the availability and use of ICP has been rising. These trends have been particularly striking in the United States, where more than half of the world's Internet servers hosting ICP have been located (Quayle et al. 2008) but where a decline of 53 percent in substantiated sexual abuse has been reported from 1992 to 2007 (Jones and Finkelhor 2009). Less dramatic downward trends in contact sexual abuse have also been reported over similar time periods elsewhere, including Canada (Trocme, Fallon, MacLaurin, and Copp 2002) and Australia (Dunne, Purdie, Cook, Boyle, and Najman 2003). We do not believe these trends indicate some kind of sublimation effect, whereby offenders who would otherwise have abused an actual child instead satisfy their deviant desires with ICP. Rather, we believe these epidemiological trends are consistent with our argument that the unprecedented availability of child pornography afforded by the Internet has tapped latent sexual interests that exist but are usually very well controlled in a large proportion of the (otherwise normal) population, particularly adult and adolescent males.

PROFESSIONAL IMPACTS

Law enforcement efforts to combat ICP have increased, particularly over the last decade, and this has led to increasing numbers of police and other investigators and analysts being exposed to ICP. Exposure may occur in a variety of tasks, including searching for and locating ICP on the Internet, searching confiscated computers and other devices, classifying seized material, identifying victims, preparing prosecution cases, and serving as a witness. Some of this work continues to be performed by general duties police and others involved in the investigation and prosecution of ICP offenders, but in recent years, many specialized Internet child exploitation (ICE) units have been established. Many members of these units will have an intensive and prolonged exposure to ICP. It is these groups that have been the main focus of a small but growing body of research concerned with understanding and managing the occupational health impacts of exposure to ICP. The main focus of these concerns has been on the potential for trauma-like reactions. A less discussed concern is how these personnel manage their own sexual responses to ICP.

Trauma-Related Effects

Police are routinely exposed directly to many stressful situations that most people would rarely or never encounter, including road and other accidents, violence, homicide, drug overdoses, and suicide. They are also often exposed indirectly to crime and its aftermath, including dealing with perpetrators and victims of violent and sexual offenses. Violanti and Aron (1995) reported that police ranked as the top four operational stressors: a fatal shooting; the death of a fellow officer; the aftermath of a physical attack; and exposure to images and audio of abused and suffering children. Such experiences have been linked to posttraumatic stress disorder (PTSD) and, in the case of indirect exposure to victimization, secondary traumatic stress disorder (STSD) (Brown, Fielding, and Grover 1999; Hallett 1996).

Burns et al. (2008) found that ICE investigators experienced intrusive images, hypervigilance (with regard to children's safety), nightmares, and moodiness—all of which are recognized symptoms of PTSD and STSD. Bokelberg (n.d.) reported that ICE investigators experienced other PTSD-related symptoms—namely, physical complaints (headaches and stomach ailments) and irritability as well as discomfort when interacting with children. Two female officers felt they had generalized their negative feelings about male offenders to all men, and one male officer reported a decline in physical intimacy with his wife because "everything was seeming dirty" (8). It is difficult to draw firm conclusions from these studies because the sample sizes are small, the frequency of various problems are generally not reported, and neither reported any comparison with a control group or population norms.

Perez et al. (2010) used a standardized measure of STSD with 28 ICE investigators. Mean scores were just under the criteria for moderate STSD, with 18 percent of the sample in the moderate range and a further 18 percent in the high range. High levels of emotional exhaustion and cynicism were also reported. Both emotional exhaustion and cynicism were positively correlated with heightened protectiveness of loved ones (particularly children) as well as reliance on coworker social support and distrust of the general public.

Wolak and Mitchell (2009) surveyed 511 Internet Crimes Against Children (ICAC) commanders and affiliated law enforcement agencies from across the United States. Ninety percent of ICAC agencies and 48 percent of affiliates were somewhat or very concerned about the effects of exposure to ICP. Thirty-five percent of ICAC task forces and 10 percent of affiliates reported that they had seen actual problems arising from such exposure. The most serious problems directly witnessed were personal, family, and social problems (e.g., hypervigilance concerning children, emotional distance), and work-related problems (e.g., anger, loss of objectivity, declines in productivity). Twenty-three percent of ICAC agencies reported having intervened with ICE personnel as a result of their work (e.g., referral to counseling, dealing with transfer requests). However, the majority of respondents (57% of ICAC agencies and 84% of affiliates) reported having seen no problems related to exposure to ICP. Indeed, in general, these studies suggest that ICE investigators are quite resilient. A number of authors have noted that many of these personnel are protected at least to some extent by a sense of purpose in their work and by supportive relationships at work and at home (Burns et al. 2008; Perez et al. 2010).

Sexual-Related Effects

Jewkes and Andrews (2005) point out that an investigator can be exposed to a great mass of ICP material even if he or she only worked on an ICE investigation for one day. Specialist ICE personnel generally have a much higher and more prolonged exposure to ICP than other law enforcement officers (Wolak and Mitchell 2009). Indeed, because of the sheer volume of detected material and the detailed investigations they are required to undertake, many ICE personnel will be exposed at a much greater level than many—and perhaps most—ICP offenders. Concerns about the harmful effects of viewing ICP on offenders may therefore also be relevant for others exposed legitimately in the course of their work.

The issue of whether ICP investigators may experience sexual arousal or even over time develop unhealthy and inappropriate interests in ICP is rarely raised; most of the commentary on the impact on investigators instead emphasizes the distressing and aversive aspects of the work. Where the problem is mentioned at all, it is framed in terms of the (presumably very remote) possibility that persons with already-established deviant sexual preferences may infiltrate an ICE unit so as to satisfy their deviant desires (e.g., Edelman 2010). Our view is that a greater (although still probably small) risk is that the exposure itself causes sexually deviant responses.

The task of ICP classification involves discriminating between legal and illegal pornographic images and making judgments about which illegal material deserves the greatest priority for investigation. Investigators are therefore routinely exposed to legal or legally or morally ambiguous pornography as part of their work. Descriptions of ICP often highlight the worst cases involving violence and/or very young children, which rightly deserve special attention and clearly cause the greatest concern for investigators. Nevertheless, these are probably the least common types of images viewed by investigators. The worst images are therefore likely to be viewed alongside many nonviolent images of older children (in many jurisdictions, up to 17 years of age) and legal images of young adults—all of which are intended to be sexually appealing.

A key psychological task for ICP investigators is to maintain a boundary between appropriate and inappropriate sexual material—a task likely to be made difficult by the repeated association of graphic sexually aversive and sexually pleasurable images. On one hand, this association may cause ordinary sexual situations to become difficult or aversive. A number of cases of this kind of problem have been noted in research studies (Bockelberg n.d.; Wolak and Mitchell 2009). The association may also have the converse effect—that is, becoming sexually aroused to illegal sexual images. Perez et al. (2010) reported that some investigators made unsolicited comments expressing concern about the onset of inappropriate sexual thoughts, and one participant in Wolak and Mitchell's (2009) study was concerned about an employee who had "what was perceived as an overly intense attraction to the images" (3). Others have noted that some investigators may feel anxious or guilty about being sexually aroused to some images or may fear becoming aroused to ICP images because of this association (Edelman 2010).

CONCLUSION

ICP is usually but not always produced as part of ongoing physical sexual abuse—often by older males who are well known to the victim. Sexual abuse has been empirically associated with a range of negative short- and long-term outcomes for victims, and it is not yet known whether or in what ways child pornography production may have specific effects over and above those associated with contact sexual abuse. However, whether or not the production of ICP occurs in the context of sexual abuse, victims typically experience the distribution of sexual images as abusive and harmful.

Even when they are not involved in the production or distribution of child pornography, ICP users are often held to be complicit in the sexual abuse of children because they contribute to the demand for ICP. It is true that ICP users contribute to demand, but we have argued that it is also the case that the Internet itself drives much of this demand. We have argued throughout this book that the Internet has tapped latent sexual interests that exist but are usually very well controlled in a large proportion of the (otherwise normal) population, particularly adult and adolescent males. The implications of this are wide reaching because it extends the focus of concern beyond a proportionally small group of sexually deviant individuals to a much wider population of potential offenders.

Most people will never see ICP, and very few are likely to ever see the worst images involving violence and/or very young children. Those involved in the investigation of ICP are likely to have an intensive and prolonged exposure to this material. There is evidence that this work is harmful to some investigators, but with a clear sense of purpose and supportive work and social relationships, most investigators are able to maintain good psychological health. The possibility that ICP investigation may affect sexual attitudes and behavior is an underdiscussed and underresearched problem, although at this stage, it appears that such problems are observed in only a small minority of cases.

6

Prevention: Offenders and Victims

IN THIS CHAPTER and the next, we consider how the production, distribution, and use of ICP might be prevented. We have argued in this book that the problem of ICP is best understood in terms of the person-situation interaction model of human behavior. In the present chapter, we consider prevention strategies targeting the "person" side of this equation. In the following chapter, we consider strategies aimed at changing the situational aspects of the problem—namely, the Internet and related technologies.

In the previous chapter, we examined the potential impacts on the three main groups of people involved directly with ICP: victims, offenders, and investigators. Each is involved with the problem in very different ways. Prevention efforts need to be directed primarily to reducing (and, ideally, eliminating) the production, distribution, availability, and use of ICP. Apart from situational interventions (which we will deal with in the next chapter), the main target for this is offenders and potential offenders, although separate strategies are also required to protect victims and potential victims. Borrowing from the public health prevention model, we consider strategies aimed at preventing ICP-related problems before they might otherwise occur as well as strategies aimed at responding effectively after a problem has been identified. We do not deal here with prevention strategies aimed at minimizing the potential harmful impacts on investigators. Although this is a topic worthy of attention in its own right, it is not of direct concern to the prevention of ICP. Our focus is instead on offenders and victims.

LEVELS OF PREVENTION

The public health model distinguishes three levels of prevention. Primary (or universal) prevention targets whole populations and aims to prevent a given problem from developing or occurring in the first place. Applied to ICP, primary prevention would have two main aims: to prevent children from being the subject of ICP images in the first place and to prevent potential offenders from producing, distributing, or using ICP for the first time. The advantage of primary prevention is that problems may be prevented before they might otherwise occur.

This is highly desirable in principle because, like sexual abuse more generally, the aftermath of ICP offending and victimization can be exceedingly costly in personal, social, and monetary terms. A disadvantage is that, particularly when applied to people (as opposed to situations), primary prevention can be very inefficient, especially when it is used to address relatively infrequent or low-prevalence problems, such as ICP offending, and especially when risk factors are poorly defined or understood.

Secondary (or selected) prevention targets at-risk groups and aims to prevent or slow the transition from risk to manifest problem. Secondary prevention of ICP would target potential offenders at risk of producing, distributing, or using ICP and children identified as being at risk of ICP victimization. A key advantage of secondary prevention is that it promises a far greater efficiency than would be possible with primary/universal prevention. However, identifying at-risk individuals or groups involves making judgments about who is at risk and who is not. Because such judgments are inevitably imperfect, secondary prevention introduces two types of error to the prevention task: false positive error, where individuals are identified as at risk but who would not, in fact, go on to offend or be victimized and false negative error, where individuals are judged not to be at risk but who do, in fact, go on to develop the targeted problem. At best, false positive error results in an inefficient allocation of prevention resources; at worst, it can be harmful in itself by unnecessarily and mistakenly labeling people as at risk or drawing them into intrusive and possibly even harmful interventions. Because secondary prevention targets specific groups or individuals who are thought to be at risk, secondary interventions are often more intensive and intrusive than primary/universal interventions. Therefore, it is important that secondary strategies be designed to anticipate and control for negative impacts on unintended targets (i.e., false positive cases).

Tertiary (or indicated) prevention targets those individuals identified as having already developed a given problem and aims to ameliorate associated harms and prevent further recurrences of the problem. For ICP offenders, tertiary prevention essentially involves efforts to prevent further ICP and other offending, especially contact sexual abuse. For victims, tertiary prevention principally aims to prevent any further incidents of sexual victimization. Tertiary prevention in some respects offers the greatest efficiency of the three prevention levels because it targets the fewest number of people and because it is easier to identify a problem once it exists. However, because it applies only after the fact, it also has the highest personal and social (and probably also monetary) costs. As with secondary prevention, tertiary interventions also introduce error because they are generally based on predictions or assumptions about future outcomes. Because of the high level of concern attached to these potential outcomes, a higher threshold for false positive error is typically tolerated for tertiary interventions. That is to say, policymakers and practitioners will often be more concerned about avoiding missing intended targets and less concerned about overincluding nonintended targets.

We need not be distracted by how we might precisely define these three prevention levels. In fact, we are inclined to conceptualize the model in terms of a

Table 6.1 Offender- and Victim-focused Prevention of ICP

	Primary and Secondary Prevention	Tertiary Prevention
Offenders	• Developmental prevention • General deterrence • Confidential helplines	• Specific deterrence • Correctional treatment programs • Incapacitation
Victims	• Self-protection training • Resilience building	• Facilitating disclosure • Support during prosecution • Preventing revictimization

continuum along which various prevention strategies might be located rather than as a categorical scheme. The significance of the public health model is that it provides a conceptual framework within which it is possible to envisage a wide range of potential preventive interventions, including the compelling possibility that ICP offending might be prevented before it would otherwise occur. For the purposes of organizing various strategies, we have simply separated those aimed at preventing problems before they occur (primary and secondary prevention) and those aimed at preventing further problems after the fact (tertiary prevention) (see Table 6.1).

A key limitation of the public health model is that it does not identify specific prevention targets or methods. Successful applications of the model in other areas of public health concern (e.g., heart disease) have been underpinned by extensive research that has identified risk factors associated with problem outcomes (e.g., poor diet, smoking, and so on, in the case of heart disease) as well as experimental studies showing that interventions targeting these risk factors do indeed result in reductions in problem outcomes. As we have seen in previous chapters, in the case of ICP offending and victimization, the research base is much less well developed. Nevertheless, it is possible to at least tentatively consider a range of approaches. While we do not yet have a strong basis to guide specific evidence-based prevention strategies, we are able to identify three key targets—offenders (or potential offenders), victims (or potential victims), and ICP offense settings—and to propose a number of prevention methods based on evidence from the related fields of sexual abuse and crime prevention.

How the model might be applied to offenders and victims is shown in Table 6.1 and discussed in the sections that follow. (We will elaborate on ICP offense settings as targets for prevention in the following chapter.) Examples given in each of the cells in Table 6.1 are not intended to be definitive or exhaustive.

OFFENDER-FOCUSED PREVENTION

ICP offenders differ from one another in important ways, including their personal and psychological characteristics, whether they have already been involved in contact sexual abuse, whether they are involved in the production or distribution as well as the use of ICP, and their risk of proceeding to contact abuse. Characteristics and motivations of individual offenders (or potential offenders) are also likely to change over time. For example, offending-related motivations are likely to change in more or less stable ways over the course of their offending as well as in highly dynamic ways as their personal and life circumstances change. Different preventive interventions are therefore likely to be needed for different kinds of offenders and for different stages of individual offending trajectories.

Developmental Prevention

Developmental crime prevention has generally been implemented as a primary- or secondary-level intervention, aimed broadly at reducing the prevalence of general delinquency and crime. This approach is based on established developmental theories and an extensive evidence base linking adverse developmental circumstances to later involvement in antisocial behavior (Farrington 2005). In fact, adverse early developmental circumstances have been linked empirically to a wide range of later behavioral and mental health problems, including conduct problems, school problems (e.g., truancy, suspension, early dropout, poor academic achievement), drug and alcohol problems, early sexual activity, having multiple sexual partners, teenage pregnancy, unstable relationships, personal victimization, low income, and unemployment as well as involvement in delinquency and crime.

The major empirical sources for the identification of developmental risk and protective factors associated specifically with delinquency and crime have been numerous large-scale prospective longitudinal studies (e.g., Dunedin Multidisciplinary Health and Development Study, Moffit 1990; Mater University of Queensland Longitudinal Study of Pregnancy, Najman et al. 2001; Cambridge Study in Delinquent Development, Farrington 1995; Pittsburgh Youth Study, Loeber et al. 1996). A large number of predictor variables have been identified. Meta-analytic reviews have concluded that the most significant predictors for 6 to 11-year-olds are early delinquent conduct and substance use, and for 12- to 14-year-olds are involvement with antisocial peers and weak social ties. The strongest family-level predictors are antisocial parents, low family socioeconomic status, and poor parent-child relations (e.g., harsh discipline, low parental involvement, low supervision, low warmth, and so on) (Hawkins et al. 1998; Lipsey and Derzon 1998). There is now also a substantial catalogue of successful developmental crime prevention projects demonstrating that targeting these empirically identified developmental risk factors during childhood and adolescence can produce significant reductions in later delinquency and other problems (e.g., Elmira Prenatal/Early Infancy Project, Olds 2002; High/Scope Perry Pre-School Project, Schweinhart, Barnes, and Weikhart 1993; Montreal Prevention Project, Tremblay et al. 1995).

Longitudinal delinquency studies and associated prevention programs have generally not reported outcomes specifically for sexual offending; however, retrospective studies of adolescent and adult sexual offenders indicate that, on the whole, similar developmental risk factors are associated with sexual and other offending (Smallbone 2006). Although less is known about the developmental antecedents to sexual offending, it thus seems likely that developmental crime prevention programs would reduce sexual offending as part of their more generic effects (Smallbone et al. 2008). Unfortunately, virtually nothing is known about the developmental antecedents of ICP offending. Studies of ICP offenders suggest that these offenders are less criminally involved and possess fewer psychosocial problems than contact sexual abuse offenders (see Chapter 3), so we would expect that developmental crime prevention methods would have, at best, modest effects on ICP offending. There are wide variations among ICP offenders, though, so it may be that generic developmental crime prevention programs would reduce the prevalence of some kinds of ICP offending, particularly ICP production, which typically involves contact sexual abuse and which we would therefore assume is more likely to involve antisocial motivations.

More research is needed to discover whether and to what extent ICP offending may be associated with specific developmental risk factors that could be targeted in developmental prevention programs. In the meantime, one potential direction may be to develop universal programs aimed at increasing responsible Internet use among adolescents. Programs targeting adolescents have to date been focused on alerting them to potential risks posed by others, particularly adults, who they may encounter on the Internet (Anderson 2002; Wolak, Finkelhor, and Mitchell 2004). Such programs may need to be extended to include attention to the dangers of their own irresponsible behavior, including producing, distributing, or viewing sexual images depicting young people.

General Deterrence

General deterrence is usually operationalized as the public dissemination of successful arrest and prosecution outcomes for known offenders, with the aim of dissuading would-be offenders from committing such offenses themselves. For ICP offending, the key aim of general deterrence is to establish or increase the perception among the general public that producing, disseminating, or even viewing ICP brings with it a substantial risk of detection and punishment.

Evidence suggests that general deterrence does have a substantial population-wide primary prevention effect but that the sensitivity of individuals to intended deterrence effects is highly variable. Unfortunately, those individuals who are most prone to committing crimes are often the least likely to be deterred by threats of detection and punishment (Baron and Kennedy 1998; Grasmick and Bryjak 1980). First, many crimes are committed impulsively, with little forethought or planning. In these circumstances, offenders are focused more on immediate personal gain rather than on the more distant and uncertain prospects of being caught and punished. Studies have shown that for many crimes, including presumably less impulsive crimes (such as armed robbery), offenders tend to pay more attention to the execution of the crime than to the likelihood or severity of punishment (Carroll and Weaver 1986; Light, Nee, and Ingham 1993; Morrison and O'Donnell 1994). Second, research suggests that people are more concerned about the personal costs of being caught (e.g., loss of job, reputation, family, friends, and so on) than about the objective severity of the punishment itself. Therefore, general deterrence has less effect on those with less to lose by way of valued personal and social connections (Baron and Kennedy 1998).

The implications of these general findings for deterring ICP offending are mixed. The apparently normal profile of ICP offenders suggests that, unlike many other kinds of offenders, they are characteristically neither impulsive nor socially marginalized, so we would not expect them to be especially resistant to general deterrence. However, it may be a different story for different kinds of ICP offenders. Those who produce ICP as part of their direct sexual abuse of children—particularly those whose involvement with ICP is associated with criminal or sexual abuse networks—may be emboldened by the use of more sophisticated methods to avoid detection, reassured by their knowledge that others go undetected, and perhaps more disconnected from the social norms with which general deterrence efforts are aligned. On the other hand, even though the novice ICP user may in normal circumstances be responsive to general deterrence, as we have argued in previous chapters, the ease and perceived anonymity of the Internet environment may temporarily affect their judgment about the appropriateness and risk of proceeding to download ICP images. This suggests that while population-wide interventions aimed at increasing perceived risks associated with ICP offending are important, more targeted interventions designed to deter potential or novice users at the point that they first search for or encounter ICP may be particularly effective. We will consider this latter strategy in more detail in the following chapter.

Detection and Prosecution

We observed in Chapter 4 that the more pressing problem for police is not that they cannot detect ICP users but that they are able to detect many more alleged users than they are able to pursue with full investigations. This is a serious dilemma, particularly given the strong public expectations that all detected sexual offenses should be vigorously prosecuted. Police are no doubt obliged to follow up on third-party complaints concerning ICP, but their own proactive efforts (e.g., searching the Internet, infiltrating distribution networks) are likely to present many more opportunities to detect and identify individual offenders. In the absence of substantially more resources, the pragmatic solution is to prioritize the allocation of investigative resources to the most concerning cases. This in turn presents the problem of on what basis such investigations should be prioritized. The three main concerns are whether the person of interest has been or is likely at some time in the future to be involved in contact sexual abuse; whether the person is involved in the production or distribution of ICP; and the volume and content of the ICP material itself.

There are now numerous studies in which "dual" offenders (those who have been found to possess ICP and to have committed contact sexual abuse) have been compared to ICP possession-only offenders, and a number of authors have proposed that findings from such studies may assist in the prioritizing of police investigations. However, findings have been mixed. For example, McCarthy (2010) found that dual offenders possessed a significantly larger number of ICP images than ICP-only offenders, but Long, Alison, McManus, and McCallum (2011) found the opposite, with ICP-only offenders having a significantly larger number of images. Long et al. (2011) found that dual offenders tended to possess images rated as higher severity, but this finding has not been confirmed by other studies. Most studies comparing contact and ICP offenders have focused on differences in psychological characteristics (e.g., Babchishin et al. 2011). Findings from these studies are also mixed, but even if reliable differences were found, this may be of dubious assistance to investigators.

Using a novel methodology, Smid (2011) examined whether information that could be obtained by police from a quick preliminary analysis of seized ICP material could predict the outcome of completed investigations. Two outcomes were examined: contact sexual abuse and the severity of images. The aim was to identify predictors of these outcomes that could be used by police to prioritize their investigations. A large number of potential predictors were identified from an analysis of 96 cases. Those predictors that were significantly related to contact sexual abuse, a high level of image severity, and contact abuse and image severity are listed in Table 6.2. This study was limited in a number of important respects (e.g., contact sexual abuse was found to have occurred in only 7 of 96 cases), and we do not represent the findings in Table 6.2 as reliable or valid predictors. These findings would need to be replicated with larger samples and cross-validated before they could be used in applied settings. We refer to the study here because it is a good example of the kind of work that is needed to solve an important practical problem in the investigation of ICP.

Investigations of ICP offending attract a great deal of media attention, and the detection and prosecution of ICP offenders is clearly important police work. Nonetheless, it is important to keep in mind that the number of arrests for ICP is still very small relative to the number of arrests for contact sexual offending (Wolak et al. 2011). In terms of the wider problem of child abuse, victimization studies show that the greatest harms tend to be experienced by children who are sexually abused in family settings (Hebert et al. 2006), and the great majority of these cases presumably do not involve the production or use of ICP. From a child protection perspective, familial sexual abuse should therefore remain one of the highest priorities for police and other authorities—whether or not ICP is

Table 6.2 Predictors of Contact Sexual Abuse and ICP Image Severity

Predictors of Contact Abuse	Predictors of Image Severity	Predictors of Contact Abuse and Severity
• Use of peer-to-peer network	• Use of secured data carriers	• Notification through a witness
• Notification of online grooming	• Unemployed or unskilled	• Traced through PC (e.g., repair, sale)
• Prior sexual offense charges	• Has children older than 18 years old	• No use of commercial website
• More than three computers or hard drives	• Prior suspect for sexual and nonsexual offenses	• Prior nonsexual offense charges
• Images of boys		• Offender living alone

Source: Adapted from Smid 2011.

involved. In terms of ICP investigations, the highest priority should be given to preventing or interrupting the production of ICP, especially because this so often occurs in the context of familial sexual abuse.

Specific Deterrence

Where general deterrence relies on the perceived risk of detection and punishment among the general public, specific deterrence relies on the actual detection and punishment of individual offenders. The aim of specific deterrence is to use punishment to dissuade the individual offender from reoffending. It is often assumed that the greater the severity of the sentence, the more likely the offender will be deterred from further offending, but in fact, research shows that the severity of punishments generally bears little relationship to recidivism outcomes (McGuire 2002). Indeed, severe sentences can even have apparently perverse effects by increasing recidivism, particular for young offenders (Petrosino, Turpin-Petrosino, and Beuhler 2003).

We know virtually nothing about the persistence or otherwise of undetected ICP users. Presumably, a large proportion of novice users do not continue beyond their initial encounters with ICP—either because they find the experience unappealing or aversive or because they fear the possibility of detection. Others will continue beyond the point of their initial encounter, and some will become compulsive users. We would expect occasional or one-off users to be overrepresented in the undetected ICP offender population because they are less exposed to the risk of detection in the first place and because police presumably give priority to those with significant search histories or particularly concerning collections of ICP images. Assuming, then, that a significant proportion of arrested ICP offenders have offended repeatedly before being caught and given their very low official recidivism rates (Seto et al. 2011), it seems that being arrested has a profound effect on persistence. Given the general findings on specific deterrence noted earlier, it may be the arrest itself rather than the severity of their sentence that apparently deters ICP offenders. Again, the apparently normal profile of ICP offenders suggests that they have much to lose by being detected by police. This is underscored by the unusually large number of suicides of ICP suspects that have sometimes been reported following major ICP investigations (Howie 2005; Sherriff 2004).

Treatment and Counseling

Psychological or psychiatric treatment of sexual offenders has become a cornerstone of criminal justice system efforts to prevent recidivism among convicted offenders. The development of these correctional programs has generally followed the so-called risk-needs-responsivity model of offender rehabilitation (Andrews and Bonta 2003). Essentially, the *risk principle* requires that priority be given to the highest risk offenders and that the intensity of programs (usually operationalized as the time spent engaged in program activities) should vary according to assessed risk. That is, high-risk offenders should be allocated to high-intensity programs, medium-risk offenders should be allocated to medium-intensity programs, and so on. The *needs principle* requires that programs target those factors that have been empirically or theoretically associated with recidivism—so-called criminogenic needs. The *responsivity principle* requires programs to be designed to maximize the engagement of offenders, taking account of such individual characteristics as age, intelligence, education, ethnicity, and treatment readiness. Meta-analytic reviews have concluded that cognitive behavioral and pharmacological treatments are the most effective for adult sexual offenders, and cognitive behavioral and multisystemic treatments are most effective for adolescent sexual offenders (Hanson et al. 2002; Losel and Schmucker 2005).

It is not clear whether ICP offenders should be included in standard sexual offender treatment programs, whether they require specially designed programs or whether they require formal treatment at all. There are two main problems related to the risk and needs principles. First, observed average sexual recidivism rates for ICP offenders are very low—less than 5 percent over follow-up periods between 1.5 and 6 years (Seto et al. 2011)—so very few would meet an assessed risk threshold that would warrant inclusion in high- or medium-intensity treatment programs. Such a low recidivism rate raises the question of what purpose treatment would serve. Second, studies of ICP offenders indicate that they possess few discernable psychological problems, and virtually nothing is known about factors associated with recidivism among ICP offenders, so it is also unclear exactly which criminogenic needs treatment programs would target. Both recidivism risk and criminogenic needs are likely to vary, and a small proportion of ICP offenders are therefore likely to present with very significant risk and complex needs. The most sensible approach at this point may be to base decisions about treatment on careful individualized assessments and, where necessary, to provide individually tailored treatment and risk management interventions. Such interventions should address the original motivations for and the psychological and behavioral effects of using ICP.

A more recent development has been the establishment of confidential telephone hotlines targeting adults concerned with their own or others' sexual abuse behavior. The first of note was the Stop It Now! hotline in Vermont. In its first four years (from 1995 to 1999), 657 calls were received. About half of these were from adults who knew either a suspected abuser or a suspected victim, and an additional 99 calls (15%) were from self-identified sexual abusers themselves (Stop It Now! 2006). Two other hotlines have since been established: one operated by Stop It Now! UK and Ireland and one by a group at the Charite Medical University in Berlin, Germany (Prevention Project Dunkelfeld: see Beier et al. 2009). The most recent report on the UK hotline indicates that more than 50 percent of some 12,000 calls received between June 2005 and December 2009 were from adults concerned about their own behavior. In 2009 alone, the hotline received 1,259 calls from persons concerned about their own ICP-related behavior. Most of these callers (85%) were seeking assistance following their arrest, but 162 (15% of callers) had not had any contact with police (Stop It Now! UK and Ireland 2010). The Dunkelfeld project has received calls from approximately 1,500 individuals since its inception in 2005 (K. Beier, pers. comm., Dec. 2011). Of 137 men who attended the project's clinic during 2005 to 2007, 42 (30.6%) disclosed ICP offenses only and 50 (36.5%) disclosed ICP and contact sexual abuse offenses (Neutze et al. 2010).

These UK and German projects have a different scope and very different theoretical approaches but both target undetected or potential ICP offenders and both demonstrate that at least some of these target groups are willing to seek assistance concerning their ICP- and other abuse-related behavior without necessarily having been arrested. These hotlines shift the usually exclusive focus on tertiary-level intervention with ICP offenders to a mix of secondary- and tertiary-level intervention.

Incapacitation

Incapacitation essentially involves the removal of offenders from opportunities to commit further offenses. The ultimate form of incapacitation is execution, but it is hard to conceive that, except perhaps in the most unusual of circumstances, ICP-related offending would attract capital punishment, even in jurisdictions that still allow such practices. A far more popular method of incapacitation is imprisonment, and even here for ICP offenders, retribution and deterrence are probably the more dominant rationales for sentencing judges. As with other kinds of crime, a small proportion of persistent ICP offenders is likely to be responsible for the larger part of the problem. Selective incapacitation of the highest-risk offenders may therefore be justifiable—at least hypothetically. The main problem with operationalizing selective incapacitation is the poor reliability of risk prediction methods, particularly when applied to individual cases. Nevertheless, perhaps as a last resort option, selective incapacitation of persistent ICP offenders may be a necessary component of a broader prevention strategy.

VICTIM-FOCUSED PREVENTION

The problem of ICP begins with its production. While the great majority of offenders may be users who never have direct sexual contact with children, the use of ICP nevertheless relies on its availability. We have noted that ICP is generally originally produced in the context of contact sexual abuse—often involving as perpetrators adults with familial or other close personal or social connections to the victim. As we saw in Chapter 5, while victims are typically further aggrieved by the distribution of their sexual images, the harms associated with their direct sexual abuse can be particularly devastating. Even though some ICP may be produced in originally nonabusive settings, it therefore makes sense for ICP prevention efforts to primarily target sexual abuse itself. In this section, we consider a number of prevention strategies focused at three points along the abuse continuum: preventing abuse before it occurs (i.e., primary and secondary prevention), ending ongoing abuse, and preventing revictimization.

Self-Protection

Personal safety programs aim to prevent sexual abuse by teaching children skills to recognize and avoid risky situations and to physically and verbally resist sexual advances by potential abusers. This approach began to emerge in the 1970s and is now the most prominent primary prevention strategy for sexual abuse. Programs generally target school children from kindergarten to the sixth grade and typically aim to teach participants: definitions of sexual abuse and how to recognize sexually inappropriate behavior; strategies to avoid risky situations and to resist sexual advances of offenders; and to tell a trusted adult if any inappropriate advances have been made or if actual abuse has occurred (Sanderson 2004; Taal and Edelaar 1997).

Reviews have found personal safety programs to be generally effective in teaching sexual abuse concepts and skills to children (MacIntyre and Carr 2000; Rispens et al. 1997). There is also evidence, albeit more limited, that these programs increase disclosure rates (Finkelhor and Dziuba-Leatherman 1995; MacIntyre and Carr 2000). Few studies have tested whether participation results in a lower incidence of actual abuse, and fewer still have reported positive results. The only study to date to have found evidence of reduced victimization was by Gibson and Leitenberg (2000). They surveyed 825 female undergraduates on their prior participation in protective behaviors programs and their self-reported experience of sexual victimization in childhood. Eight percent of program participants said they had been sexually abused, compared with 14 percent who had not participated in a program.

Concerns about the potentially harmful effects of engaging children in these programs have been largely allayed. Some studies have found modest increases in discomfort, anxiety, and wariness about being touched among participants, particularly older children (MacIntyre and Carr 2000; Taal and Edelaar 1997), but others have found little evidence of negative effects (Sarno and Wurtele 1997). Doubts remain about whether children can ever be in a position to negotiate their own safety in the face of complex and often (from the victim's viewpoint) highly ambiguous abuse situations, although some experts argue that children can avoid at least some situations, such as encounters with youthful offenders and with adult offenders who may be tentative in their approach or public encounters where the child may be able to elicit assistance from bystanders (Finkelhor 2010). We are not aware of any programs specifically targeting ICP, but given the increased media attention to the problem in recent years, it would be surprising if this were not now incorporated into at least some programs. Particularly for young adolescents, self-protection programs may present an opportunity to talk through the risks associated with the production of sexual images with peers.

Resilience Building

An alternative or adjunct to self-protection programs are strategies aimed at strengthening victim resilience. This approach involves targeting the characteristics of children and of their family and social circumstances that may increase the risks of sexual victimization. Most estimates indicate that girls are generally at greater risk of contact sexual abuse than boys (Finkelhor and Dzuiba-Leatherman 2001), and this seems to also be the case for ICP victimization (Svedin and Back 2003; von Weiler et al. 2010). For girls and boys, general psychological vulnerabilities (e.g., low self-esteem, emotional neediness) seem to increase risk for contact abuse, as do general difficulties (including neglect and other forms of abuse) in the home. While individual offenders may be attracted to specific physical and psychological features, offenders are generally more likely to target children who are alone, have family problems and lack confidence, and who the offender regards as physically attractive, innocent, curious, trusting, and vulnerable (Conte et al. 1989; Elliot et al. 1995).

Some of these risk factors involve otherwise positive individual (e.g., innocence, curiosity, trustfulness) and interpersonal characteristics (e.g., dependence on and emotional closeness with adults), and it would be sensible to avoid interventions that may diminish these qualities in children. Other risk factors involve unambiguously negative features (e.g., low confidence and self-esteem, excessive emotional neediness, family problems), and it is these factors that would be the most appropriate targets, particularly for secondary-level prevention interventions. Apart from primary guardians, schools, child protection services, and general and mental health services are probably best placed to identify these risk factors and to deliver remedial interventions. Interventions may directly target at-risk children—for example, by providing them with self-esteem programs (Daro and Salmon-Cox 1994)—or operate indirectly by providing services and resources to at-risk families (Larner, Stevenson, and Behrman 1998).

Facilitating Disclosure

A longer duration of sexual abuse is associated with more adverse outcomes for victims (Hebert et al. 2006), and facilitating early detection is therefore an important tertiary-level prevention goal. In one study, just over half of substantiated CSA cases came to light through disclosure by the victim, with the rest through discovery by an adult (Sauzier 1989). However, most victims do not tell others about their abuse. In their review, London, Bruck, Ceci, and Shuman (2005) reported a modal self-disclosure rate of 33 percent. Even when self-disclosure does occur, it is often delayed until after the abuse itself has ceased, thus missing an important prevention opportunity. Ussher and Dewberry (1995) found that only about half of disclosures occur during the victim's childhood, with the mean age at disclosure of 26 years, a delay of some 12 years on average from the time of the abuse.

It can be very difficult for child victims to recognize sexual abuse and then to confide in a trusted adult. The child may also be deterred from reporting because of the loyalty felt to the offender or the shame and embarrassment felt about the sexual abuse. Shame and embarrassment may be exacerbated in cases where the victim is aware that the offender possesses images of the abuse or where they are aware that these images have been distributed on the Internet (Leonard 2010). Svedin and Back (2003) found that many ICP victims remained reluctant to discuss their experience with professionals even after investigations were well advanced. Lawson and Chaffin (1992) found that the disclosure of contact abuse increased with the level of caregiver support. Several studies have found that disclosure rates are lower in cases where the victim is related to the offender (e.g., Hanson et al. 1999; Wyatt and Newcomb 1990), but others have not supported this finding (e.g., Arata 1998; Kellog and Hoffman 1995). Victim age, gender, ethnicity, and abuse severity do not seem systematically related to the likelihood of disclosure (London et al. 2005).

While a supportive family environment appears to facilitate disclosure, a supportive response following disclosure is also associated with more positive adjustment (Arata 1998; Harvey, Orbuch, Chwalisz, and Garwood 1991; Testa, Miller, Downs, and Paneck 1992). In fact, victims who receive a nonsupportive response can fare worse than those who do not disclose in the first place (Everill and Waller 1994). Heriot (1996) found that in around a quarter of substantiated familial sexual abuse cases, the child's mother did not believe the accusation. Almost a third of mothers failed to take action to protect the child, and roughly the same number withdrew maternal support from the child.

As we noted earlier, teaching children to disclose through self-protection programs has a positive but limited effect. The strongest predictor of disclosure is a supportive family environment, and this suggests the need to invest in family-level interventions to create environments in which children feel confident to talk about sensitive issues.

Reporting to Authorities

Victimization surveys indicate that only between 3 percent and 15 percent of sexual abuse cases are reported to authorities (Finkelhor and Dziuba-Leatherman 1994; Kilpatrick and Saunders 1999). Even when nonoffending parents become aware of the abuse, many are reluctant to involve outside authorities. For example, Finkelhor (1984) found that only 42 percent of sexual abuse cases known to nonoffending parents were reported to police. Surveys of legal and mental health professionals—those who are perhaps most familiar with how such reports are actually handled—also suggest a widespread reluctance to initiate formal investigations (Besharov 1994; Eastwood 2003; Pence and Wilson 1994). In an effort to increase reporting rates, many jurisdictions have introduced mandatory reporting laws. In some jurisdictions, these laws apply only to certain professionals (e.g., doctors and teachers), while in others, all citizens are legally obliged to report suspected sexual abuse (Higgins, Bromfield, and Richardson 2007; Pence and Wilson 1994). Mandatory reporting generally results in an immediate and substantial increase in official notifications (Besharov 1994). However, much of this increase is accounted for by an increase in unsubstantiated cases, thus putting further pressure on already heavily burdened child protection services with sometimes marginal gains.

Even when additional substantiated cases are identified, mandatory reporting does not necessarily improve outcomes for the children concerned. However, along with efforts to increase reporting rates, many police and child protection agencies have introduced improved practices for dealing with victims and their families. Berliner and Conte (1995) found that while children experienced the reporting process as daunting and humiliating, they mostly felt that they were being treated with respect and accepted the process as a necessary and ultimately helpful one. Victims have more positive views on reporting if interviews are handled sensitively, if they are not required to give multiple interviews, and if they develop a trusting relationship with the investigating professional (Eastwood, Patton, and Stacy 2000; Henry 1997).

Prosecution

We noted in Chapter 5 that the existence of ICP images can sometimes provide forensic evidence that is otherwise rarely available in investigations of contact sexual abuse. Nevertheless successful prosecutions will still rely to a significant extent on obtaining reliable and accurate accounts from victims. A number of forensic interviewing techniques have been suggested for abuse cases. For example, structured interviewing protocols using open-ended questions have been found to elicit more accurate responses than unstructured methods and the use of closed or focused questions (Memon and Vartoukian 1996; Sternberg et al. 2001). However, in practice, forensic interviews do not always adhere to best-practice principles, with many interviewers continuing to rely on techniques that may contaminate the accuracy of responses (Hershkowitz, Lamb, Sternberg, and Esplin 1997).

In many cases, successful prosecutions also rely on the testimony of victims. Testifying in court is potentially very stressful for victims, who may be required to come face-to-face with the accused and to endure vigorous cross-examination. Many jurisdictions have now introduced reforms to courtroom practices to protect victims from further distress. These include reducing waiting times to go to trial, allowing victims to testify remotely via closed circuit television, allowing the use of prerecorded testimony, and imposing limits on the cross-examination process (Eastwood 2003; Myers 1994; Sas, Wolfe, and Gowdey 1996). These modifications may not always be utilized even if they are technically available, and there is undoubtedly room for further improvements in this regard. Some studies have shown that many victims and their parents still regret their decision to take the matter to court (Eastwood 2003), but others indicate that, albeit in difficult circumstances, victims often appreciate the opportunity to testify in court (Berliner and Conte 1995).

Preventing Revictimization

Among the more concerning long-term outcomes for sexual abuse victims, particularly female victims, is a significantly increased risk to be sexually victimized again—often later in life and in circumstances apparently unrelated to the original abuse. Estimates of sexual revictimization rates range from 15 percent to as high as 72 percent (Roodman and Clum 2001; Van Bruggen, Runtz, and Kadlec 2006). In one study, women who had experienced sexual abuse as a child were twice as likely as women who had not been sexual abused to be raped, even when controlling for the presence of other kinds of childhood maltreatment (Messman-Moore and Brown 2004). Risk factors for sexual revictimization seem to be much the same as for other negative outcomes of sexual abuse (e.g., duration, severity, and familial context of the original abuse) (Van Bruggen et al. 2006). It is not known whether ICP victimization has any specific association with revictimization, but because ICP abuse typically involves contact abuse, we would expect there to be similar risks.

Along with the increased attention to sexual abuse in recent years has come an increase in the availability of professional services for victims, although there have been some observations that even within these specialist victim services, expertise in understanding and responding to the newer problem of ICP victimization may still be lacking (von Weiler et al. 2010). Most interventions with sexual abuse victims aim to assist victims and their families with dealing with the immediate impact of the abuse and to reduce negative long-term impacts. However, despite the widespread recognition of the problem of revictimization, there has been surprisingly little published research on the effects of victim services in reducing revictimization. Nevertheless while victim interventions may be driven largely by a therapeutic concern with ameliorating harm, there are clear overlaps between this objective and revictimization prevention. Victim services provide an important opportunity to address some of the personal and environmental factors that may have caused the initial abuse and which, if left unaddressed, may also facilitate revictimization. In addition, in addressing the negative consequences of the original abuse, victim services may also be addressing some of the risks of revictimization. Treating such issues as feelings of powerlessness, diminished self-esteem, self-blame, sexualized behavior, stigmatization, and social isolation—all of which may follow the experience of sexual abuse—is likely to have harm minimization and prevention benefits. Improvements may nevertheless be achieved by more directly targeting risks for revictimization and by including revictimization outcomes as a critical component of program evaluations.

CONCLUSION

In this chapter, we examined potential prevention strategies targeting offenders (or potential offenders) and victims (or potential victims). Different prevention strategies are required for different kinds of ICP offenders and for different stages in individual offender trajectories. Developmental crime prevention approaches may produce modest reductions in those kinds of ICP offending that involve general criminality, dispositions to violence, disturbed sexuality, or other development-related problems, but the general profile of ICP offenders indicates that these are not common features. Indeed, the absence of general criminality and other disturbances in much of this population suggests that they may be particularly responsive to general and specific deterrence strategies. There are wide variations in offender characteristics and behavior, and investigations should give priority to cases where contact sexual abuse may be involved, where the offender may be involved in the production or distribution of ICP, and where particularly concerning images are found. Few ICP offenders would meet assessed risk thresholds to be prioritized for standard treatment programs, although treatment may be effective for those who do present with high risk and complex needs. Even though most ICP offenders apparently do not reoffend, a serious risk potential nevertheless exists within this population. Therefore, careful individualized assessments are needed to make informed judgments about whether and what kinds of treatment or risk management may be required.

Because ICP is usually produced in the context of contact sexual abuse, victim-focused strategies should primarily target sexual abuse itself. Although we have some reservations about personal safety programs, especially for young children, there is no reason why ICP-related topics could not be incorporated into such programs. Strategies aimed at strengthening resilience in children may be an effective alternative or adjunct to these programs, particularly for already-vulnerable children. Once ICP abuse has occurred, it is important that every opportunity is made available for early and safe disclosure. Police and child protection authorities and the courts have special responsibilities to ensure that the outcomes of disclosure, reporting, and prosecution are positive for victims. Finally, high-quality counseling and support services should be made available to victims, and these services should explicitly target the prevention of further victimization.

No one strategy is likely to be sufficient. Nor will a suite of strategies focused only on offenders and victims be sufficient. Rather, a comprehensive and multifaceted prevention strategy is required. In the next chapter, we examine a range of additional strategies focused on the situational aspects of the problem—namely, the Internet and related technologies.

7

Prevention: The Internet and Related Technologies

IN THIS CHAPTER, we shift our attention from prevention efforts targeting offenders and victims to efforts directed at changing those aspects of the Internet that facilitate ICP offending. Borrowing the language of economics, we move from examining attempts to reduce the demand for ICP to attempts to reduce the supply of ICP. The rationale for this shift in focus is the principle that all behavior occurs as a result of the interaction between personal characteristics of the actor and the situational characteristics of the setting in which the action takes place. If ICP offending is a product of the offender and the Internet, then prevention of ICP requires attention to be paid to both sides of the equation. We examine Internet focused interventions from the perspective of situational crime prevention. Applied to the problem of ICP, the situational prevention approach requires strategies that make it more difficult for offenders to access images on the Internet ("increasing the effort"); make it more likely that their online behavior will be detected ("increasing the risks"); frustrate attempts by offenders to derive benefits from ICP ("reducing rewards"); allow offenders fewer opportunities to minimize the seriousness of ICP ("removing excuses"); and remove situational factors that might trigger the impulse to view ICP ("reduce provocations").

THE PERSON-SITUATION INTERACTION REVISITED

We introduced the person-situation interaction in Chapter 1 when we set out the general rationale for the approach adopted in this book. While the idea of the person-situation interaction sounds straightforward enough, the full implications of the concept are often surprisingly difficult for people to accept. Interpreting the causes of behavior in terms of individual dispositions comes naturally to humans. We typically downplay the role that situational factors play in behavior in favor of explanations based around internal factors, such as the actor's attitudes, personality, and psychological disorder. Psychologists have a term for this phenomenon: fundamental attribution error (Jones 1979; Ross 1977). It seems that we are hard-wired to interpret our social world from the perspective of actors. We like to reduce the behavior of others to a few salient traits—someone is confident, friendly, cheerful, and so on. These traits are then assumed to cause their behavior more or less independently of the situational context. It is thought that the tendency to reduce complex behavior to a few dispositional categories has evolved as an efficient information processing strategy to help people make sense of their social world. However, fundamental attribution error can fool us into thinking that behavior is more stable than it really is and can make it difficult for us to accept that situational factors play anything other than a trivial role in behavior.

A moment's thought should reveal just how important situations are in behavior. We behave differently depending on where we are and who we are with. We might be confident when we are talking to friends but lack confidence when talking to someone in authority. At times, we are also capable of doing things that are out of character and of which we feel ashamed. When this happens, we tell ourselves that our behavior was a product of the particular circumstances. If we become aggressive, it is because we have had a bad day, someone has provoked us, we have had too much to drink, or we are feeling frustrated. Perhaps not surprisingly, fundamental attribution error only applies when we interpret the behavior of others, not ourselves. When someone else gets aggressive, it is because he or she is an aggressive person.

To see how the person-situation interaction might apply to behavior on the Internet, consider the inventive study carried out by Demetriou and Silke (2003). They established a website that offered legal shareware, and people were directed to the website if they searched for "shareware," "freeware," "free," "free games," and "free software." However, once visitors arrived at the site, in addition to legal shareware, they were offered purported links (that did not work) to illegal and obscene sites, offering commercial games, commercial software, hardcore pornography, and stolen passwords. The hardcore pornography link was by far the most popular of all the links, clicked by 483 visitors, while the softcore pornography link, with 358 clicks, was the second-most popular. Tracking the keywords used to arrive at the site, Demetriou and Silke found that of 803 visitors, only 26 were looking for pornography. Legal shareware—the reason the vast majority of people went to the site in the first place—was the least popular link, with only 268 clicks. Most people did not visit the website with the formed intention of viewing hardcore pornography, but they responded to the opportunity when it was offered.

Demetriou and Silke interpreted their findings in terms of the psychological construct of deindividuation. As we saw in Chapter 5, deindividuation is the reduced capacity of individuals to self-regulate their behavior under conditions of anonymity and heightened arousal. Disinhibition is produced not just by a perceived freedom from the censure of others but, more fundamentally, by freedom from self-censure. In a deindividuated state, we lose sense of our own standards of behavior and can do things that we would ordinarily never consider doing. In the Demetriou and Silke study, the majority of visitors to the site—freed from the personal and social controls that might otherwise have inhibited them from viewing hardcore pornography—chose to satisfy their sexual curiosities. While clearly ethically problematic, it is intriguing to ponder what Demetriou and Silke might have found if they had included a purported link to a child pornography site on the shareware site.

As we have outlined in earlier chapters, it is not our contention that ICP offenders are hapless victims of circumstance. Undoubtedly many ICP offenders have a preferential sexual attraction to children and actively seek out ICP images. Nevertheless, even the behavior of highly motivated individuals is limited by the situational context. Internet-focused interventions make sense when we understand the dynamic relationship between individuals and their immediate environment. If we see ICP offending solely in terms of the aberrant sexual motivations of offenders, then we are likely to regard any attempts to reduce the opportunities for offenders to access ICP images as largely futile—we will believe that offenders will always find a way to offend no matter what we do. This sort of pessimistic view is all too common in the ICP literature. On the other hand, if ICP offending is seen to be the product of the person-situation interaction, then we will understand that reducing the opportunities for ICP can significantly slow down prolific offenders and may completely deter those less determined offenders.

SITUATIONAL PREVENTION OF ICP

The best-known model for organizing supply-side prevention strategies is Clarke's (1997; 2008) situational crime prevention (SCP). SCP is a criminological model that is more usually applied in physical environments to reduce such crimes as burglary, vandalism, and sexual assault but that has been increasingly used to explain illegal activity on the Internet (Newman and Clarke 2003; Taylor and Quayle 2006). Clarke viewed offender behavior in terms of the rational choice perspective (Cornish and Clarke 1986, 2008; see also Chapter 3). According to Clarke, offenders make a judgment about whether to commit crime based on their perception of the costs and benefits that criminal behavior will deliver. These judgments are made utilizing situational cues provided at the crime scene. SCP involves altering those aspects of the immediate environment that facilitate the occurrence of crime, and this is achieved by increasing the perceived costs of offending and reducing the perceived benefits. In SCP, it is the crime event rather than the offender that is the object of analysis. By carefully analyzing the situational characteristics of the crime event, the prevention practitioner is in a position to develop environmental counterstrategies. As far as the offender is concerned, SCP is only interested in his thoughts and behaviors at the time of the offense; little consideration is given to developmental factors in the offender's life that might have caused his criminal motivations. The object of situation interventions is to inhibit unwanted behavior in specific contexts, not to cure individuals.

There is an accumulating body of evidence showing that situational interventions can be highly successful in reducing specific crimes in specific contexts

(Clarke 1997; Welsh and Farrington 2000). Moreover, it has been consistently found for a wide variety of crimes that situational interventions do not just move crime to different locations or targets (a process known as displacement) but result in a net reduction of crime (Bowers et al. 2011; Guerette and Bowers 2009). Clarke has outlined five broad strategies for implementing situational interventions: increasing the effort of offending; increasing the risks of offending; reducing the rewards from offending; removing excuses for offending; and reducing provocations to offend. As we go through and apply each of these strategies to the problem of ICP in the following sections, it will also become clear that there are a variety of groups that have a role to play in the prevention of ICP. Law enforcement agencies, the Internet industry (ISPs, domain name registrars, and web-hosting companies), nongovernment organizations, workplace managers, the business community (credit card companies, banks, and advertisers), parents, legislators, and even offenders themselves can contribute to the prevention of ICP. A summary of prevention strategies and the groups that have a role in implementing them are shown in Table 7.1.

Increasing the Effort

All things being equal, offenders will select crimes that are easy to commit, and they may impulsively commit crimes just because they require so little effort. At a trivial level, we can observe the effect of effort on our own behavior when we decide we cannot be bothered to get up from the couch to make ourselves a cup of coffee. However, effort plays a significant role in even deeply motivated behavior. Consider the classic study by Clarke and Mayhew (1988) on suicide patterns in Britain. They discovered that when nontoxic natural gas replaced toxic coal gas for domestic use, there was a dramatic reduction in the number of suicides, roughly equal to the number of individuals who ordinarily would have committed suicide by gassing themselves. Gassing is a relatively convenient and easy method of suicide, requiring little in the way of skill or planning, and was (before the conversion to natural gas) the most popular method of suicide in Britain. It seems that many potential suicide victims who might have selected gassing as their method of choice abandoned their suicide attempt when that option was denied rather than seek out other less convenient methods.

Increasing effort is the rationale for crime prevention strategies that make it more difficult for offenders to commit crime. The best-known strategy is target-hardening, in which potential crime targets are protected by barriers, locks, or toughened materials. For example, Webb (1997) found that the introduction of steering locks for cars in Germany, Britain, and the United States resulted in immediate and long-term reductions in car theft. In the context of Internet child pornography, increasing the effort involves making it more difficult for offenders to access child pornography images. Note that increasing effort does not mean making it *impossible* for offenders to access ICP; simply making access to ICP more difficult has the potential to significantly reduce the volume of ICP offending.

Table 7.1 Summary of Situational Prevention Strategies for ICP

	Increase Effort	Increase Risks	Reduce Rewards	Remove Excuses	Reduce Provocations
Police	NTD orders	Stings		Stop messages	Targeting embedded ICP
Internet Industry	Removing ICP Filters Deregistration of ICP domains	Identity verification		Service agreements	
Business	Blocking online payments for ICP		Blocking online payments for ICP Advertising boycotts		
Workplaces	Filters	Audits of Internet use		Codes of conduct	
NGOs	Hotlines				
Parents	Filters	House rules			
Offenders		e-Safety software House rules			Relapse prevention
Legislators	Mandating/ reporting/ filtering of ICP	Regulating remailers Key escrowed encryption			

Removing ICP

As we discussed in Chapter 4, one goal of law enforcement is to reduce the amount of child pornography on the Internet, and this might involve police agencies issuing a notice and takedown (NTD) order to relevant ISPs and other web-hosting companies in their jurisdiction. The police are aided in this task by information from ICP hotlines run by such nongovernment organizations as the Internet Watch Foundation (IWF) and the CyberTipline. In addition, ISPs may independently take down ICP of which they become aware—either because of legal obligations or because they have voluntarily subscribed to an industry code of practice. While not legally obliged to do so, ISPs may have active "cyber patrols" involving automated software that searches for illegal sites.

Arguably, there has been considerable success in reducing the volume of child pornography in open areas of the Internet, such as the World Wide Web. Calder (2004) estimated that ISPs removed more than 20,000 ICP images between 1996–2004. More recently, the Internet Watch Foundation (2010) reported that they took action against nearly 17,000 ICP URLs in 2010 and that it has on average 500 URLs on its ICP blacklist at any one time. It also reported a significant increase in the speed with which illegal URLs were taken down. Where in previous years it may have taken months or even years for a site to be removed, this period has been typically reduced to weeks or days. Eighty-one percent of sites are taken down within 100 days (Internet Watch Foundation 2008). There was a particular improvement in the cooperation of international agencies in acting on information from the IWF.

Just the same, removing all child pornography from the Internet is an enormous and, frankly, impossible task. Distributors of ICP have responded with counterstrategies, such as splitting collections into many small collections that are then hosted on a temporary basis across numerous sites (Internet Watch Foundation 2010). There is also no guarantee that taken-down images will not reappear on a new site. Furthermore, active policing of the web has had the consequence of driving dedicated offenders to deeper levels of the Internet, where they trade images in specific child pornography chat rooms and newsgroups. While commercial servers may block access to such sites, they are much more difficult to regulate.

In SCP terms, these counterstrategies are examples of offender adaptation. Offender adaptation is to be expected and should not discourage efforts to reduce access to ICP. The principle of increasing effort is to keep forcing offenders to adopt new, nonpreferred strategies. Each forced switch of tactic involves a cost to offenders. The more hidden ICP becomes, the more difficult it is for the offenders themselves to access. Offenders require the knowledge of where to locate child pornography sites and the technical skill to access them. Many child pornography chat rooms and newsgroups are secured sites; that is, a password is required in order to gain access to them. Passwords, in turn, can be difficult to obtain. Because of the risk that these sites will be infiltrated by undercover police, potential users are carefully vetted before being allowed to join. Thus, the movement of child pornography activity to these hidden areas of the Internet has significantly increased the effort offenders must expend in order to locate ICP images.

Filtering ICP

There are numerous methods of filtering Internet content and various levels of the Internet at which the filter may be applied. In the case of the NTDs discussed in the previous section, if it is not possible to take down offending sites (because the server is outside of the police agency's jurisdiction and local police will not take action), in some countries, ISPs can apply a filter that stops the designated URLs from being accessed by its customers. Typically, where ISP filtering occurs, blacklisted URLs are compiled manually based on reports from police agencies, nongovernment organizations concerned with ICP, and ICP hotlines. All sites are visually checked by police to verify that they contain illegal images.

However, manually compiled blacklists are time consuming to construct and by their nature always based on historical data (Lee and Luh 2008). Alternatively, it is possible for filtering algorithms to block access to sites automatically on the basis of a range of other specified rules. For example, filters may block the use of certain search terms. They may also examine incoming data and block access to sites that contain flagged keywords or images. In these cases, it is not necessary to know the particular URL or to visually check site content; the filter is applied to types of sites determined by the algorithm. However, using these filtering methods, there is the potential for innocuous sites to be erroneously blocked (known as "false positive error") as well as for offending sites to slip through the filter (known as "false negative error").

Filters can be applied either at the server level or the client level. Apart from filtering associated with police blacklists, some ISPs offer content-limited services that filter "inappropriate" material. These ISPs are often selected by parents to help control their children's Internet use. Filters can also be used on servers within LANs in specific locations, such as schools, libraries, and workplaces. For example, it is not uncommon for organizations to restrict the types of sites employees may access on their work computers. Client-level filters are installed on home computers and have been found to significantly reduce exposure to unwanted sexual material (Ybarra et al. 2009). They are password protected and govern URLs that can be accessed from that computer. The major search engines (e.g., Google) also allow home users to block the use of certain search terms.

Whether ISPs should be legally required to filter ICP is controversial (Maurushat and Watt 2009; Sandy 2009; Stol et al. 2009). Those opposed to mandatory filtering argue that it is an infringement on the right to freedom of speech, arguing that there will inevitably be a process of net widening, whereby an increasing number of non-ICP sites will be deliberately or inadvertently blocked. Doubt has also been raised about the effectiveness of filters in blocking access to ICP sites. Certainly, filters are not foolproof, and blocks placed on sites can be thwarted by determined and savvy offenders. However, as with other strategies designed to increase the effort expended by offenders, the goal of filtering is to make the access of ICP more difficult by disrupting criminal activities.

Deregistration of ICP Domains

All websites—even illegal ones—require domain registration. You will recall from Chapter 2 that it is the registration of domain names that allows DNS servers to locate the desired information on the Internet. The process for registering domain names is devolved to accredited domain registrars. Different countries have their own accreditation system, but the process is coordinated internationally by the Internet Corporation for Assigned Names and Numbers (ICANN). Research by the Internet Watch Foundation (2008) revealed that 10 domain registrars accounted for 76 percent of all commercial ICP domains. Working with registrars and registries, the IWF is exploring strategies to deregister the domain names used by commercial producers of ICP. Deregistration of the domain name would prevent access to the relevant website even if server hosting arrangements were changed.

Increasing the Risks

The risk of detection is perhaps the most salient consideration in the decision to offend, and situations can provide important cues to potential offenders on the likelihood of getting away with criminal acts. Crime rates can escalate dramatically when the chances of detection and punishment are reduced, such as during police strikes (Nagin 1978), riots (Rosenfeld 1997), blackouts (Muhlin, Cohen, Struening et al. 1981), and natural disasters (LeBeau 2002; Teh 2008). On the other hand, potential crime sites that are well guarded or under surveillance are less likely to be subject to crime than are sites that are not. The installation of closed-circuit TV cameras can reduce crime is car parks (Poyner 1991), town centers (Brown 1996), and buses (Poyner 1988); improved street lighting can reduce theft, vandalism, and vehicle crime by up to 45 percent (Painter and Farrington 1999); the use of radar to detect speeding can result in crash reductions of up to 30 percent (Cameron and Delaney 2008; Mountain, Hirst and Maher 2005; Novoa, Pérez, Sanatamariña-Rubio et al. 2010); and random breath testing can reduce car accidents by 17 percent (Erke, Goldenbeld and Vas 2009).

As we have discussed, a driving factor in ICP offending is the perception of anonymity on the Internet and the belief that it is a risk-free environment in which to offend. In this section, we discuss strategies designed to increase the real and the perceived risks associated with ICP offending.

Stings

We discussed sting operations in Chapter 4 in the context of the investigation of ICP. There are two basic types of ICP sting. In one approach, law enforcement officers operate undercover in chat rooms, newsgroups, and P2P networks, infiltrating offender networks and interacting directing with individual offenders in an attempt to gather incriminating evidence on them. In the other approach, websites purporting to contain ICP are established and the details captured of the individuals who visit the site. In fact, both of these strategies result in few arrests relative to the hundreds of thousands of individuals estimated to be involved in ICP. Police and offenders know that the sheer volume of traffic in ICP makes the task of prosecuting all offenders impossible and that, in truth, the chances of an ICP offender being arrested are very small. However, risk and perceived risk are two different things. The chief purpose of sting operations is not so much to catch offenders as it is to create the *perception* that the Internet is an unsafe environment in which to access child pornography images. Far from keeping sting operations secret in order to maximize the number of offenders they may catch, many police departments have learned to use the media to good effect to publicize their ICP stings in advance in order to maximize the general deterrent effect (BBC 2001; BBC 2002; BBC 2003). The goal of publicizing stings is to create uncertainty in the mind of a potential ICP offender each time he contemplates downloading an ICP image from a website or trading images with someone he has contacted online.

Identity Verification

We have noted that the perception of anonymity is a key driver of misbehavior on the Internet. Anonymity is accentuated in real terms by the lack of effective verification of the identity of those who use the Internet. Identity verification is a problem with the distributors and users of ICP. In terms of distribution, one area of concern is the registration of domain names. While ICANN requires domain name registrars to provide certain personal information on registrants (e.g., name and address), there is no requirement at present that domain name registrars verify those details. Hence, it is quite possible to register a domain name by using an alias, making it almost impossible to trace who posted the illegal content on the Internet (House Standing Committee on Communications 2009).

There is a similar lack of regulation requiring ISPs to verify the identities of people who open Internet accounts. Currently, in most jurisdictions, accounts may be opened by using false names and addresses, and this makes it difficult to trace individuals who engage in illegal Internet activity. In addition, without verifying users' ages, there is no way of knowing if children are operating Internet accounts without adult supervision. This problem of Internet anonymity has increased because accessing the Internet via mobile phones has become commonplace, and ISPs and mobile phone networks need to strengthen procedures for user verification (Carr 2004).

Auditing Workplace Internet Use

The traffic through most work-based servers is less than that for commercial ISPs, making auditing by the system administrator of employee Internet use more feasible. Because companies own the LAN, they also have a legal right to control the sites that employees access. Work computers have been implicated in a number of child pornography cases (Ferraro and Casey 2005).

Regulating "Crime Facilitators"

In situational crime prevention, crime facilitators are tools that offenders use to help them commit their crimes. Guns used in robberies and aerosol paint cans used for graffiti are crime facilitators. Controlling access to facilitators (e.g., tighter gun laws, bans on the sale of aerosol paint cans to juveniles) can make it more difficult for offenders to carry out their crimes. In the case of ICP, some facilitators are used by offenders to help them avoid detection. Two ICP facilitators we have discussed are anonymous remailers and encryption software. Remailers are servers that forward e-mails after stripping them of sender identification; encryption allows people to store files in ways so they cannot be accessed without a key. Looking at data from 2001, Wolak et al. (2005b) found that roughly 3 percent of offenders encrypted their ICP files and 1 percent used anonymous remailers. While these figures are small, those who use these strategies are likely to be among the most serious offenders, and law enforcement agencies have complained about the frustration that these technologies pose for them. It has been argued that much tighter regulation of remailers and encryption software is necessary. In the case of remailers, some have advocated making remailer administrators legally responsible for knowingly forwarding illegal material, while others have called for a complete ban on remailers (Mostyn 2000). In the case of encryption, there have been calls for the introduction of key escrow. Key escrowed encryption would require anyone selling encryption software to supply a trusted third party with a key to the code (Graham 2000). Both proposals are controversial and are strongly resisted by the computer industry and those who are opposed to Internet regulation on privacy and freedom of speech grounds.

Monitoring Known Offenders

Situational crime prevention is usually conceptualized as primary prevention—that is, as involving strategies that reduce opportunities for offending on a population-wide basis to stop crime before it occurs. However, situational prevention strategies can also be applied at a tertiary level with known offenders in order to stop them from reoffending. Elliott et al (2010) describe a UK program that uses e-Safety software to monitor Internet use by convicted sex offenders. e-Safety software is installed on the participant's home computer. The software monitors the use of prohibited words or phrases drawn from a customized library stored on a centralized secure server. If any blacklisted terms are used by the offender, a snapshot is taken of the screen and other evidentiary information, such as date and time, is recorded and transmitted to the secure server. In a six-month pilot study, the Internet use of 11 volunteer offenders was monitored. No major violations occurred during the study period. From the participants' perspective, knowing that their Internet behavior was closely monitored was like having the sword of Damocles hanging over them. However, feedback from participants indicated that they generally welcomed the opportunity to take part in the program, believing that it helped them control their behavior and that it also allowed them to prove to others that they were not offending. A full program is now in operation. It takes in volunteers who want assistance managing their offending behavior and offenders who have received a court-mandated Sexual Offender Prevention Order requiring them to have the e-Safety software installed. The program offers courts the option of allowing offenders to continue using their computers for legitimate purposes rather than banning their use of a computer outright. Of the first 18 participants, two were found to have accessed ICP during the surveillance period (Elliott and Findlater 2010).

House Rules

Situational strategies can be applied not just to the Internet but also to the physical and social environment in which the Internet is accessed. House rules may be set to govern computer use within the home. The rules may be particularly relevant to children but, in some cases, may also be useful to help manage inappropriate Internet behavior by adults. This may involve secondary prevention, where an at-risk individual seeks assistance to manage pedophilic urges, or as tertiary prevention as part of a postrelease management plan for offenders. Rules are designed to increase the level of surveillance over computer use. For example, rules may specify time periods in which the computer may be used or require that the computer is installed in a public area of the house (Dombroski et al. 2007; Young 2008). However, as Young (2008) notes, such rules will be increasingly difficult to enforce as smartphones and other wireless devices become standard.

Reducing Rewards

According to the situational crime prevention model, offenders are motivated to commit crimes because they are seeking to benefit themselves in some way. Reducing the perceived rewards of offending requires the implementation of strategies that deny offenders the rewards they are seeking. We see many examples of this strategy applied to everyday crime. Some strategies attempt to reduce rewards directly at the point of offending. For example, many shops display signs announcing "No Cash (or Drugs) Held on Premises" in order to reduce the motivation for burglaries and robberies from those premises (Hunter and Jeffery 1992). Similarly, prepaid phone cards have reduced vandalism of public phones because there is less cash in the money box to steal (Bridgeman 1997). Other strategies to reduce rewards seek to disrupt the markets that support illegal activity more broadly. For example, metal thieves need to find a compliant scrap metal dealer who will purchase their stolen metal. Clamping down on illegal scrap metal dealers can have the effect of suppressing the value of stolen metal and thus reducing the motivation for metal theft (Sidebottom et al. 2011).

In the case of ICP, there are two basic motivations for offending: sexual gratification and money. For the offender sitting at his computer and downloading ICP, the reward is sexual gratification. Reducing rewards for these offenders involves reducing their access to ICP. We have already examined earlier in this chapter some strategies for reducing access to ICP under the heading of increasing the effort. For commercial producers and distributors of ICP, the rewards are largely monetary. In this section, we examine ways of disrupting the economics of the ICP business by reducing the financial rewards to producers and distributors, which in turn will make it more difficult for end users to purchase images.

Blocking Online Payments

In many cases, child pornography has to be purchased by the user. Payment for ICP may involve credit cards, prepaid cards, or other e-payment systems (Internet Watch Foundation 2010). Launched in 2006, the Financial Coalition Against Child Pornography (FCACP) is a grouping of 35 ISPs, credit card companies, banks, and other companies providing online payment services. Prominent members of FCACP include American Express, Bank of America, MasterCard, and PayPal. The goal of FCACP is to undermine the commercial viability of ICP. This is achieved by tracking the flow of money in ICP transactions and blocking payments for illegal downloads. Companies may use keywords and web crawlers to proactively identify suspected illegal transactions (Financial Coalition Against Child Pornography 2008).

Trends in the purchase of commercial ICP published by the FCACP (2011) suggest that denying ICP offenders access to legitimate financial services is having an effect. ICP websites have had to adopt new and convoluted strategies to obtain payments. For example, when the attempt to use a credit card fails, purchasers may be directed to send an e-mail to a specified address in order to receive instructions for using alternative non–credit card payment methods (e.g., mailing cash). Still other sites refuse to accept U.S. credit cards altogether. Incidentally, these strategies also have the effect of increasing the effort for the offender. It is claimed that since the operation of the FCACP, there has been a 50 percent drop in the number of commercial ICP sites reported to the CyberTipline. There has also been a dramatic increase in the cost of commercial ICP. Monthly subscriptions have risen from about $30 per month in 2006 to as much as $1,200 per month. FCACP interprets this rise as evidence that the costs of business have risen sharply as a result of the financial squeeze that has been applied.

Advertising Boycotts

There are two competing commercial forces acting on the Internet industry with respect to hosting ICP. On the one hand, if an Internet company actively screens for child pornography on its server, it may lose out financially to other companies that do not. Therefore, it will always be possible for offenders to find a company that will store or provide access to child pornography sites. On the other hand, Internet companies also have their commercial reputation to protect, and it is often in their best interests to cooperate with law enforcement agencies. Most major ISPs have shown a commitment to tackling the problem of child pornography, partly motivated by the desire to protect the reputation of their brand name. In some cases, direct economic pressure may be applied to companies to encourage them to monitor illegal content. In one example of applying pressure to the Internet industry, major brands withdrew advertising from P2P networks that carried ICP (Adegoke 2003).

Removing Excuses

We have a stereotype of offenders as holding deviant attitudes and as positively valuing the crimes they commit. However, there is considerable research evidence to show that many offenders know only too well that their behavior is morally wrong and that they experience shame and guilt for their actions. In order to resolve the dissonance between their behavior and their values, offenders may attempt to minimize their criminality by invoking various excuses to free themselves from the inhibitory effects of self-blame (Bandura 1976; Sykes and Matza 1957). They may minimize the validity of the rule ("I didn't know it was wrong"), their personal responsibility for the behavior ("I couldn't help myself"), the negative consequences of the behavior ("I didn't hurt anyone"), and the worth of the victim ("They deserved it"). To counter excuse-making of this sort, situational strategies seek to reinforce the illegitimacy of the contemplated behavior. For example, the presence of formal codes of conduct can reduce company thefts (Parilla et al. 1988), bullying in schools (Elliot 1991), and workplace aggression (Randall 1997).

Like other offenders, many child sexual offenders experience a tension between their behavior and their moral standards. For example, it has been found that up to a quarter of callers to child sexual abuse hotlines are from men expressing concern about their own sexual feelings toward children (Chasan-Taylor and Tabachnick 1999). It is also noteworthy that in the aftermath of Operation Ore, which saw the arrest of 1,300 suspected ICP offenders in Britain (see Table 4.3), there were more than 30 suicides among suspects (Howie 2005; Sherriff 2004). Many ICP offenders may find solace in the belief that viewing child pornography does no harm (e.g., "They are just images, not real people") (Burke et al. 2002; Quayle and Taylor 2003) and even that it is not illegal (McCabe 2000).

Service Agreements and Codes of Conduct

One way to clarify expected standards of behavior is to require individuals to explicitly agree to a code of conduct that sets out a list of unacceptable behaviors.

There are a number of opportunities where this can occur on the Internet. When customers sign up for Internet access, their ISPs may include requirements that they do not access illegal websites containing ICP. Likewise, web-hosting companies can make it clear that they will not accept ICP content on their servers. Finally, organizations that provide access to the Internet at work can require employees to sign workplace codes of conduct that prohibit them from using work computers or accounts for ICP.

Warning Messages

We discussed in Chapter 4 the filtering of illegal websites, and in the current chapter, we picked up on ICP filtering as a strategy to increase the effort of offending. There is an additional element to ICP filtering as it is implemented in some countries that relates to removing excuses for offending. A feature of the Child Sexual Abuse Anti-Distribution Filter (CSAADF) implemented in Europe by the Cospol Internet Related Child Abusive Material Project (CIRCAMP) is the potential to insert a "stop page"—rather than the usual 500-code server-error message (e.g., a "503 Service Unavailable")—once access to the requested website is denied. The stop page used in Norway (where the CSAADF originated) reads as follows:

Stop!

Your Internet browser is trying to contact an Internet site that is used in connection with the distribution of photos depicting sexual abuse of children, which is a criminal offence in accordance with the Norwegian Penal Code section §204a (previously known as child pornography).

If you have any objections to these pages being blocked from access, or you believe that the blocking is incorrect, please contact the National Criminal Investigation Service Norway at +47 23 20 80 00, or send us an email.

No information about your IP address or any other information that can be used to identify you will be stored when this page is displayed. The purpose of blocking access to these pages is only to prevent the commission of criminal dissemination of documented sexual abuse, and to prevent the further exploitation of children who have already been abused and photographed.

If you have want more information, or if you wish to forward a tip to NCIS Norway, please go to NCIS tip receival or phone us at 09989.

In the Norwegian example, the clear intention of the stop page is to alert the potential offender's conscience rather than to increase the perceived risks of ICP offending. Potential offenders are explicitly told that no personal information about them has been captured (although seeing the stop page might give them pause to realize that they are not anonymous on the Internet and that is quite possible for information about them to be collected). As far as we know, there is no research that examines the effectiveness of stop pages. The Norwegian message is in our view perhaps rather bland and does not fully exploit the potential of this strategy. We can envisage experimenting with different sorts of messages to examine what wording has the greatest effect (see also Williams 2005). There would seem to us to be three possible types of messages that might be usefully displayed: conscience-raising messages, involving messages that stress the harm to children portrayed in the images; deterrence-focused messages, emphasizing the potential to capture personal details in future; and therapeutically oriented messages, directing the potential offender to services where he might address his sexual attraction to children. One advantage of messages of these sorts is that the offender encounters them at the very moment he is attempting to engage in illegal activity. As such, they have the potential to challenge directly the sense of anonymity that offenders experience as they interact on the Internet.

Reducing Provocations

The situational strategies we have examined so far are based on the rational choice perspective. Rational decision-making models are concerned with the perceived consequences of behavior. Offenders will decide not to proceed with a contemplated crime if it is judged to be too difficult or risky to carry out or if the outcome fails to deliver adequate rewards or induces feelings of guilt. The final column of Clarke's situational crime prevention model is based on a different logic. Reducing provocations seeks to address factors that stimulate the motivations to offend and that induce individuals to commit crimes that they might not have otherwise considered committing. Wortley (2001) uses the term "crime precipitators" rather than "provocations" to capture more generally the wide range of environmental factors that can trigger offending. Crime precipitators can affect people at a subcognitive level, and they need not even recognize that they are being influenced. For example, Homel and colleagues (Homel and Clark 1994; Homel, Hauritz, Wortley, McIlwain, and Carvolth 1997; Macintyre and Homel 1997) found that nightclub violence was related to a range of aggravating environmental features, such as the amount of cigarette smoke, the lack of ventilation, poor lighting, overcrowding, and the demeanor of security staff. Patrons may visit a nightclub with no formed intention of engaging in violence, only to become progressively more frustrated and aggressive as the night unfolds.

We have argued elsewhere (Smallbone, Marshall and Wortley 2008; Wortley and Smallbone 2006) that immediate environments might be particularly important in precipitating child sexual abuse. The sexual impulse is often triggered during intimate care-giving activities—bathing, dressing, comforting, tucking into bed, roughhousing, and so on—which the offender experiences as stimulating. Likewise, accessing ICP is likely to be triggered by particular situational events.

Targeting Embedded ICP

There is little research on the circumstances surrounding ICP offenders' onset offense—that is, the very first time that they accessed ICP. However, it is likely that the decision to actively seek out ICP would have been for many offenders a significant psychological threshold to cross. Involvement in ICP offending may be an insidious, progressive process (Quayle and Taylor 2003). One pathway to ICP may have been through legal adult-focused pornography. Pornography has been found to have a habituating effect. Repeated exposure to sexually explicit material reduces its psychological impact on the viewer (Ceniti and Malamuth 1984; Howard, Reifler, and Liptzin 1971; Zillman and Bryant 1984). Viewers may respond to habituation in one of two ways: They may become bored with pornography and stop viewing it or they may seek out more extreme forms of pornography to increase the stimulation they receive. In the second scenario, ICP embedded in legal adult sites becomes particularly problematic. Individuals may first encounter ICP without having to actively seek it out and when they are already sexually aroused. Not unreasonably, law enforcement agencies focus resources on the most serious forms of ICP, which typically appears on dedicated sites. However, if embedded ICP is a pathway to more serious offending, then serious attention should also be given to it.

Managing Environmental Triggers

The role of situational precipitators has been recognized for some time in the sex offender treatment field. In relapse prevention, offenders are taught to analyze the environmental context of their offending in order to recognize and manage situations they might find sexually stimulating that might set in motion an offending cycle (Pithers, Marques, Gibat, and Marlatt 1983). For example, if walking past a school is likely to trigger thoughts of offending, then that behavior should be avoided as part of a self-management plan. The relapse prevention model has also been suggested for ICP offending (Elliott and Beech 2009). However, at this stage, there appears to be little research that identifies specific ICP offending triggers. To the extent that research has considered the issue, the focus has been on psychological states prior to offending. For example, it has been found that ICP offenders report feeling angry, anxious, depressed, or lonely prior to offending (Quayle and Taylor 2002, 2003). We suggest that identifying triggers for ICP offending in more concrete, environmental terms may be a useful avenue for future research. It is likely that there will be generic triggers that affect most ICP offenders and that can be used broadly as a situational prevention strategy as well as triggers that are specific to particular ICP offenders and that may form the basis of a tailored relapse prevention plan.

CONCLUSION

All behavior is the result of a person-situation interaction. Accordingly, the Internet is not just an alternative platform that dedicated pedophiles happen to use to view child pornography; the Internet is a contributing cause of child pornography. This means we cannot rely solely on the arrest and rehabilitation of offenders to solve the problem of ICP. Certainly, offenders—especially those at the more serious end of the offending spectrum involved in producing and distributing child pornography—should be targeted by law enforcement personnel and arrested where possible. But there are many more people accessing child pornography via the Internet than can ever be arrested. Fewer still ICP offenders will receive the benefits of participating in a rehabilitation program. If, as we have argued, the proliferation of child pornography is a function of increased opportunity offered by the Internet, then a comprehensive approach to tackling ICP must by include reducing that opportunity.

Admittedly, the task is not a simple one. As we have discussed in earlier chapters, the structure of the Internet makes the control of child pornography very difficult. Because of the difficulties policing the Internet, it is easy to be pessimistic about the prospects of controlling ICP. There is especially the danger of interpreting partial success as complete failure. It is undoubtedly true that none of the situational strategies that have been discussed in this chapter will work perfectly. Offenders vary considerably in the strength of their attraction to child pornography and the technological sophistication they are able to employ to access images and to avoid detection. Whatever we do, there will a core of dedicated offenders who possess the determination and technical skills to thwart prevention attempts. But we must keep the task in proper perspective. Imagine if we did nothing to inhibit access to child pornography on the Internet—that there were no efforts to take down child pornography sites, no search filters, no police stings, no clampdown on online payments, and so on. Would there be more child pornography on the Internet and more offenders accessing that pornography?

While it is impossible to know the answer for certain, common sense tells us that if child pornography were freely available on the Internet, then the problem would be significantly greater than is currently the case. Situational strategies have the potential to slow down determined offenders and to completely deter less determined ones. But it important to recognize that the battle to prevent ICP is not one that can ever be won once and for all. Rather, it is an ongoing arms race characterized by a cycle involving the deployment of prevention strategies, the adaptation of offenders to those strategies, and the deployment of new prevention strategies to counter offender adaptation.

8

Conclusion

CHILD PORNOGRAPHY IS a topic that generates strong emotions. The thought of innocent and vulnerable children being callously exploited in such debased ways elic-
its our compassion for the victims and anger toward those who are responsible
for the exploitation—whether they produce and distribute the abuse images or
help perpetuate the abuse by viewing the images. Our collective abhorrence of
child pornography is a relatively modern phenomenon and contrasts with the situation in previous ages in which the sexual exploitation of children was often
disbelieved, ignored, tolerated, or even condoned. The discovery of child pornography as a serious social problem has resulted in the creation of specific child
pornography legislation, significant investment in law enforcement resources to
rescue victims and catch offenders, the forming of numerous nongovernment
advocacy organizations dedicated to raising awareness, and the emergence of
child pornography as an active area of academic interest.

Along with strong emotional reactions to child pornography comes the danger of polarized views. In our fervent desire to "do something" about the problem
of ICP, we risk falling victim to a moral panic in which the Internet is portrayed
as awash with ICP, and our responses are dominated by the stereotype of the ICP
offender as a cunning and remorseless deviant. Inevitably, some have reacted
against the attention now given to ICP by claiming that the extent of the problem
has been grossly exaggerated, warning of the threats to liberty posed by Internet
controls designed to prevent ICP and, in some cases, defending the rights of individuals to access to ICP.

We have endeavored in this book to present a balanced view of the ICP
problem. We have acknowledged that child pornography is a serious social issue
that has been dramatically exacerbated by the advent of the Internet. We regard
the sexual exploitation of children as morally indefensible and do not doubt the
devastating psychological and physical effects that ICP can have on many victims. We also believe that there is a core of persistent, technically skilled, and
well-organized offenders who are consumed by a sexual attraction to children
and who are very difficult to catch or deter. At the same time, we need to treat
with caution claims that are made about the size of the ICP problem. Most of
the figures in circulation concerning the extent of ICP are little more than

guesses—made in some cases, one suspects, by those with a vested interest in stressing the seriousness of the problem.

We also need to try to separate our moral outrage about ICP offenders from our efforts to understand their behavior. With this, we believe, comes the uncomfortable acceptance that there is a widespread potential to become sexually aroused by ICP and that what defines many ICP offenders is their ordinariness, not their deviance. Characterization of ICP material itself in terms of its worst and most unusual examples—involving violent sexual degradation of very young children—makes it all the more difficult to see this. To be sure, such terrible images exist, and the knowledge that some offenders derive sexual pleasure from them stretches our sense of the bounds of human behavior. But the truth is that the severity of ICP images ranges along a continuum, ultimately toward the legally and morally ambiguous. Fundamentally, we have argued that effective responses to ICP must be based on a dispassionate analysis, not on myths and moral assumptions.

The idea that ICP use is not limited to an easily definable group of sexual deviants presents us with a double-edged sword when it comes to dealing with the problem. On the one hand, it can make the control of ICP seem all the more challenging. If the potential to be sexually responsive to images of children and young people is endemic—a component of male human nature—then how can we hope to contain the ICP problem? The Internet has placed child pornography within the reach of any individual who has so much as a fleeting thought about children as sexual objects. Indeed, the problem we have with child pornography today—as opposed to the situation pre-1980—exists precisely because the Internet has made it so easy for individuals to act on their latent sexual desires. On the other hand, we can draw some comfort from the fact that the majority of ICP offenders do not have a deep-seated sexual attraction to children nor are they particularly sophisticated in their offending strategies. The stereotypical compulsive offender is the extreme end of a continuum. There may be more child pornography offenders than ever before, but controlling the behavior of many of these offenders may not be as challenging as is often assumed.

This interpretation of the dynamics of ICP offending has important implications for how we need to respond to the problem. First and foremost, it reinforces the view that the prevention of ICP offending *before it occurs* must be our priority. The apparatus of law enforcement and of the criminal justice system more broadly are designed to react to the commission of crime. That is, our dominant crime-response strategies are to catch and punish known offenders. To the extent that these activities have a prevention function, it is largely in terms of reducing reoffending by incapacitating the offender for some period of time, during which they are restrained from offending (e.g., imprisonment), and/or by hoping that the received punishment will serve as a deterrent against future criminality. Of course, we believe that ICP offenders should be held accountable for their crimes and prosecuted if they are apprehended, and the evidence suggests that the reconviction rates for ICP offenders are low. We have also argued that publicizing the risk of arrest may have general deterrent effects, helping to counter perceptions by potential offenders that the Internet is an anonymous and safe environment in which to offend. However, the growth of the child pornography problem since the Internet began means that the arrest of a few thousand individuals each year will have a trivial impact on the overall numbers of ICP offenders. Even with a considerable increase to resources now devoted to policing ICP, the number of potential arrestees and the time, effort, and logistic difficulties involved in securing convictions makes the arrest of anything approaching a significant proportion of offenders simply not viable.

For similar reasons, we should not place too much faith in rehabilitation—the traditional focus of most psychological approaches to ICP—to make any significant dent in the problem. If few offenders are arrested for ICP, fewer still are offered places in a rehabilitation program. Even the best rehabilitation programs, in turn, are never completely effective in eliminating reoffending. There are no figures available for the success rates of ICP treatment programs in particular, but based on research examining general offender treatment programs, the best that could be hoped for is a reduction in recidivism of between 12 percent (Redondo, Sánchez-Meca, and Garrido 1999) and 25 percent (Landenberger and Lipsey 2005). In any case, based on Seto et al.'s (2011) findings, the reoffending rates for untreated ICP offenders are so low that any additional benefit that might be derived from rehabilitation would seem negligible. Concentrating rehabilitation resources on the most persistent and disturbed ICP offenders would seem to be the most sensible approach, although assistance should also be made available for those willing to self-refer.

A central thread in our analysis of ICP has been the crucial role of the person-situation interaction in offending, and it is this that provides the key to devising effective preventative strategies. The person side of the equation refers to the psychological capacity to gain sexual gratification from sexual images of children. At a community level, we need to continue to reinforce the abhorrent nature of ICP and challenge perceptions that downloading images is a victimless crime. Beyond this, the apparently ordinary profile of the ICP offender presents special challenges to the usual offender-focused prevention strategies of early intervention and detection. Focusing prevention efforts on those most at risk of becoming ICP offenders makes sense, but more needs to be known about how ICP offending more commonly begins and progresses. Because ICP is usually produced in the context of contact sexual abuse, prevention efforts also need to focus on victims and potential victims and on the settings in which such abuse occurs.

The situation side of the equation refers to the opportunity to access such images provided by the Internet. Here, the goal is clearer, although the task is not unproblematic. If increased opportunity is responsible for the proliferation of ICP, then reducing opportunity must be a major part of any prevention effort. We need to continue in the efforts to make ICP offending more difficult to carry out, to entail greater risks of detection, to deliver fewer rewards, to be less excusable in the eyes of the offender, and to be less likely to be triggered by environmental cues or stresses.

However, the person-situation interaction means more than that each factor is individually important in behavior; it is the way that personal and situational factors combine that is often the most interesting. In the case of ICP offending, we saw how interacting in a virtual environment can profoundly affect an individual's sense of self and his perceptions of risk. The Internet has a disinhibiting effect, and people will behave in ways online that they would not behave in "real life." Thus, for example, situational strategies do not just need to increase the risk of offending; they need to increase the risk of offending as it is *perceived* by the individual interacting online.

There are difficulties in implementing person-focused and Internet-focused interventions, and neither guarantee the elimination of ICP. It is easy to feel overwhelmed by the size of the ICP problem and to be pessimistic about the prospects for success. It is certainly unlikely that we will ever be able to make the confident assertions about having broken the back of the child pornography problem as were made in the report by the General Accounting Office some 30 years ago (Ahart 1982) and quoted at the beginning of this book. However, we believe there are encouraging signs of success and that without the efforts currently being made, the ICP problem would be far greater than it is. At the same time, offenders are adaptable, and we are locked in an ongoing struggle to keep one step ahead. To tip the battle in our favor, it is vital that our approach to the prevention of ICP derives from a sound research base.

THE WAY AHEAD: WHAT DO WE NEED TO KNOW?

It has become a cliché to end academic works with a call for more research. Be that as it may, there is much we do not know about ICP offending. There is surprisingly little empirical research; moreover, much of the limited research activity is, in our view, misdirected and contributes little to a prevention agenda. In the following sections, we list some areas we see as priorities for future research.

The Behavior of Offenders

Much of the available empirical research on ICP offenders comes from the behavioral sciences and sets out to identify stable trait differences between offenders and nonoffenders and among different types of offenders. As we have detailed, few distinguishing psychological features of ICP offenders have been found. But even if certain psychological peculiarities were to be identified, one must ask the question of the usefulness of such information and how exactly might it be used to help reduce offending? What is desperately lacking is research on the *behavior* of ICP offenders—how they go about the task of offending. Situational prevention involves countering the strategies employed by offenders. More needs to be known about when and where offenders access ICP, the emotional and environmental triggers for offending, the Internet search strategies employed, the security precautions taken, and the way that risk is perceived and responded to. This information may be obtained by asking offenders about their behavior and/or directly examining records of online offending. The research design developed by Demetriou and Silke (2003), which examined responses on a bogus website, offers a model for directly examining online behavior under experimental conditions.

Offending Onset

In particular, as we explore the behavior of offenders, we need to know more about the dynamics of the onset of offending. We have made the point elsewhere (Smallbone, Marshall, and Wortley 2008) that for contact child sexual abuse, the dynamics surrounding the very first offense are likely to be very different from those surrounding subsequent offending. The first offense is special. At this point, the offender has no routine modus operandi and may not even have formed an established sexual attraction toward children; that may come as a consequence of offending. Therefore, preventing the onset offense is particularly important, and it may also be the easiest offense to prevent. We think the same principles are likely to apply to ICP offenders. Research needs to establish how and why people commit their first ICP offense and to track the psychological and behavioral progression—where progression does occur—to pathological levels of offending.

Nontreatment and Nonprisoner Samples

Almost all the information we have on ICP offenders comes from studies involving incarcerated samples—often comprising prisoners in treatment. There is a danger that what we think we know about ICP offenders is based on a narrow band of serious offenders, giving us a highly skewed picture of the dynamics of ICP offending. The confidential hotlines we described in Chapter 6 may provide an unusual opportunity to learn about how ICP offenders begin, progress, and desist from their offending behavior, but even these help-seeking offenders are unlikely to be representative. In one of the few studies involving a community sample of Internet users, Seigfried et al. (2008) found that roughly 15 percent of males had accessed ICP, supporting our contention that there is likely to be a great deal of opportunistic and undetected ICP offending. Particularly surprising was the finding that about 5 percent of females had also viewed ICP, a level of offending that greatly exceeds the levels found in official arrest figures. It seems there may be much more to learn about the individuals who comprise this "gray area" of offending.

Getting Specific

ICP offending is a term that covers a diverse range of behaviors involving the production, distribution, and downloading of images. In addition, there is a range of related crimes that come under the more general heading of Internet child exploitation (ICE), and that includes the online sexual grooming of children, cyberstalking and sexual harassment, child sexual tourism, and the trafficking of children. While the same offender may be involved in multiple types of ICE offending, in many cases, each type of offense comprises distinct populations of offenders. For example, some offenders who download ICP are also involved in its production by recording their own sexual abuse of children, but the majority of those downloading ICP are not involved in contact child sexual abuse. The prevention strategies—person centered and situational—required for the production of ICP are very different from those required for the downloading of ICP. Very often, however, research on Internet child exploitation fails to make distinctions between different types of online offenders or between different types on online offending. If we are to develop effective interventions, we need to unpack online child exploitation and produce research findings that are specific to the different types of exploitation. Making clear the distinctions between various types of Internet child exploitation also allows us to better prioritise our prevention efforts, focusing particularly on offenses that involve contact sexual abuse.

Joining Up Research Efforts

We conclude by returning to our central theme—that of the person-situation interaction. In this book, we have reviewed research that has addressed both sides of this dynamic. What was striking to us is that this research exists essentially as two separate literatures. One source of research is the behavioral sciences, which, as previously noted, focus on the characteristics of offenders. The other source of research is computer science, which focuses on the technical aspects of detecting, tracking, and blocking illegal Internet use. It is apparent how little each of the literatures refers to or even shows any awareness of the other. Furthermore, in many cases, research papers are written in technical terms that assume prior disciplinary knowledge and that make the findings largely inaccessible to those outside the discipline. What is lacking is research that brings behavioral and computer science perspectives together. Behavioral scientists and computer scientists have much to learn from each other, and the contributions of both are required. It seems to us that the behavioral scientist cannot fully understand how to prevent the behavior of ICP offenders unless he or she also has some understanding of how the Internet is used in offending; likewise, the computer scientist must be proficient not just in the technical aspects of the Internet but must also appreciate how the individual experiences the Internet at a psychological level. For example, the rational choice perspective that underpins situational crime prevention is a product of behavioral science, but many of the strategies required to implement situational crime prevention require the expertise of the computer scientist. Like calls for more research, calls for greater levels of multi-disciplinary research are so frequent as to be almost cliché. Multidisciplinarity is often held as an aspiration, but it is difficult to achieve in practice. However, ICP is an area where the need for a multidisciplinary approach and the benefits that such an approach may yield would seem to be self-evident.

References

ABC News. 2006. "Teen Tells How He Was Lured into Child Porn." *ABC News*. Available at http://abcnews.go.com/GMA/story?id=1803413 (accessed on December 12, 2011).

Adegoke, Yinka. 2003. "Top Brands Start to Pull Ads from P2P Networks." *New Media Age*, p. 1, April 24.

Ahart, Gregory J. 1982. "Sexual Exploitation of Children—A Problem of Unknown Magnitude." *Report to the Chairman, Subcommittee on Select Education, House Committee on Education and Labor*. Gaithersburg, MD: U.S. General Accounting Office.

Ahmed, Murad. 2009. "Teen 'Sexting' Craze Leading to Child Porn Arrests in US." *The Times*. Available at http://technology.timesonline.co.uk/tol/news/tech_and _web/article5516511.ece (accessed on December 12, 2011).

Akdeniz, Yaman. 2008. *Internet Child Pornography and the Law: National and International Responses*. Surrey, UK: Ashgate Publishing.

American Psychiatric Association. 2000. *Diagnostic and Statistical Manual of Mental Disorders* (4th ed.). Washington, DC: American Psychiatric Association.

Analdo, Carlos A. 2001. *Child Abuse on the Internet: Ending the Silence*. Paris: UNESCO/Berghahn Books.

Anderson, Ronald E. 2002. "Youth and Information Technology." In Jeylan T. Mortimer & Reed W. Larson (eds.), *The Changing Adolescent Experience: Societal Trends and the Transition to Adulthood*, pp. 175–207. New York: Cambridge University Press.

Andrews, D. A., and James Bonta. 2003. *The Psychology of Criminal Conduct* (3rd ed.). Cincinnati: Anderson.

Angelides, Steven. 2005. "The Emergence of the Paedophile in the Late Twentieth Century." *Australian Historical Studies*, 36(126): 272–95.

Anonymous. 1648. *Aristotle's Masterpiece*. Available at http://www.exclassics.com/arist/ariintro.htm (accessed on December 12, 2011).

Arata, Catalina M. 1998. "To Tell or Not to Tell: Current Functioning of Child Sexual Abuse Survivors Who Disclosed Their Victimization." *Child Maltreatment, 3*(1): 63–71.

Ariès, Philippe. 1962. *Centuries of Childhood: A Social History of the Family*. London: Jonathan Cape.

Artur, Patrick. 2010. "Software Helps Law Enforcement Officers Track Child Pornography." *Criminal Law*. Available at http://www.hg.org/article.asp?id=18952 (accessed on December 12, 2011).

Ashcroft v. Free Speech Coalition. 535 U.S. 234. 2002.

Avert. n.d. *World Wide Ages of Consent*. Available at http://www.avert.org/age-of-consent.htm (accessed on December 12, 2011).

Babchishin, Kelly M., R. Karl Hanson, and Chantal A. Hermann. 2011. "The Characteristics of Online Sex Offenders: A Meta-Analysis." *Sexual Abuse: A Journal of Research and Treatment, 23*(1): 92–123.

Bandura, Albert. 1976. "Social Learning Analysis of Aggression." In Emillio Ribes-Inesta and Albert Bandura (eds.), *Analysis of Delinquency and Aggression*. Hillsdale, NJ: Erlbaum.

Baron, Stephen W., and Leslie W Kennedy. 1998. "Deterrence and Homeless Male Street Youths." *Canadian Journal of Criminology, 40*(1): 27–60.

Bates, Andrew, and Caroline Metcalf. 2007. "A Psychometric Comparison of Internet and Non-Internet Sex Offenders from a Community Treatment Sample." *Journal of Sexual Aggression, 13*(1): 11–20.

BBC News. 1999. "UK Glitter Jailed Over Child Porn". *BBC Online Network*. Available at http://news.bbc.co.uk/1/hi/uk/517604.stm (accessed on December 12, 2011).

BBC News. 2001. "Tackling Online Child Pornography." *BBC Online Network*. Available at http://news.bbc.co.uk/1/hi/uk/1166135.stm (accessed on December 12, 2011).

BBC News. 2002. "Operation Avalanche: Tracking Child Porn." *BBC Online Network*. Available at http://news.bbc.co.uk/1/hi/uk_news/2445065stm (accessed on December 12, 2011).

BBC News. 2003. "Police Trap Online Paedophiles." *BBC Online Network*. Available at http://news.bbc.co.uk/1/hi/uk/3329567.stm (accessed on December 12, 2011).

Beech, Anthony R., Ian A Elliott, Astrid Birgden, and Donald Findlater. 2008. "The Internet and Child Sexual Offending: A Criminological Review." *Aggression and Violent Behavior, 13*(3): 216–28.

Beier, Klaus M., Christoph J. Ahlers, David Goecker, Janina Neutze, Ingrid A. Mundt, Elena Hupp, and Gerard A. Schaefer. 2009. "Can Pedophiles be Reached for Primary Prevention of Child Sexual Abuse? First Results of the Berlin Prevention Project Dunkelfeld (PPD)." *Journal of Forensic Psychiatry & Psychology, 20*(6): 851–67.

Berliner, Lucy, and Jon R. Conte. 1995. "The Effects of Disclosure and Intervention on Sexually Abused Children." *Child Abuse and Neglect, 19*(3): 371–84.

Besharov, Douglas J. 1994. "Responding to Child Sexual Abuse: The Need for a Balanced Approach." *The Future of Children, 4*(2): 135–155.

Blundell, Barry, Michael Sherry, Anne Burke, and Shawn Sowerbutts. 2002. "Child Pornography and the Internet: Accessibility and Policing." *Australian Police Journal, 56*(1): 59–65.

Bokelberg, George A. n.d. *Stress Associated with Investigating and Working in Support of Investigations of Internet Sexual Crimes Against Children.* (Unpublished study). Washington DC: Federal Bureau of Investigation.

A Book Named "John Cleland's Memoirs of a Woman of Pleasure" v. Attorney General. 383 U.S. 413, 86 S. Ct. 975, 16 L. Ed. 2d 1. 1966.

Bourke, Michael L., and Andres E. Hernandez. 2009. "The 'Butner Study' Redux: A Report of the Incidence of Hands-on Child Victimization by Child Pornography Offenders" *Journal of Family Violence, 24*(3): 183–91.

Bowers Kate, Shane Johnson, Rob T. Guerette, Lucia Summers, and Susanne Poynton. 2011 "Spatial Displacement and Diffusion of Benefits Among Geographically Focused Policing Initiatives. A Meta-analytic Review." *Journal of Experimental Criminology, 7*: 347–374.

Bridgeman, Cressida. 1997. "Preventing Pay Phone Damage." In Marcus Felson and Ronald V. Clarke (eds.), *Business and Crime Prevention.* Monsey, NY: Criminal Justice Press.

Briere, John, and Diana M. Elliot. 2001. "Immediate and Long-Term Impacts of Child Sexual Abuse." In Kris Franey, Robert Geffner, and Robert. Falconer (eds.), *The Cost of Child Maltreatment: Who Pays? We All Do*, pp. 121–36. San Diego, CA: Family Violence and Sexual Assault Institute.

Brown, Ben. 1996. *CCTV in Town Centres: Three Case Studies. Police Research Group Crime Detection and Prevention Series Paper 68.* London: Home Office.

Brown, Jennifer, Jane Fielding, and Jennifer Grover. 1999. "Distinguishing Traumatic, Vicarious and Routine Operational Stressor Exposure and Attendant Adverse Consequences in a Sample of Police Officers." *Work & Stress, 13*(4): 312–25.

Bullough, Vern. L. 2004. "Children and Adolescents as Sexual Beings: A Historical Overview." *Child and Adolescent Psychiatric Clinics of North America, 13*: 447–59.

Burgess, Ann W. 1984. *Child Pornography and Sex Rings.* Lexington, MA: DC Heath.

Burke, Anne, Shawn Sowerbutts, Barry Blundell, and Michael Sherry. 2002. "Child Pornography and the Internet: Policing and Treatment Issues." *Psychiatry, Psychology and Law, 9*(1): 79–84.

Burns, Carolyn M., Jeff Morley, Richard Bradshaw, and José Domene. 2008. "The Emotional Impact on and Coping Strategies Employed by Police Teams Investigating Internet Child Exploitation." *Traumatology, 14*(2): 20–31.

Buss, David M. 1994. *The Evolution of Desire: Strategies of Human Mating.* New York: Basic Books.

Calder, Martin C. 2004. "The Internet: Potential, Problems and Pathways to Hands-on Sexual Offending." In Martin C. Calder (ed.) *Child Sexual Abuse and the Internet: Tackling the New Frontier*, pp. 1–23. Lyme Regis, UK: Russell House Publishing.

Cameron, May H., and Amanda K. Delaney. 2008. *Speed Enforcement—Effects, Mechanisms, Intensity and Economic Benefits of Each Mode of Operation.* Presentation to Joint Australasian College of Road Safety and Queensland Parliamentary Travelsafe Committee conference, Brisbane 18–19 September.

Carr, John. 2001. *Theme Paper on Child Pornography for the 2nd World Congress on Commercial Sexual Exploitation of Children.* Paper presented at the Second World Congress against the Commercial Sexual Exploitation of Children, Yokahama, Japan. Available at http://www.childcentre.info/robert/extensions/robert/doc/67ba32d30c03c842b7032932f2e6ce74.pdf (accessed on December 12, 2011).

Carr, John. 2004. *Child Abuse, Child Pornography and the Internet*. London: NCH.

Carroll, John, and Frances Weaver. 1986. " 'Shoplifters' Perceptions of Crime Opportunities: A Process-Tracing Study." In Derek B. Cornish and Ronald V. Clarke (eds.), *The Reasoning Criminal: Rational Choice Perspectives on Offending*, pp. 19–38. New York: Springer-Verlag.

Casey, Eoghan. 2004. "Network Traffic as a Source of Evidence: Tool Strengths, Weaknesses, and Future Needs." *Digital Investigation, 1*: 28–43.

Cassell, Justine, and Meg Cramer. 2008. "High Tech or High Risk: Moral Panics about Girls Online." In Tara McPherson (ed.), *Digital Youth, Innovation, and the Unexpected*, pp. 53–76. The John D. and Catherine T.MacArthur Foundation Series on Digital Media and Learning. Cambridge, MA: The MIT Press. Available at https://netfiles.uiuc.edu/rfouche/www/readings/cassell.pdf (accessed on December 12, 2011).

Ceniti, Joseph, and Neil M. Malamuth. 1984. "Effects of Repeated Exposure to Sexually Violent and Non-Violent Stimuli on Sexual Arousal to Rape and Nonrape Depictions." *Behaviour Research and Therapy, 22*(5): 535–48.

Chandy, Joseph M., Robert Wm. Blum, and Michael D. Resnick. 1997. "Sexually Abused Male Adolescents: How Vulnerable Are They?" *Journal of Child Sexual Abuse, 6*(2): 1–16.

Chapman, Cameron. 2009. *The History of the Internet in a Nutshell. Six Revisions*. Available at http://sixrevisions.com/resources/the-history-of-the-internet-in-a-nutshell/ (accessed on December 12, 2011).

Chasan-Taber, Lisa, and Joan Tabachnick. 1999. "Evaluation of a Child Sexual Abuse Prevention Program." *Sexual Abuse, 11*(4): 279–92.

Child Pornography Protection Act. 1996a. 18 U.S.C. §§ 2252A, 2256(8).

Child Pornography Protection Act. 1996b. 18 U.S.C. §§ 2251, 2252, et seq.

Child Protection and Obscenity Enforcement Act. 1988. Amending §§ 2251, 2252.

Child Protection Act. 1984. 18 U.S.C. 2251–2255.

Child Protector and Sexual Predator Punishment Act. 1998. 42 U.S.C. §§ 13032.

CIRCAMP. No Date. *"Child pornography" versus "Child sexual abuse material."* COSPOL Internet Related Child Abusive Material Project. Available at http://circamp.eu/index.php?option=com_content&view=article&id=10:child-pornography-versus-child-sexual-abuse-material&catid=1:pr (accessed on December 12, 2011).

Clarke, Ronald V., ed. 1997. *Situational Crime Prevention: Successful Case Studies* (2nd ed). Albany, NY: Harrow and Heston.

Clarke, Ronald V. 2008. "Situational Crime Prevention." In Richard Wortley and Lorraine Mazerolle (eds.), *Environmental Criminology and Crime Analyses*, pp. 178–94. Cullompton, UK: Willan.

Clarke, Ronald V., and Pat Mayhew. 1988. "The British Gas Suicide Story and its Criminological Implications." In Michael Tonry and Norval Morris (eds.), *Crime and Justice, Volume 10: An Annual Review of Research*. Chicago, IL: University of Chicago Press.

Cohen, Stanley. 1972. *Folk Devils and Moral Panics*. London, UK: MacGibbon and Kee.

Conte, Jon, Steven Wolfe, and Tim Smith. 1989. "What Sexual Offenders Tell Us About Prevention Strategies" *Child Abuse and Neglect, 13*(2): 293–302.

Cooper, Alvin, Dana E. Putnam, Lynn A. Planchon, and Sylvain C. Boies. 1999. "Online Sexual Compulsivity: Getting Tangled in the Net." *Sexual Addiction and Compulsivity*, *6*(2): 79–104.

Cornish, Derek B., and Ronald V. Clarke. 1986. "Introduction." In Derek B. Cornish and Ronald V. Clarke (eds.), *The Reasoning Criminal: Rational Choice Perspectives on Offending*. New York: Springer-Verlag.

Cornish, Derek B., and Ronald V. Clarke. 2008. "The Rational Choice Perspective." In Richard Wortley and Lorrane Mazerolle (eds.), *Environmental Criminology and Crime Analyses*, pp. 21–47. Cullompton, UK: Willan.

Crewdson, John. 1988. *By Silence Betrayed: Sexual Abuse of Children in America*. Boston: Little Brown.

Daro, Deborah, and Sara Salmon-Cox 1994. *Child Sexual Abuse Prevention Programs: Do They Work*? Englewood, CO: National Resource Center on Child Abuse and Neglect.

Deane, Elicia C. 2011. *The Relationship between Indecent Image Offending and Child Sexual Abuse*. Unpublished Masters Dissertation. Department of Security and Crime Science, University College London.

Dedman, Bill, and Bob Sullivan. 2008. "ISPs Are Pressed to Become Child Porn Cops". *Security on MSNBC.com*. October 16. Available at http://www.msnbc.msn.com/id/27198621/ns/technology_and_science-security/t/isps-are-pressed-become-child-porn-cops/#.Tu3HM0rkI3Y (accessed on December 12, 2011).

DeLamater, John, and William N. Friedrich. 2002. "Human Sexual Development." *Journal of Sex Research, 39*(1): 10–14.

DeMarco, Robert T. 2005. *Technology and the Fight Against Child Pornography. Watch Right*. Available at http://blog.watchright.com/?itemid=337 (accessed on December 12, 2011).

deMause, Lloyd. 1988. ed. *The history of childhood: The untold story of child abuse*. New York, US: Peter Bedrick Books.

deMause, Lloyd. 1991. "The universality of incest." *The Journal of Psychohistory*, 1991 19(2). Available at http://www.thebirdman.org/Index/Others/Others-Doc-Sex/+Doc-Sex-Pedophilia&Incest/UniversalityOfIncest.htm (accessed on December 12, 2011).

deMause, Lloyd. 1997. "The history of child abuse." *The Journal of Psychohistory, 25*(3): 216–36.

Demetriou, Christina, and Andrew Silke. 2003. "A Criminological Internet 'Sting': Experimental Evidence of Illegal and Deviant Visits to a Website Trap." *British Journal of Criminology, 43*(1): 213–22.

Diener, Edward. 1980. "Deindividuation: The Absence of Self-Awareness and Self-Regulation in Group Members." In Paul B. Paulus (ed.), *Psychology of Group Influence*, pp. 209–42. Hillsdale, NJ: Erlbaum.

Dombrowski, Stefan C, Karen L. Gischlar, and Theo Durst. 2007. "Safeguarding Young People from Cyber Pornography and Cyber Sexual Predation: A Major Dilemma of the Internet." *Child Abuse Review, 16*(3): 153–70.

Dunne, Michael P., David M. Purdie, Michelle D. Cook, Frances M. Boyle, and Jake M. Najman. 2003. "Is Child Sexual Abuse Declining? Evidence from a Population-Based Survey of Men and Women in Australia." *Child Abuse & Neglect, 27*(2): 141–52.

Eastwood, Christine. 2003. "The Experiences of Child Complainants of Sexual Abuse in the Criminal Justice System." *Trends and Issues in Crime and Criminal Justice, No. 250.* Canberra: Australian Institute of Criminology. Available at http://www .aic.gov.au/documents/1/8/F/%7B18FF5A71-2773-4BC8-BC93-933DD57A5BDD %7Dti250.pdf (accessed on December 12, 2011).

Eastwood, Christine, Wendy, Patton, and Helen, Stacy. 2000. "Children Seeking Justice: Surviving Child Sexual Abuse and the Criminal Justice System." *Queensland Journal of Educational Research, 16*(2): 158–82.

ECPAT. 2008. Regional overview on Child Sexual Abuse Images through the Use of Information and Communication Technologies in Belarus, Moldova, Russia and Ukraine. Bangkok. Thailand: ECPAT International.

Edelmann, Robert J. 2010. "Exposure to Child Abuse Images as Part of One's Work: Possible Psychological Implications." *Journal of Forensic Psychiatry & Psychology 21*(4): 481–89.

Elliot, Michelle, ed. 1991. *Bullying: A Practical Guide to Coping for Schools.* Harlow: Longman.

Elliott Ian A., and Anthony R. Beech. 2009. "Understanding Online Child Pornography Use: Applying Sexual Offense Theory to Internet Offenders." *Aggression and Violent Behavior, 14*(3): 180–93.

Elliott, Ian A., Anthony R. Beech, Rebecca Mandeville-Norden, and Elizabeth Hayes. 2009. "Psychological Profiles of Internet Sexual Offenders: Comparisons With Contact Sexual Offenders." *Sexual Abuse: A Journal of Research and Treatment, 21*(1): 76–92.

Elliott, Michelle, Kevin Browne, and Jennifer Kilcoyne. 1995. "Child Sexual Abuse Prevention: What Offenders Tell Us." *Child Abuse and Neglect, 19*(5): 579–94.

Elliott, Ann N., and Connie N. Carnes. 2001. "Reactions of Non-Offending Parents to the Sexual Abuse of their Child: A Review of the Literature." *Child Maltreatment, 6* (4): 314–31.

Elliott, Ian A., and Donald Findlater. 2010. *A review of a 'Managed Service' for the home computer use of Registered Sex Offenders.* Hampshire Constabulary & The Lucy Faithfull Foundation.

Elliott, Ian A., Donald Findlater, and Teresa Hughes. 2010. "Practice Report: A Review of e-Safety Remote Computer Monitoring for UK Sex Offenders." *Journal of Sexual Aggression, 16*(2): 237–48.

Endrass, Jérôme, Frank Urbaniok, Lea C. Hammermeister, Christian Benz, Thomas Elbert, Arja Laubacher, and Astrid Rossegger. 2009. "The Consumption of Internet Child Pornography and Violent and Sex Offending." *BMC Psychiatry, 9*(43). Available at http://www.biomedcentral.com/1471-244X/9/43 (accessed on December 12, 2011).

Erke, Alena, Charles Goldenbeld, and Truls Vas. 2009. "The Effects of Drink-Driving Checkpoints on Crashes—A Meta-Analysis." *Accident Analysis and Prevention, 41*(5): 914–23.

Everill, Joanne, and Glenn Waller. 1994. "Disclosure of Sexual Abuse and Psychological Adjustment in Female Undergraduates." *Child Abuse and Neglect, 19*(1): 93–100.

Farrington, David P. 1995. "The Development of Offending and Antisocial Behaviour From Childhood: Key Findings from the Cambridge Study in Delinquent Development." *Journal of Child Psychology and Psychiatry and Allied Disciplines, 36*(6): 929–64.

Farrington, David P. 2005. "Childhood Origins of Antisocial Behavior." *Clinical Psychology and Psychotherapy, 12*(3): 177–90.

Ferraro, Monique M., and Eoghan Casey. 2005. *Investigating Child Exploitation and Pornography: The Internet, the Law and Forensic Science.* London: Elsevier Academic Press.

Ferraro, Monique M., Eoghan Casey, and Michael McGrath. 2005. *Investigating Child Exploitation and Pornography: The Internet, the Law and Forensic Science.* Boston, MA: Elsevier/Academic.

Festinger, L., A. Pepitone, and T. Newcomb. 1952. "Some Consequences of Deindividuation in a Group." *Journal of Abnormal and Social Psychology, 47*(supplement 2): 382–89.

Financial Coalition against Child Pornography. 2008. "Trends in Migration, Hosting and Payment for Commercial Child Pornography Websites." *Technology Challenges Working Group Report 2008.* Available at http://www.missingkids.com/missingkids/servlet/PageServlet?LanguageCountry=en_US&PageId=3703 (accessed on December 12, 2011).

Financial Coalition against Child Pornography. 2011. *Report on Trends in Online Crime and Their Potential Implications in the Fight Against Commercial Child Pornography.* Available at http://www.missingkids.com/missingkids/servlet/PageServlet?LanguageCountry=en_US&PageId=3703 (accessed on December 12, 2011).

Finkelhor, David. 1984. *Child Sexual Abuse: New Theory and Research.* New York: Free Press.

Finkelhor, David. 2010. *The Internet, Youth Deviance and the Problem of Juvenoia.* Video of presentation at University of New Hampshire, October 22. Available at http://vimeo.com/16900027 (accessed on December 12, 2011).

Finkelhor, David, and Jennifer Dziuba-Leatherman. 1994. "Victimization of Children." *American Psychologist, 49*(3): 173–83.

Finkelhor, David, and Jennifer Dziuba-Leatherman. 2001. "Victimization of Children." In Ray Bull (ed.), *Children and the Law: The Essential Readings*, pp. 5–28. Oxford: Blackwell Publishing.

Fournier de Saint Maur, Agnes. 1999. *Sexual Abuse of Children on the Internet: A New Challenge for INTERPOL.* Expert Meeting on Sexual Abuse of Children, Child Pornography and Paedophilia on the Internet: an International Challenge. UNESCO, Paris, Room II, 18–19 January 1999.

GAO. 2004. "File Sharing Programs: Users of Peer-to-Peer Networks Can Readily Access Child Pornography." *Testimony Before the Subcommittee on Commerce, Trade, and Consumer Protection, Committee on Energy and Commerce, House of Representatives.* Washington, DC: United States General Accounting Office.

Gibson, Laura E., and Harold Leitenberg. 2000. "Child Sexual Abuse Prevention Programs: Do They Decrease the Occurrence of Child Sexual Abuse?" *Child Abuse and Neglect, 24*(9): 1115–25.

Graham, William R., Jr. 2000. "Uncovering and Eliminating Child Pornography Rings on the Internet: Issues Regarding and Avenues Facilitating Law Enforcement's Access to 'Wonderland'." *The Law Review of Michigan State University-Detroit College of Law, 2*: 457–84.

Grasmick, Harold G., and George J. Bryjak. 1980. "The Deterrent Effect of Perceived Severity of Punishment." *Social Forces, 59*(2): 471–91.

Griffith, Gareth, and Kathryn Simon. 2008. *Child Pornography Law Briefing Paper No 9/ 08* Sydney: NSW Parliamentary Library Research Service. Available at http:// www.parliament.nsw.gov.au/prod/parlment/publications.nsf/0/289C584B88554B CBCA2574B400125787/$File/Child%20pornography%20law%20and%20index .pdf (accessed on December 12, 2011).

Gottfredson, Michael R., and Travis Hirschi. 1990. *A General Theory of Crime A General Theory of Crime*. Palo Alto, CA: Stanford University Press.

Guerette, R. T., and Bowers, K. J. (2009) "Assessing the Extent of Crime Displacement and Diffusion of Benefits: A Review of Situational Prevention Evaluations," *Criminology, 47*: 1331–68.

Hafner, Katie, and Mathew Lyon. 1998. *Where Wizards Stay Up Late: The Origins Of The Internet*. New York, NY: Simon & Schuster.

Hallett, S. (1996). "Trauma and Coping in Homicide and Child Sexual Abuse Detectives." *Dissertation Abstracts International, 57*(3-B). (UMI No. 9623716).

Hanson, R. Karl, and Monique T. Bussière. 1998. "Predicting Relapse: A Meta-Analysis of Sexual Offender Recidivism Studies." *Journal of Consulting and Clinical Psychology, 66*(2): 348–62.

Hanson, R. Karl., Arthur Gordon, Andrew J. R. Harris, Janice K. Marques, William Murphy, Vernon L. Quinsey, and Michael C. Seto. 2002. "First Report of the Collaborative Outcome Data Project on the Effectiveness of Psychological Treatment of Sex Offenders." *Sexual Abuse: A Journal of Research and Treatment, 14*(2): 169–95.

Hanson, Rochelle F., Heidi S. Resnick, Benjamin E. Saunders, Dean G. Kilpatrick, and Connie Best, 1999. 'Factors Related to the Reporting of Childhood Rape." *Child Abuse and Neglect, 23*(6): 559–69.

Harvey, John H., Terri L. Orbuch, Kathleen D. Chwalisz, and Gail Garwood. 1991. "Coping with Sexual Assault: The Roles of Account-Making and Confiding." *Journal of Traumatic Stress 4*(4): 515–31.

Hawkins, J. D., T. L. Herrenkohl, D. P. Farrington, D. Brewer, R. F Catalano, and T. W. Harachi. 1998. "A Review of Predictors of Youth Violence." In R. Loeber & D. P. Farrington (eds.), *Serious and violent juvenile offenders: Risk factors and successful interventions*, pp. 106–46. Thousand Oaks, CA: Sage Publications.

Hébert, Martine, Nathalie Parent, Isabelle V. Daignault, and Marc Tourigny. 2006. "A Typological Analysis of Behavioral Profiles of Sexually Abused Children." *Child Maltreatment, 11*: 203–16.

Henry, Jim. 1997. "System Intervention Trauma to Child Sexual Abuse Victims Following Disclosure." *Journal of Interpersonal Violence, 12*(4): 499–512.

Henry, Olivia, Rebecca Mandeville-Norden, Elizabeth Hayes, and Vincent Egan. 2010. "Do Internet-Based Sexual Offenders Reduce to Normal, Inadequate and Deviant groups?" *Journal of Sexual Aggression, 16*(1): 33–46.

Heriot, Jessica K. 1996. "Maternal Protectiveness Following the Disclosure of Intrafamilial child sexual abuse." *Journal of Interpersonal Violence, 11*(2): 181–94.

Hershkowitz, Irit, Micahle E. Lamb, Kathleen J. Sternberg, and Phillip W. Esplin. 1997. "The Relationships Among Interviewer Utterance Type, CBCA Scores, and the Richness of Children's Responses." *Legal and Criminological Psychology, 2*: 169–76.

Hickey, William. 1995. *Memoirs of a Georgian Rake*, ed. Roger Hudson. London, UK: Folio Society.

Higgins, Daryl. J., Leah M. Bromfield, and Nick Richardson. 2007. *Mandatory Reporting of Child Abuse*. Available at: http://www.aifs.gov.au/nch/pubs/sheets/rs3/rs3.html (accessed on December 12, 2011).

Homel, Ross, and Clark, Jeff. 1994. "The Prediction and Prevention of Violence in Pubs and Clubs." In Ronald V. Clarke (ed.), *Crime Prevention Studies Volume 3*, pp. 1–46. Monsey, NY: Criminal Justice Press.

Homel, Ross, Marg Hauritz, Richard Wortley, Gillian McIlwain, and Russell Carvolth. 1997. "Preventing Alcohol-Related Crime Through Community Action: The Surfers Paradise Safety Action Project." In Ross Homel (ed.), *Policing for Prevention: Reducing Crime, Public Intoxication and Injury*, pp. 35–90. Monsey, NY: Criminal Justice Press.

Hoover, J. Nicholas. 2006. As Child Porn Industry Grows, Coalition Launches Counterattack. *Information Week*. Available at http://www.informationweek.com/news/183700580 (accessed on December 12, 2011).

Horton, Merlyn. 2001. *Places of Risk, Places of Help, Internet Exploitation: An Overview of Existing Technology*. Available at http://www.safeonlineoutreach.com/pdf/Places_of_Risk_Help.pdf (accessed on December 12, 2011).

House Standing Committee on Communications. 2009. *Enquiry into Cybercrime. Supplementary Submission No. 34.1*. Available at http://www.aph.gov.au/house/committee/coms/cybercrime/ (accessed on December 12, 2011).

Howard, James L., Clifford B. Reifler, and Myron B.Liptzin. 1971. "Effects of Exposure to Pornography." *Technical Reports of the Commission on Obscenity and Pornography, Volume 8*, pp. 97–132. Washington, DC: US Government Printing Office.

Howie, Michael. 2005. "Doubts Cast Over Success of Child Porn Inquiry." *News. Scotsman.com*. Available at http://www.scotsman.com/news/scottish-news/edinburgh-east-fife/doubts_cast_over_success_of_child_porn_inquiry_1_1098485 (accessed on December 12, 2011).

Howitt, Dennis and Kerry Sheldon. 2007. "The Role of Cognitive Distortions in Paedophilic Offending: Internet and Contact Offenders Compared." *Psychology, Crime & Law, 13*(5): 469–86.

Hunter, Ronald D., and C. Ray Jeffery. 1992. "Preventing Convenience Store Robbery Through Environmental Design." In Ronald V. Clarke (ed.), *Situational Crime Prevention: Successful Case Studies*, pp. 194–204. Albany, NY: Criminal Justice press.

International Centre for Missing & Exploited Children. 2008. *Child Pornography: Model Legislation & Global Review* (5th ed). Available at http://www.icmec.org/missingkids/servlet/PageServlet?LanguageCountry=en_X1&PageId=4348 (accessed on December 12, 2011).

Internet Watch Foundation. 2007. *2007 Annual and Charity Report*. Available at http://www.iwf.org.uk/accountability/annual-reports/2007-annual-report (accessed on December 12, 2011).

Internet Watch Foundation. 2008. *2008 Annual and Charity Report*. http://www.iwf.org.uk/accountability/annual-reports/2008-annual-report (accessed on December 12, 2011).

Internet Watch Foundation. 2010. *2010 Annual and Charity Report*. Available at http://www.iwf.org.uk/accountability/annual-reports/2010-annual-report (accessed on December 12, 2011).

Internet World Stats. 2011 *Internet Growth Statistics*. Available at http://www.internetworldstats.com/emarketing.htm (accessed on December 12, 2011).

Jayachandran, C. R. 2003. "World Wide Porn: 260 mn, Growing." *Times of India*. Available at http://timesofindia.indiatimes.com/World-wide-porn-260-mn-growing/articleshow/203486.cms (accessed on December 12, 2011).

Jenkins, Philip. 2001. *Beyond Tolerance: Child Pornography on the Internet*. New York: New York University Press.

Jewkes, Yvonne. 2010. "Much Ado About Nothing? Representations and Realities of Online Soliciting of Children." *Journal of Sexual Aggression, 16*(1): 5–18.

Jewkes, Yvonne, and Carol Andrews. 2005. "Policing the Filth: The Problems of Investigating Online Child Pornography in England and Wales." *Policing and Society, 15*(1): 42–62.

Joinson, Adam N. 1998. "Causes and Implications of Disinhibited Behaviour on the Net." In Jayne Gackenbach (ed.), *Psychology and the Internet: Intrapersonal, Interpersonal, and Transpersonal Implications*. California. Academic Press.

Jones, Edward E. 1979. "The Rocky Road from Acts to Dispositions." *American Psychologist, 34*(2): 107–17.

Jones, Lisa, and David Finkelhor. 2009. *Updated trends in child maltreatment, 2007*. Durham: University of New Hampshire: Crimes against Children Research Center.

Kellogg, Nancy D., and Thomas J Hoffman. 1995. "Unwanted and Illegal Sexual Experiences in Childhood and Adolescence." *Child Abuse and Neglect, 19*(9): 1457–68.

Kendall-Tackett, Kathleen A., Linda M. Williams, and David Finkelhor. 1993. "Impact of Sexual Abuse on Children: A Review and Synthesis of Recent Empirical Studies." *Psychological Bulletin, 113*(1): 164–80.

Kilpatrick, Dean G., and Benjamin E. Saunders. 1999. *Prevalence and Consequences of Child Victimization: Results from the National Survey of Adolescents: Final Report* (NIJ Grant No. 93-IJCX-0023). Charleston, SC: Author.

Krafft-Ebing, R.v. 1886. Psychopathia Sexualis, (English translation), New York: Rebman Company. Available at http://www.archive.org/details/psychopathia sexu00krafuoft (accessed on December 12, 2011).

Krone, Tony. 2004. "A Typology of Online Child Pornography Offending." *Trends & Issues in Crime and Criminal Justice, No 279*. Canberra, Australia: Australian Institute of Criminology. Available at http://www.aic.gov.au/documents/4/F/8/%7B4F8B4249-7BEE-4F57-B9ED-993479D9196D%7Dtandi279.pdf (accessed on December 12, 2011).

Krone, Tony. 2005. "International Police Operations Against online Child Pornography." *Trends & Issues in Crime and Criminal Justice, No. 296*. Canberra, Australia: Australian Institute of Criminology. Available at http://www.aic.gov.au/documents/3/C/E/%7B3CED11B0-F3F4-479C-B417-4669506B3886%7Dtandi296.pdf (accessed on December 12, 2011).

Landenberger, Nana A., and Mark W. Lipsey. 2005. "The Positive Effects of Cognitive–Behavioral Programs for Offenders: A Meta-Analysis of Factors Associated with Effective Treatment." *Journal of Experimental Criminology, 1*(4): 451–76.

Larner, Mary B., Carol S. Stevenson, and Richard E. Behrman, 1998. "Protecting Children from Abuse and Neglect: Analysis and Recommendations." *The Future of Children, 8*(1): 4–22.

Latapy, Matthieu, Cl´emence Magnien, and Raphäel Fournier. 2009. *Quantification of Paedophile Activity in a Large P2P System.* Available at http://antipaedo.lip6.fr (accessed on December 12, 2011).

Lawson, Louanne, and Mark Chaffin. 1992. "False Negatives in Sexual Abuse Disclosure Interviews: Incidence and Influence of Caretaker's Belief in Abuse in Cases of Accidental Abuse Discovery of STD." *Journal of Interpersonal Violence, 7*(4): 532–42.

LeBeau, James L. 2002. "The Impact of a Hurricane on Routine Activities and on Calls For Police Service: Charlotte, North Carolina, and Hurricane Hugo." *Crime Prevention and Community Safety: An International Journal, 4*: 53–64.

Lee, Lung-Hao, and Cheng-Jye Luh. 2008. "Generation of Pornographic Blacklist and its Incremental Update Using an Inverse Chi-Square Based Method." *Information Processing and Management, 44*(5): 1698–706.

Leiner, Barry M., Vinton G. Cerf, David D. Clark, et al. 2011. *Brief history of the Internet.* Internet Society. Available at http://www.internetsociety.org/internet/internet-51/history-internet/brief-history-internet (accessed on December 12, 2011).

Lemos, Robert. 2008. "P2P Investigation Leads to Child-Porn Busts." *Security Focus, August 19.* Available at http://www.securityfocus.com/brief/801 (accessed on December 12, 2011).

Leonard, Marcella M. 2010. "I did What I Was Directed To Do But He Didn't Touch Me: The Impact of Being a Victim of Internet Offending." *Journal of Sexual Aggression, 16*(2): 249–56.

Leyden, John. 2008. "P2P Searches Touted as Tool Against Child Abuse." *The Register.* Available at http://www.theregister.co.uk/2008/04/21/child_abuse_clampdown/ (accessed on December 12, 2011).

Licklider, J. C. R. 1960. "Man-Computer Symbiosis." *IRE Transactions on Human Factors in Electronics*, volume HFE-1(1): 4–11.

Light, Roy, Claire Nee, and Helen Ingham. 1993. *Car Theft: The Offender's Perspective. Home Office Research Study No. 130.* London: HMSO.

Linz, Daniel., and Dorothy Imrich. 2001. "Child Pornography." In Susan O. White (ed.), *Handbook of Youth and Justice*, pp. 79–114. New York: Kluwer Academic/Plenum.

Lipsey, Mark W., and James H. Derzon. 1998. "Predictors of Serious Delinquency in Adolescence and Early Adulthood: A Synthesis of Longitudinal Research." In R. Loeber and D. P. Farrington (eds.), *Serious and violent juvenile offenders: Risk factors and successful interventions*, pp. 86–105. Thousand Oaks, CA: Sage Publications.

Loeber, R., W. B. Van Kammen, and M. Fletcher. 1996. *Serious, Violent and Chronic Offenders in the Pittsburgh Youth Study: Unpublished Data.* Pittsburgh, PA: Western Psychiatric Institute and Clinic.

London, Kamala, Maggie Bruck, Stephen J. Ceci, and Daniel W. Shuman. 2005. "Disclosure of Child Sexual Abuse: What Does the Research Tell Us About the Ways that Children Tell?" *Psychology, Public Policy, and Law, 11*(1): 194–226.

Lösel, Freidrich, and Martin Schmucker. 2005. "The Effectiveness of Treatment for Sexual Offenders: A Comprehensive Meta-Analysis." *Journal of Experimental Criminology, 1*(1): 117–46.

Maalla, Najat M'jid. 2009. *Promotion and Protection of All Human Rights, Civil, Political, Economic, Social and Cultural Rights, Including the Right to Development.* Report of the Special Rapporteur on the sale of children, child prostitution and child pornography. United Nations, General Assembly, Human Rights Council

MacIntyre, Deirdre, and Alan Carr. 2000. "Prevention of Child Sexual Abuse: Implications of Programme Evaluation Research." *Child Abuse Review, 9*(3): 183–99.

Macintyre, Stuart and Ross Homel. 1997. "Danger on the Dance Floor: A Study of Interior Design, Crowding and Aggression in Nightclubs." In Ross Homel (ed.) *Policing for Prevention: Reducing Crime, Public Intoxication and Injury,* pp. 91–114. Monsey, NY: Criminal Justice Press.

Maurushat, Alana, and Renee Watt. 2009. "Clean Feed: Australia's Internet Filtering Proposal." *University of New South Wales Faculty of Law Research Series, Paper 7.* Available at http://law.bepress.com/unswwps/flrps09/art7 (accessed on December 12, 2011).

McCabe, Kimberley A. 2000. "Child Pornography and the Internet." *Social Science Computer Review, 18*(1): 73–76.

McCarthy, Jennifer A. 2010. Internet Sexual Activity: A Comparison Between Contact and Non-Contact Child Pornography Offenders." *Journal of Sexual Aggression, 16*(2): 181–95.

McCullagh, Declan. 2008. *FBI Posts Fake Hyperlinks to Snare Child Porn Suspects.* CNET, March 20. Available at http://news.cnet.com/8301-13578_3-9899151-38.html (accessed on December 12, 2011).

McEwen v. Simmons & Anor. 2008. *NSWSC 1292.*

McGloin, Jean M., and Cathy S. Widom. 2001. "Resilience Among Abused and Neglected Children Grown up." *Development and Psychopathology, 13*(4): 1021–38.

Mehta, Michael D., Don Best, and Nancy Poon. 2002. "Peer-to-Peer Sharing on the Internet: An Analysis of How Gnutella Networks Are Used to Distribute Pornographic Material." *Canadian Journal of Law and Technology, 1*(1). Available at http://cjlt.dal.ca/vol1_no1/articles/01_01_MeBePo_gnutella.pdf (accessed on December 12, 2011).

Memon, Amina, and Rita Vartoukian. 1996. "The Effect of Repeated Questioning on Young Children's Eyewitness Testimony." *British Journal of Psychology, 87*(3): 403–15.

Messman-Moore, Terri L., and Amy L. Brown. 2004. "Child Maltreatment and Perceived Family Environment as Risk Factors for Adult Rape: Is Child Sexual Abuse the Most Salient Experience?" *Child Abuse and Neglect, 28*: 1019–34.

Middleton, David, Ian A. Elliott, Rebecca Mandeville-Norden, and Anthony R. Beech. 2006. "An Investigation into the Applicability of the Ward and Siegert Pathways Model of Child Sexual Abuse with Internet Offenders." *Psychology, Crime & Law, 12*(6): 589–603.

Mitchell, Kimberly J., David Finkelhor, and Janis Wolak. 2007. "Online Requests for Sexual Pictures from Youth: Risk Factors and Incident Characteristics." *Journal of Adolescent Health, 41*: 196–203.

Moffitt, Terrie E. 1990. "Juvenile Delinquency and Attention Deficit Disorder: Developmental Trajectories from Age 3 to 15." *Child Development, 61*(3): 893–910.

Morrison, Shona, and Ian O'Donnell. 1994. *Armed Robbery: A Study in London.* Oxford: Centre for Criminological Research.

Mostyn, Micahel M. 2000. "The Need for Regulating Anonymous Remailers." *International Review of Law Computers & Technology, 14*(1): 79–88.

Moultrie, Denise. 2006. "Adolescents Convicted of Possession of Abuse Images of Children: A New Type of Adolescent Sex Offender?" *Journal of Sexual Aggression, 12*(2): 165–74.

Mountain, L. J., W. M. Hirst, and M. J. Maher. 2005. "Are Speed Enforcement Cameras More Effective Than Other Speed Management Measures? The Impact of Speed Management Schemes on 30 mph Roads." *Accident Analysis and Prevention, 37*(4): 742–54.

Muhlin, Gregory L., Patricia Cohen, Elmer L. Struening, Louis E. Genevie, Seymour R. Kaplan, and Harris B. Peck. 1981. "Behavioral Epidemiology and Social Area Analysis: The Study of Blackout Looting." *Evaluation and Program Planning, 4*(1): 35–42.

Myers, John E. B. 1994. "Adjudication of Sexual Abuse Cases." *The Future of Children, 4*(2): 84–101.

Nagin, Daniel. 1978. "Crime Rates, Sanction Levels, and Constraints on prison Population." *Law & Society Review, 12*(3): 341–66.

Najman, J. M., G. M. Williams, J. Nikles, S. Spence, W. Bor, M. O'Callaghan, R. Le Brocque, M. J. Andersen, and G. J. Shuttlewood. 2001. "Bias Influencing Maternal Reports of Child Behaviour and Emotional State." *Social Psychiatry and Psychiatric Epidemiology, 36*(4): 186–94.

National Campaign to Prevent Teen and Unplanned Pregnancy. 2008. *Sex and Tech: Results From a Survey of Teens and Young Adults*. Available at http://www .thenationalcampaign.org/sextech/PDF/SexTech_Summary.pdf (accessed on December 12, 2011).

National Center for Missing and Exploited Children. 2005. *Child Porn Among Fastest Growing Internet Businesses*. Available at http://www.missingkids.com/ missingkids/servlet/NewsEventServlet?LanguageCountry=en_US&PageId=2064 (accessed on December 12, 2011).

Neutze, Janina, Michael C. Seto, Gerard A. Schaefer, Ingrid A. Mundt, and Klaus M. Beier. 2011. "Predictors of Child Pornography Offenses and Child Sexual Abuse in a Community Sample of Pedophiles and Hebephiles." *Sexual Abuse: A Journal of Research and Treatment, 23*: 212–42.

Newman Graeme R., and Ronald V. Clarke. 2003. *Superhighway Robbery: Preventing e-commerce Crime*. Cullompton UK: Willan.

NewsFlavor. 2011. "British Man in Possession of The Largest Collection of Child Pornography in History" *NewsFlavor*. Available at http://newsflavor.com/alternative/ british-man-in-possession-of-the-largest-collection-of-child-pornography-in-history/ #ixzz1ZRvZUZ6k (accessed on December 12, 2011).

New York v. *Ferber*. 1982. (458 U.S. 747).

Novoa, Ana M., Katherine Pérez, Elena Santamariña-Rubio, Marc Marí-Dell'Olmo, and Aurelio Tobías. 2010. "Effectiveness of Speed Enforcement by Fixed Speed Cameras: A Time Series Study." *Injury Prevention, 16*(1): 12–16.

O'Donohue, William T., and James H. Geer. 1985. "The Habituation of Sexual Arousal." *Archives of Sexual Behavior, 143*: 233–46.

Office of the United Nations High Commissioner for Human Rights. 2002. *Optional Protocol to the Convention on the Rights of the Child on the Sale of Children, Child*

Prostitution and Child Pornography, G. A. Res. 54/263, Annex II, U.N. Doc. A/54/49, Vol. III, art. 2, para. c, *entered into force* January 18, 2002. Available at http://www2.ohchr.org/english/law/crc-sale.htm (accessed on December 12, 2011).

Olds, David L. 2002. "Prenatal and infancy home visiting by nurses: From Randomised Trials to Community Replication." *Prevention Science, 3*(3): 153–72.

Osborne v. *Ohio*. 1990. 495 U.S. 103.

Painter, Kate A., and David P. Farrington. 1999. "Street Lighting and Crime: Diffusion of Benefits in the Stoke-on-Trent Project." In Kate. A. Painter and Nick Tilley (eds.), *Surveillance of Public Space: CCTV, Street Lighting and Crime Prevention Crime Prevention Studies*, vol. 10. Monsey, NY: Criminal Justice Press.

Panksepp, Jaak. 1998. *Affective Neuroscience: The Foundations of Human and Animal Emotions*. New York, New York: Oxford University Press.

Parilla, Peter F., Richard C. Hollinger, and John P. Clark. 1988. "Organizational Control of Deviant Behavior: The Case of Employee Theft." *Social Science Quarterly, 69*(2): 261–80.

Pence, Donna M., and Charles A. Wilson. 1994. "Reporting and Investigating Child Sexual Abuse." *The Future of Children 4*(2): 70–83.

Perez, Lisa M., JeremyJones, David R. Englert, and Daniel Sachau. 2010. "Secondary Traumatic Stress and Burnout among Law Enforcement Investigators Exposed to Disturbing Media Images." *Journal of Police and Criminal Psychology, 25*(2): 113–24.

Petit, Juan M. 2006. Rights of the Child. Report of the Special Rapporteur on the Sale of Children, Child Prostitution and Child Pornography. United Nations. Economic and Social Council.

Petrosino, Anthony, Carolyn Turpin-Petrosino, and John Buehler. 2003. "Scared Straight and Other Juvenile Awareness Programs for Preventing Juvenile Delinquency: A Systematic Review of the Randomized Experimental Evidence." *Annals of the American Academy of Political and Social Science, 589*(1): 41–62.

Pithers, W. D., J. K. Marques, C. C. Gibat, and G. A. Marlatt. 1983. "Relapse Prevention with Sexual Aggressives: A Self-Control Model of Treatment and Maintenance of Change." In J. G. Greer and I. R. Stuart (eds.), *The Sexual Aggressor: Current Perspectives on Treatment*, pp. 214–39. New York: Van Nostrand-Reinhold.

Postmes, Tom, and Russell Spears. 1998. Deindividuation and Antinormative Behavior: A Meta-Analysis. *Psychological Bulletin, 123*(3): 238–59.

Potter, Roberto Hugh, and Lyndy A. Potter. 2001. "The Internet, Cyberporn, and Sexual Exploitation of Children: Media Moral Panics and Urban Myths For Middle -Class Parents?" *Sexuality & Culture, 5*(3): 31–48.

Poyner, B. 1988. "Video Cameras and Bus Vandalism." *Security Administration, 11*: 44–51.

Poyner, B. 1991. "Situational Crime Prevention in Two Parking Facilities." *Security Journal, 2*: 96–101.

Quayle, Ethel, Lars Loof, and Tink Palmer. 2008. *Child Pornography and Sexual Exploitation of Children Online: A Contribution of ECPAT International to the World Congress 111 Against Sexual Exploitation of Children and Adolescents*. ECPAT International. Available at http://www.ecpat.net/WorldCongressIII/PDF/Publications/ICT_Psychosocial/Thematic_Paper_ICTPsy_ENG.pdf (accessed on December 12, 2011).

Quayle, Ethel, and Max Taylor. 2002. "Child Pornography and the Internet: Perpetuating a Cycle of Abuse." *Deviant Behavior, 23*(4): 331–61.

Quayle, Ethel, and Max Taylor. 2003. "Model of Problematic Internet Use in People with a Sexual Interest in Children" *Cyberpsychology and Behavior, 6*(1): 93–106.

Randall, Peter. 1997. *Adult Bullying: Perpetrators and Victims*. London: Routledge.

Redondo, Santiago, Julia Sánchez-Meca, and Vicente Garrido. 1999. "The Influence of Treatment Programmes on the Recidivism of Juvenile *and A*dult offenders: An European Meta-Analytic Review." *Psychology, Crime and Law, 5*(3): 251–78.

Reijnen, Lotte, Erik Bulten, and Henk Nijman. 2009. "Demographic and Personality Characteristics of Internet Child Pornography Downloaders in Comparison to Other Offenders." *Journal of Child Sexual Abuse, 18*(6): 611–22.

Rind, Bruce, Philip Tromovitch, and Robert Bauserman. 1998. "A Meta-Analytic Examination of Assumed Properties of Child Sexual Abuse Using College Samples." *Psychological Bulletin 124:* 22–53.

Rispens, Jan, Andre Aleman, and Paul P. Goudena. 1997. "Prevention of Child Sexual Abuse Victimization: A Meta-Analysis of School Programs." *Child Abuse and Neglect, 21*(10): 975–87.

Robertson, Stephen. No Date. "Age of Consent Laws," in *Children and Youth in History*, *Item #230*. Available at http://chnm.gmu.edu/cyh/teaching-modules/230 (accessed on December 12, 2011).

Rogers, Marcus K., Kathryn Seigfried, and Kirti Tidke. 2006. "Self-reported Computer Criminal Behavior: A Psychological Analysis." *Digital Investigation, 3*: 116–20.

Roodman, Alison A., and George A. Clum. 2001. "Revictimization Rates and Method Variance: A Meta-Analysis." *Clinical Psychology Review, 21*(2): 183–204.

Ropelato, Jerry. 2003. *Pornography Statistics 2003*. Available at http://web.archive.org/web/20030621095030/http://www.internetfilterreview.com/internet-pornography -statistics.html (accessed on December 12, 2011).

Ropelato, Jerry. 2011. "Internet Pornography Statistics." *Top Ten Reviews*. Available at http://internet-filter-review.toptenreviews.com/internet-pornography-statistics.html (accessed on December 12, 2011).

Rosenfeld, Michael J. 1997. Celebration, Politics, Selective Looting and Riots: A Micro Level Study of the Bulls Riot of 1992 in Chicago." *Social Problems, 44*(4): 483–502.

Ross, Lee. 1977. "The Intuitive Psychologist and his Shortcomings: Distortions in the Attribution Process." In Leonard Berkowitz (ed.), *Advances in Experimental Psychology* (vol. 10), pp. 174–214. New York: Academic Press.

Sanderson, Jennifer. 2004. "Child-Focussed Sexual Abuse Prevention Programs: How Effective Are They in Preventing Child Abuse?" *Research and Issues Paper Series, No. 5*. Brisbane: Crime and Misconduct Commission.

Sandy, Geoffrey A. 2009. "Mandatory ISP Filtering for a Clean Feed to Australian Internet Subscribers." *AMCIS 2009 Proceedings. Paper 779*. Available at http://aisel .aisnet.org/amcis2009/779 (accessed on December 12, 2011).

Sarno, Julie A., and Sandra K. Wurtele. 1997. "Effects of a Personal Safety Program on Preschoolers' Knowledge, Skills, and Perceptions of Child Sexual Abuse." *Child Maltreatment, 2*(1): 35–46.

Sas, Louise D., David A. Wolfe, and Kevin Gowdey. 1996. "Children and the Courts in Canada." *Criminal Justice and Behavior, 23*(2): 338–57.

Sauzier, M. 1989. "Disclosure of Child Sexual Abuse: For Better or Worse." *Psychiatric Clinics of North America, 12*(2): 455–69.

Schotenfield, Dara L. 2007. "Witches and Communists and Internet Sex Offenders, Oh My: Why it is Time to Call Off The Hunt." *ST. Thomas Law Review, 20*: 359–86.

Schwartz, Mark F., and Stephen Southern. 2000. "Compulsive Cybersex: The New Tea Room." *Sexual Addiction & Compulsivity, 7*(1–2): 127–44.

Schweinhart, Lawrence J., Helen V. Barnes, and David P. Weikhart. 1993. *Significant Benefits: The High/Scope Perry Preschool Study through Age 27.* Ypsilanti, MI: High/Scope Educational Research Foundation.

Seate, Mike. 2009, February 3. "Sexting arrests provide warning". Tribune-Review. Available at http://www.pittsburghlive.com/x/pittsburghtrib/opinion/columnists/seate/s_609935.html (accessed on December 12, 2011).

Seigfried, Kathryn C., Richard W. Lovely, and Marcus K. Rogers. 2008. "Self-Reported Online Child Pornography Behavior: A Psychological Analysis." *International Journal of Cyber Criminology, 2*(1): 286–97.

Sentencing Guidelines Council. 2007. *Sexual Offences Act 2003: Definitive Guideline.* London, UK: Sentencing Guidelines Council.

Seto, Michael C., James M. Cantor, and Ray Blanchard. 2006. "Child Pornography Offenses Are a Valid Diagnostic Indicator of Pedophilia." *Journal of Abnormal Psychology, 115*(3): 610–15.

Seto, Michael C., Hanson, R. Karl, and Kelly M. Babchishin. 2011. "Contact Sexual Offending by Men with Online Sexual Offenses." *Sexual Abuse: A Journal of Research and Treatment, 23*(1): 124–45.

Sexual Exploitation of Children Act. 1978. Pub.L. 95-225, 92 Stat. 7

Sherriff, Lucy. 2004. "Child Porn Suspect Suicide Tally Hits 32." *The Register.* December 21. Available at http://www.theregister.co.uk/2004/12/21/child_porn_suicide_shame/ (accessed on December 12, 2011).

Shuler, Rus. 2005. *How Does the Internet Work?* Available at http://www.theshulers.com/whitepapers/internet_whitepaper/index.html (accessed on December 12, 2011).

Sidebottom, A., J. Belur, K. Bowers, L. Tompson, and S. D. Johnson. 2011. Theft in Price-Volatile Markets: On the Relationship between Copper Price and Copper Theft. *Journal of Research on Crime & Delinquency, 48*(3): 396–418.

Silbert, Mimi H. 1989. "The Effects on Juveniles of Being Used for Pornography and Prostitution." In Dolf Zillman and Jennings Bryant (eds.), *Pornography: Research Advances and Policy Considerations*, pp. 215–34. Hillsdale, NJ: Lawrence Erlbaum and Associates.

Simon, Leonore M. J., and Kristen Zgoba. 2006. "Sex Crimes Against Children: Legislation, Prevention and Investigation." In Richard Wortley and Stephen Smallbone (eds.), *Situational prevention of Child Sexual Abuse*, pp. 65–100. Monsey NY: Criminal Justice Press.

Smallbone, Stephen. 2006. "An Attachment Theoretical Revision of Marshall and Barbaree's Integrated Theory of the Etiology of Sexual Offending." In William L. Marshall, Yolanda M. Fernandez, and Liam E. Marshall (eds.), *Sexual Offender Treatment: Controversial Issues*, pp. 93–108. Hboken, NJ: Wiley.

Smallbone, Stephen, William L Marshall, and Richard Wortley. 2008. *Preventing Child Sexual Abuse: Evidence, Policy and Practice.* Cullompton, UK: Willan Publishing.

Spaccarelli, Steve. 1994. "Stress, Appraisal, and Coping in Child Sexual Abuse: A Theoretical and Empirical Review." *Psychological Bulletin, 116*(2): 340–62.

Stanley, Janet. 2001. "Child Abuse and the Internet." *National Child Protection Clearinghouse*, vol. 115 (Summer). Melbourne: Australian Institute of Family Studies. Available at www.aifs.org.au/nch/ (accessed on April 19, 2010).

Steel, Chad M. S. 2009. "Web-Based Child Pornography: Quantification and Qualification of Demand." *International Journal of Digital Crime and Forensics, 1*(4): 58–60.

Sternberg, Kathleen J., Micahel E. Lamb, Yael Orbach, Phillip W. Esplin, and Susanne Mitchell. 2001. "Use of Structured Investigative Protocol Enhances Young Children's Responses to Free-Recall Prompts in the Course of Forensic Interviews." *Journal of Applied Psychology, 86*(5): 997–1005.

Stol, W. Ph., H. K. W. Kaspersen, J. Kerstens, E. R. Leukfeldt, and A. R. Lodder. 2009. Governmental filtering of websites: The Dutch case. *Computer Law and Security Review, 25*(3): 251–62.

Stop It Now! 2006. *The Campaign to Prevent Child Sexual Abuse*. Available at http://www.stopitnow.org/about.html (accessed on December 12, 2011).

Stop It Now! UK and Ireland. 2010. *Stop it Now Helpline Report 2005-2009*. Available at http://www.stopitnow.org.uk/files/Helpline%20Report%2009%20SM.pdf (accessed on December 12, 2011).

Suler, John. 2004. "The Online Disinhibition Effect." *CyberPsychology & Behavior*, 7(3): 321–26.

Sullivan, Joe and Anthony, Beech. 2004. "Assessing Internet Sex Offenders." In Martin C. Calder (ed.) *Child Sexual Abuse and the Internet: Tackling the New Frontier*, pp. 69–83. Lyme Regis, UK: Russell House Publishing.

Svedin, Carl G., and Christina Back. 2003. *Why Didn't They Tell Us? Sexual Abuse in Child Pornography*. Stockholm, Sweden: Save the Children Sweden. Available at http://158.126.240.41/pages/13265/Report%20Save%20the%20Children_okt-11.pdf (accessed on December 12, 2011).

Sykes, Gresham M., and David Matza. 1957. "Techniques of Neutralization: A Theory of Delinquency." *American Sociological Review, 22*(6): 664–70.

Taal, Margot, and Edelaar, Monique. 1997. "Positive and Negative Effects of a Child Sexual Abuse Prevention Program." *Child Abuse and Neglect, 21*(4): 399–410.

Tate, Tim. 1990. *Child Pornography: An Investigation*. London, UK: Methuen.

Taylor, Max, and Ethel Quayle. 2003. *Child Pornography: An Internet Crime*. London: Brunner-Routledge.

Taylor, Max, and Ethel Quayle. 2006. "The Internet and Abuse Images of Children: Search, Precriminal Situations and Opportunity." In Richard Wortley and Stephen Smallbone (eds.), *Situational Prevention of Child Sexual Abuse. Crime Prevention Studies*, vol. 19, pp. 169–96. Monsey, NY: Criminal Justice Press.

Taylor, Max, Ethel Quayle, and Gemma Holland. 2001. "Child Pornography, the Internet and Offending". *The Canadian Journal of Policy Research* (ISUMA) *2*(2): 94–100.

Teh, Yik, Koon. 2008. "The Abuses and Offences Committed During the Tsunami Crisis." *Asian Criminology, 3*: 201–11.

Testa, Maria, Belinda A. Miller, William R. Downs, and Denise Paneck. 1992. "The Moderating Impact of Social Support Following Childhood Sexual Abuse." *Violence and Victims, 7*(2): 173–86.

Thomas, Daphne S. 1997. "Cyberspace Pornography: Problems with Enforcement." *Internet Research: Electronic Networking Applications and Policy, 7*(3): 201–7.

Thornhill, Randy, and Nancy W Thornhill, N. 1987. "Human Rape: The Strengths of the Evolutionary Perspective." In Charles B. Crawford, Martin Smith and Dennis L. Krebbs (eds.), *Sociobiology and Psychology: Ideas, Issues, and Applications*, pp. 269–92. Hillsdale, NJ: Lawrence Erlbaum.

Thornhill, R. and N. Thornhill. 1992. "The Evolutionary Psychology of Men's Coercive Sexuality." *Behavioral and Brain Sciences, 15*: 363–75.

Tomak, Sheri, Frederick S. Weschler, Marjan Ghahramanlou-Holloway, Thomas Virden, and Mahsaw E. Nademin. 2009. "An Empirical Study of the Personality Characteristics of Internet Sex Offenders." *Journal of Sexual Aggression, 15*: 139–48.

Tremblay, Richard. E., Linda Pagani-Kurtz, Louise C. Masse, Frank Vitaro, and Robert O. Phil. 1995. "A Bimodal Preventive Intervention for Disruptive Kindergarten Boys: It's Impact Through Mid-Adolescence" *Journal of Consulting and Clinical Psychology, 63*(4): 560–68.

Trocmé, Nico, Barbara Fallon, Bruce MacLaurin, and Barbara Copp. 2002. *The Changing Face of Child Welfare Investigations in Ontario: Ontario Incidence Studies of Reported Child Abuse and Neglect (OIS 1993/1998)*. Toronto, ON: Centre of Excellence for Child Welfare, Faculty of Social Work, University of Toronto.

Tyler, R. P. "Toby", and Lore E. Stone. 1985. "Child Pornography: Perpetuating the Sexual Victimisation of Children." *Child Abuse & Neglect, 9*: 313–18.

Tyson, Jeff. 2004. *How Internet Infrastructure Works*. How Stuff Works. Available at http://computer.howstuffworks.com/internet/basics/internet-infrastructure.htm (accessed on December 12, 2011).

UNICEF. 2009. *Handbook on the Optional Protocol on the Sale of Children, Child Prostitution and Child Pornography*. Florence, Italy: UNICEF Innocenti Research Centre.

United States v. Borowy, 2010 WL 537501 (U.S. Court of Appeals for the 9th Circuit 2010).

United States v. *Dost*. 1986. 636 F.Supp. 828, 832 (S.D. Cal. 1986), aff 'd sub nom.

United States v. *Knox*. 1995. 32 F.3d 733 (3d Cir. 1994), cert denied, 513 U.S. 1109.

U.S. Department of Justice. 2004. *Law Enforcement Initiative Targets Child Pornography Over Peer-to-Peer Networks*. Available at http://www.fbi.gov/dojpressrel/pressrel04/p2p051404.htm (accessed on December 12, 2011).

U.S. Department of Justice. 2007. *Crime in the United States, 2006*. Available at http://www2.fbi.gov/ucr/cius2006/index.html (accessed on December 12, 2011).

U.S. Department of Justice. 2010. *Crime in the United States 2009*. Available at http://www2.fbi.gov/ucr/cius2009/data/table_65.html (accessed on December 12, 2011).

Ussher, Jane M., and Christopher, Dewberry. 1995. "The Nature and Long-Term Effects of Childhood Sexual Abuse: A Survey of Women Survivors in Britain." *British Journal of Clinical Psychology, 34*(2): 177–92.

Van Bruggen, Lisa K., Marsha G. Runtz, and Helena Kadlec. 2006. "Sexual Revictimization: The Role of Sexual Self-Esteem and Dysfunctional Sexual Behaviors." *Child Maltreatment, 11*(2): 131–45.

Verisign. 2011. *The Domain Name Industry Brief*, 8(3). Available at http://www.verisigninc.com/en_US/why-verisign/research-trends/domain-name-industry-brief/index.xhtml (accessed on December 12, 2011).

Violanti, John M., and Fred Aron. 1995. "Police Stressors: Variations in Percpetion Among Police Personnel." *Journal of Criminal Justice, 23*(3): 287–94.

von Weiler, Julia, Annette Haardt-Becker, and Simone Schulte. 2010. "Care and Treatment of Child Victims of Child Pornographic Exploitation (CPE) in Germany." *Journal of Sexual Aggression, 16*(2): 211–22.

Ward, Tony, and Anthony Beech 2006. "An Integrated Theory of Sexual Offending." *Aggression and Violent Behavior, 11*: 44–63

Ward, Tony, and Richard J. Siegert. 2002. "Toward a Comprehensive Theory of Child Sexual Abuse: A Theory Knitting Perspective." *Psychology, Crime & Law, 8*(4): 319–51.

Wardwell, James, and G. Stevenson Smith. 2008. "Recovering Erased Digital Evidence from CD-RW Discs in a Child Exploitation Investigation." *Digital Investigation, 5*: 6–9.

Webb, Barry. 1997. "Steering Column Locks and Motor Vehicle Theft: Evaluations from Three Countries." In Ronald V. Clarke (ed.), *Crime Prevention Studies*, vol. 2, pp. 46–59. Monsey, NY: Criminal Justice Press.

Webb, L., J. Craissati, and S. Keen. 2007. "Characteristics of Internet Child Pornography Offenders: A Comparison with Child Molesters." *Sexual Abuse: A Journal of Research and Treatment, 19*(4): 449–65.

Wellard, Sarah. 15th–21st March, 2001. "Cause and Effect." *Community Care, 1364*: 26–27.

Welsh, Brandon C., and David P. Farrington. 2000. "Monetary Benefits of Crime Prevention Programs." *Crime and Justice, 27*: 305–61.

Williams, Katherine S. 2003. "Controlling Internet Child Pornography and Protecting the Child." *Information & Communication Technology Law, 12*(1): 3–24.

Williams, Katherine S. 2005. "Facilitating Safer Choices: Use of Warnings to Dissuade Viewing of Pornography on the Internet." *Child Abuse Review, 14*(6): 415–29.

Wolak, Janis, David Finkelhor, and Kimberley J. Mitchell. 2004. "Internet-Related Sex Crimes Against Minors: Implications for Prevention Based on Findings from a National Study." *Journal of Adolescent Health, 35*(5): 424 e11–424 e20.

Wolak, Janis, David Finkelhor, and Kimberley J. Mitchell. 2005a. "The Varieties of Child Pornography Production." In Max Taylor and Ethel Quayle (eds.), *Viewing Child Pornography on the Internet: Understanding the Offence, Managing the Offender, Helping the Victims*, pp. 31–48. Dorset, England: Russell House.

Wolak, Janis, David Finkelhor, and Kimberley J. Mitchell. 2005b. *Child Pornography Possessors Arrested in Internet-Related Crimes: Findings From the National Juvenile Online Victimisation Study*. Alexandria, VA, US: Department of Justice, National Center for Missing and Exploited Children.

Wolak, Janis, David Finkelhor, and Kimberly J. Mitchell. 2011. "Child Pornography Possessors: Trends in Offender and Case Characteristics." *Sexual Abuse: A Journal of Research and Treatment, 23*(1): 22–42.

Wolak, Janis, David Finkelhor, Kimberly J. Mitchell, and Michele L. Ybarra. 2008. "Online "Predators" and Their Victims: Myths, Realities, and Implications for Prevention and Treatment." *American Psychologist, 63*(2): 111–28.

Wolak, Janis, and Kimberly J. Mitchell. 2009. *Work exposure to child pornography in ICAC task forces and affiliates*. University of New Hampshire Crimes against Children Research Center. New Hampshire, United States: Available at http://www.unh.edu/ccrc/pdf/Law%20Enforcement%20Work%20Exposure%20to%20CP.pdf (accessed on December 12, 2011).

Wolak, Janis, Kimberly Mitchell, and David Finkelhor. 2003. *Internet Sex Crimes against Minors: The Response of Law Enforcement*. University of New Hampshire Crimes against Children Research Center. New Hampshire, United States. Available at http://www.unh.edu/ccrc/pdf/jvq/CV70.pdf (accessed on December 12, 2011).

Wortley, Richard. 2001. "A Classification of Techniques for Controlling Situational Precipitators of Crime." *Security Journal, 14*(4): 63–82.

Wortley, Richard, and Stephen Smallbone. 2006a. *Child Pornography on the Internet. Problem-Oriented Guides for Police. Problem-Specific Guides Series No. 41.* U.S. Department of Justice. Available at http://www.popcenter.org/problems/child_pornography/ (accessed on December 12, 2011).

Wortley, Richard, and Smallbone, Stephen. 2006b. "Applying Situational Principles to Sexual Offending Against Children." In Richard Wortley and Stephen Smallbone (eds.), *Situational Prevention of Child Sexual Abuse. Crime prevention studies, Volume 19R.* Monsey, NY: Criminal Justice Press.

Wyatt, Gail E., and Michael Newcomb. 1990. "Internal and External Mediators of Women's Sexual Abuse in Childhood." *Journal of Consulting and Clinical Psychology, 58*(6): 758–67.

Ybarra, Michelle, L., and Mitchell, Kimberley J. 2005. "Exposure to Internet Pornography Among Children and Adolescents: A National Survey." *CyberPsychology & Behavior, 8*(5): 473–87.

Ybarra, Michele L., David Finkelhor, Kimberly J. Mitchell, and Janis Wolak. 2009. "Associations Between Blocking, Monitoring, and Filtering Software on the Home Computer and Youth-Reported Unwanted Exposure to Sexual Material Online." *Child Abuse and Neglect, 33*(12): 857–69.

Young, Kimberley. 2008. "Understanding Sexually Deviant Online Behavior: From an Addiction Perspective." *International journal of Cyber Criminology, 2*(1): 298–307.

Zauner, Christoph. 2010. *Implementation and Benchmarking of Perceptual Image Hash Functions.* Masters Thesis, Secure Information Systems, Upper University of Applied Sciences, Hagenberg Campus.

Zillmann, Dolf, and Jennings Bryant. 1984. "Effects of Massive Exposure to Pornography." In Neil M. Malamuth and Edward I. Donnerstein (eds.), *Pornography and Sexual Aggression*, pp. 115–38. New York: Academic Press.

Zillmann, Dolf, and Jennings Bryant. 1986. "Shifting Preferences in Pornography Consumption." *Communication Research, 13*(4): 560–78.

Zimbardo, Philip G. 1969. "The Human Choice: Individuation, Reason, and Order Versus Deindividuation, Impulse, and Chaos. In W. D. Arnold and D. Levine (eds.), *Nebraska Symposium on Motivation*, pp. 237–307. Lincoln: University of Nebraska.

Index

Abpep-t, 29
Adolescent ICP offenders, 44–45
Age: adolescent offenders, 44–45; and
    demographic characteristics of offen-
    ders, 35–36; developmental protection
    and, 92–93; model children and, 52–53;
    and origins of sexual interest in
    children, 46–47; and production of ICP,
    71–72; of victims, 31–32
Age of consent: historically, 10; selected
    countries, 4–5
Alice's Adventures in Wonderland
    (Carroll), 11
Anonymous remailers, 23
Aristotle's Masterpiece, 10
Arpanet, 17, 19
Ashcroft v. Free Speech Coalition, 5, 7
*Attorney General, A Book Named "John
    Cleland's Memoirs of a Woman of
    Pleasure" v.*, 6–7
Authentication servers, 23–24

*A Book Named "John Cleland's Memoirs
    of a Woman of Pleasure" v. Attorney
    General*, 6–7
Boycotts, 117–18
Broad Street Magazine, 12

Browsers of child pornography, 42–43
Bulletin boards, 29

Camera, impact on child
    pornography of, 1, 11
Candyman, 66
Carroll, Lewis, 11
Chat rooms, 19, 29–30
Child Behavior Checklist (CBCL),
    74–75
Child Exploitation and Obscenity Section
    (CEOS), 56–57
Child Exploitation Tracking System
    (CETS), 63–64
Childhood experiences, ICP and, 15
Child pornography: COPINE scale of
    severity of, 6, 8; definition (legal), 4–7;
    definition (nonlegal), 6–9; impact of
    camera (mid-1800s) on, 1; virtual, 4–5
Child Pornography Protection
    Act 1996, 5, 7
Child prostitution: historically, 9–11;
    media and, 12; online solicitations, 33
Child Protection Act (1984), 7
Child Protection and Obscenity
    Enforcement Act (1988), 7
Child Protection Operations (CPO), 57

Child Protector and Sexual Predator Punishment Act (1998), 7

Children-Love, 12

Child Sexual Abuse Anti-Distribution Filter (CSAADF), 58, 61–62; warning messages and, 119–20

Codes of conduct, 118–19

Communication protocols, 18–19, 21

Computer-generated images, 5

Confidential telephone hotlines, 97

Contact sexual abuse, 39–41, 95–96

COPINE scale, as ranges of severity, 6, 8

Cospol Internet Related Child Abusive Material Project (CIRCAMP): and filtering as investigative tool, 61; organization investigating ICP, 57–58; on terminology, 8; warning messages and, 119–20

Crimes Against Children Research Center (CACRC), 35–36, 41

Cyber Crimes Center (C3), 56–57

CyberTipline, 58, 110–11

Data linking as investigative technique, 63–64

Deindividuation, 80, 107–8

Demographics: characteristics of offenders, 35–37, 91–92; Internet usage, 17; and measurement of ICP, 30–33; of offenders, 35–37; sex crimes and, 14; sexual status of children (historically) and, 9–10; and social liberalization of 1960s, 11–12; of those arrested for online pornography, 3

Denmark, 11–12

Detection/prosecution as prevention of ICP, 94–96, 102–3

Developmental prevention of ICP, 92–93

Diagnostic and Statistical Manual of Mental Disorders (APA), 13

Diagnostic and Statistical Manual of Mental Disorders (DSM) (APA), 46–47

Distribution of pornographic images: CIRCAMP and, 58; contact sexual abuse/ICP overlap and, 39; Internet's exacerbation of, 26–27; and production of ICP, 72

Dodgson, Charles Lutwidge, 11

Domain names, 19, 21–22, 112–13

Domain Name Service (DNS), 22

Dost, United States v., 7

Dunkelfeld project, 98

Economics: ICP/year, 31; money as ICP motivation, 117–18; United States (1976–1977) child prostitution and, 12

eDonkey, 33

E-mail: ICP distribution via, 29; servers for, 23

End Child Prostitution, Child Pornography and Trafficking of Children for Sexual Purposes (ECPAT), 58

Environment and ICP: managing environmental triggers, 121; and reduction of provocations, 120

Europol, 58

Facebook, origin of, 20

Facilitating disclosure as prevention of ICP, 101–2

Federal Bureau of Investigations (FBI), 12, 56–57, 66

Ferber, New York vs., 7

File Transfer Protocol (FTP): definition, 23; webcams and, 28–29

Filtering software, 61–62

Fingerprint, 62

Free Speech Coalition, Ashcroft v., 5, 7

Fundamental attribution error, 106–7

Future priorities of research: behavioral/computer science research and, 128–29; and behavior of offenders, 126–27; nontreatment/nonprisoner sample studies, 127; and onset of offending, 127

Gender: and arrested offenders by type of images, 32; and demographic characteristics of offenders, 35–36; effects of child pornography victimization and, 76; evolutionary history and, 46; evolutionary terms of males' attraction to children, 14; gender differences in offenders, 47–48; males' viewing of children as sexual objects, 3; and reasons people use pornography, 47–48; of undetected ICP offenders, 37; of victims, 30

General deterrence as prevention of ICP, 93–94

Glitter, Gary, 64

Global nature of ICP. *See also* Demographics: age of consent and, 4–5; coordinated operations targeting covert groups and, 66–67; coordinated operations targeting websites and, 67–68; Denmark/Sweden and, 11–12; illegal ICP websites, 28; impact of standardized protocol (1983) on, 2; international investigations and, 56–59; legal definitions and, 6; sexual status of children (historically) and, 9–10; working across jurisdictions, 51

Groomers of child pornography, 43–44

Harris's List of Covent Garden Ladies, 10–11

Hebephilia, 13

Hickey, William, 10

Historical aspects: of child pornography, 13–15; clinical conceptualizations of offenders, 12–13; impact of camera (mid-1800s), 1; impact of Scandinavian obscenity laws, 1; importance of, 13–15; production of pornography, 10–12; sexual status of children, 9–10; and variations of legal definition, 6–9

Honeypot traps, 60–61, 68–69

Hotlines, 97

Hypertext Transfer Protocol (HTTP), 20, 22

ICP offending, 128

Images of child pornography: access to, 125–26; arrested offenders by type, 32; and distribution of ICP, 26–27, 39, 58; effects of child pornography distribution, 77–79; effects of child pornography victimization and, 74–76; image recognition as a tool, 62–63; image/robust hash, 62; impact of volume of activity, 54–55; and overlap with contact sexual abuse offending, 39–41; and production of ICP, 72; seized ICP images by Internet Watch Foundation, 31

Immigration and Customs enforcement Service, 56

Impacts of ICP on offenders: disinhibiting effects of Internet, 80–82; habituation due to viewing ICP, 83–84; relationship problems due to viewing ICP, 82–83; transition to contact abuse due to viewing ICP, 84–85

Impacts of ICP on victims: effects of child pornography distribution, 77–79; effects of child pornography victimization, 73–76; effects of child sexual victimization, 72–73; prevention of ICP, 99–104

Incapacitation as prevention of ICP, 98–99

INHOPE (International Association of Internet Hotlines), 58–59

Innocent Images task force, 56–57

International Centre for Missing and Exploited Children (ICMEC), 52–53, 59

Internet. *See also* Internet child pornography (ICP); Situational crime preventionas (SCP): as an active cause of ICP, 15; auditing workplace Internet use, 114; and challenges for investigating ICP, 50–55; communication protocols of, 18, 21; definition, 16–20; deregistration of ICP domains on, 112–13; and distribution of pornography, 26–27; domain names of, 21–22; e-mail, 23, 29; filtering ICP and, 111–12; history of, 17; honeypot traps on, 60–61, 68–69; ICP facilitation due to structure of, 50–51; impact of sophistication of technology, 54; impact of standardized protocol (1983) on, 2; impact of volume of activity, 54–55; and increased demand for child pornography, 48–49; individuals' disinhibitory behavior and, 3–4; Internet servers of, 22–24, 65, 118–19; location of child pornography on, 27–30; networks of, 24; percentage devoted to ICP, 31; and production of pornography, 26; searching as ICP investigation, 59–60; undercover ICP investigations and, 60; victimization of youth on, 33; and viewing of pornography, 27

Internet child exploitation (ICE) units, 85–86, 128

Internet child pornography (ICP), 2. *See also* Offenders; age of victims, 31–32; anonymous remailers and, 23; arrests for, 35; browsers of child pornography, 42–43; embedded, 120–21; future research priorities and, 126–29; impact of standardized protocol (1983) on, 2; impact on victims, 69; measurement of, 30–33; nongovernment organizations investigating ICP, 56–59; overlap with contact sexual abuse offending, 39–41; preconditions necessary for, 15; search terms and, 32–33; separation of ICP behavior from moral outrage, 124; as supply-led demand, 3; victim impact of. *See* Impacts of ICP on victims; violent crime and, 35; Wonderland Club, 11

Internet Corporation for Assigned Names and Numbers (ICANN), 22, 114

Internet Crimes Against Children (ICAC) task force, 56–57

Internet Message Access Protocol (IMAP), 23

Internet Protocol (IP), 21

Internet Protocol Suite, 18

Internet Relay Chat (IRC), 19

Internet servers, 22–24

Internet Service Provider (ISP), 20–21, 28

Internet Watch Foundation, (IWF), 59, 110–11; on illegal ICP websites, 28; seized ICP images by, 31

Interpol Specialized Crime Unit, 58; child pornography definition of, 6; Operation Cathedral and, 66

Interventions. *See* Investigations of ICP; Situational crime prevention (SCP)

Investigations of ICP: across jurisdictions, 51; behavioral/computer science research and, 128–29; boundary maintenance by investigators, 87; computer peripherals as evidence, 64–65; computers as evidence, 64; coordinated operations targeting covert groups, 65–67; coordinated operations targeting websites, 65, 67–68; data linking as a tool for, 63–64; filtering software as a tool for, 61–62; forensic experts and, 64; future research priorities and, 126–29; honeypot traps, 60–61, 68–69; image recognition as a tool for, 62–63; and inadequate legislation, 51–52; and inconsistent legislation, 52–53; Internet structure and, 50–51; Internet technological sophistication and, 54; and lack of enforcement, 53; offenders' expertise and, 53–54; participants, 55–59; peripherals as evidence, 65–66; remote surveillance as a tool for, 63; by searching the Internet, 59–60; servers as evidence, 66; and sexual-related effects on ICP investigators, 86–87; traditional police investigations, 61; and trauma-related effects on ICP investigators, 85–86; undercover, 60; and volume of Internet activity, 54–55

Juvenile Justice of the House Committee on Education Labor, child pornography report (1982), 1–2

Knox, United States v., 6

Krafft-Ebing, Richard von, 12–13

Landslide Productions, 67–68

Legal issues: Child Pornography Protection Act 1996, 5; computer-generated images and, 5; inadequate legislation, 51–52; inconsistent legislation, 52–53; need for global cooperation, 2; Scandinavian obscenity laws, 1; summary of court judgments, 7

Liddell, Alice, 11

Lolita, 12

Media. *See also* Images of child pornography; Internet child pornography (ICP): art/print (historically) and child pornography, 10–11; and economic in United States (1976–1977), 12; impact of Scandinavian obscenity laws, 1; and social liberalization of 1960s, 11–12

Memoirs of a Georgian Rake (Hickey), 10

Mental illness, 37

Millon Multiaxial Clinical Inventory (MCMI-III), 37

Minnesota Multiphasic Personality Inventory (MMPI), 37

Model children, 52–53

Money as ICP motivation, 117–18

Moral standards: ICP and, 15; panic and, 32–33; separation of ICP behavior from moral outrage, 124

Morphed images, 5, 32

Motivations for offending: evolutionary history and, 46; money, 117–18; and origins of sexual interest in children, 46–47

MySpace, origin of, 20

Napster, origin of, 20

National Center for Missing & Exploited Children (NCMEC), 59

National Child Exploitation Coordination Centre (NCECC), 57

Needs principle of treatment/ counseling, 97

Networks, 24

Network Service Provider (NSP), 24

Newsrooms, 29

New York vs. Ferber, 7

Nongovernment organizations investigating ICP, 56–59

Nonsecure collectors of child pornography, 43

Notice and takedown (NTD) orders, 59, 110

Nudist Moppets, 12

Obscenity: definitions, 6; impact of Scandinavian obscenity laws, 1

Offender-focused prevention of ICP: detection/prosecution, 94–96; developmental, 92–93; general deterrence, 93–94; incapacitation, 98–99; specific deterrence, 96–97; treatment/ counseling, 97–98

Offenders. *See also* Situational crime prevention (SCP): adolescent, 44–45; characteristics of, 34–35; contact sexual abuse/ICP overlap, 39–41; demographics of, 35–37; disinhibiting effects of Internet on, 80–82; expertise of, 53–54; gender differences in, 47–48; habituation due to viewing ICP, 83–84; Internet influence on, 48–49; monitoring known, 115–16; motivations of, 45–46; origins of sexual interest in children, 46–47; prevention of ICP, 92–99; psychological characteristics of, 37–39; relationship problems due to viewing ICP, 82–83; removal of excuses of, 110, 118–20; transition to contact abuse due to viewing ICP, 84–85; types (behavioral), 42–44; types (psychological), 41–42

Office of Juvenile Justice and Delinquency Prevention, 56–57

Ohio, Osborne vs., 7

Online solicitations, 33

Operation Avalanche/Ore, 65, 67–68

Operation Basket, 65, 68

Operation Candyman, 66

Operation Cathedral, 65–66

Operation Ore, 65, 67–68

Operation Pin, 68–69

Operation Rescue, 66–67

Orchid Club, 66

Osborne vs. Ohio, 7

Pedophilia, definition, 12–13

Peer-to-peer (P2P) programs: eDonkey and, 33; ICP distribution via, 30; origin of, 20; Skype and, 29

Personality Assessment Inventory (PAI) profiles, 37

Person situation interaction. *See* Situational crime prevention (SCP)

Phallometric assessment, 39
Pornography. *See also* Child pornography; Internet child pornography (ICP): reasons people use, 47–48
Postal Inspection and Customs Services, 12
Posttraumatic stress disorder (PTSD), 85–86
Pretty Baby, 12
Prevention of ICP: detection/prosecution (offender-focused), 94–96; developmental (offender focused), 92–93; facilitating disclosure (victim focused), 101–2; general deterrence (offender focused), 93–94; incapacitation (offender focused), 98–99; levels of, 89–91; as priority, 124–25; prosecution (victim focused), 94–96, 102–3; and reasons for person-situation interaction, 106–8; reporting to authorities (victim focused), 102; resilience building (victim focused), 100–101; revictimization prevention (victim focused), 103–4; self-protection (victim focused), 99–100; situational crime prevention (SCP) and, 108–22. *See also* Situational crime prevention (SCP); specific deterrence (offender focused), 96–97; treatment/counseling (offender focused), 97–98
Primary level of ICP prevention, 89–91
Production of child pornography, 26, 44
Prosecution as prevention of ICP, 94–96, 102–3
Prostitution. *See* Child prostitution
Psychological typologies of ICP offenders, 41–42
Punishment, incapacitation as, 98–99

Race and offenders, 36
Recidivism, 41, 73, 84, 125
Rehabilitation, 125
Remote surveillance as investigative technique, 63
Reporting to authorities as prevention of ICP, 102

Research: adolescent offenders, 44–45; behavioral typologies of offenders, 42–44; developmental protection, 92–93; effects of child pornography victimization, 73–76; future priorities of, 126–29; importance of, 126; longitudinal study by CACRC, 35–36, 41; longitudinal study for developmental prevention, 93; Millon Multiaxial Clinical Inventory (MCMI-III), 37; Minnesota Multiphasic Personality Inventory (MMPI), 37; online/offline offender comparisons, 36, 38–39; of overlap with contact sexual abuse offending, 39–41, 95–96; Personality Assessment Inventory (PAI) profiles, 37; person-situation interaction and, 107–8; phallometric assessment and, 39; psychological characteristics of offenders, 37–39, 41–42; sexual ICP recidivism, 41; suicide patterns in Britain (increasing effort), 109
Resilience building as prevention of ICP, 100–101
Responsivity principle of treatment/counseling, 97
Revictimization as prevention of ICP, 103–4
Risk principle of treatment/counseling, 97
Robust hash, 62

Secondary level of ICP prevention, 90–91
Secondary traumatic stress disorder (STSD), 85–86
Self-protection as prevention of ICP, 99–100
Servers, Internet, 22–24, 65, 118–19
Service agreements, 118–19
Sex crimes and evolutionary terms of males' attraction to children, 14
Sexting, 45
Sexual abuse, contact, 39–41, 95–96
Sexual deviance, 38–39, 124
Sexual Exploitation of Children Act (1978), 7, 12
Sexuality and the importance of historical aspects of child pornography, 13–15

Simple Mail Transfer Protocol (SMTP), 23
Situational crime prevention (SCP): advertising boycotts, 117–18; auditing workplace Internet use, 114; behavioral/computer science research and, 128–29; blocking online payments, 117; definition, 108; deregistration of ICP domains and, 112–13; filtering ICP, 111–12; house rules and, 116; identity verification, 114; and increasing effort of offending, 109–10; increasing risk of detection, 110, 113–14; managing environmental triggers, 121; monitoring known offenders, 115–16; reduction of provocations, 110, 120–21; regulating "crime facilitators," 115; removal of excuses of offenders, 110, 118–20; removing ICP, 110–11; reward reduction and, 110, 116–18; service agreements/codes of conduct and, 118–19; stings, 113–14; strategies, 109–10, 125–26; targeting embedded ICP, 120–21; warning messages, 119–20
Skype, 20, 29
Specific deterrence as prevention of ICP, 96–97
Sting operations: types, 113–14; websites and, 28
Stop It Now! hotlines, 97
Sweden, 11–12

Taxi Driver, 12
Telephone hotlines, 97
Terminology, 7–9, 12–13
Tertiary level of ICP prevention, 90–91
Through the Looking-Glass (Carroll), 11

Transmission Control Protocol (TCP), 21
Treatment/counseling as prevention of ICP, 97–98

Uniform Resource Locator (URL), 22, 61–62
United Nations: on lack of enforcement, 53; United Nations High Commissioner for Human Rights, 6
United States v. Dost, 7
United States v. Knox, 6
U.S. Department of Justice, 56
U.S. General Accounting Office, child pornography report (1982), 1–2
U.S. Postal Inspection Service, Landslide Productions and, 67–68

Victim-focused prevention of ICP: facilitating disclosure, 101–2; prosecution, 102–3; reporting to authorities, 102; resilience building, 100–101; revictimization prevention, 103–4; self-protection, 99–100
Victims. *See* Impacts of ICP on victims
Viewing of pornographic images, 27–28. *See also* Images of child pornography
Vigilante sites, 28–29
Virtual child pornography, 4–5
Virtual Global Taskforce (VGT), 56, 58

Webcams, 28–29
Websites, 27–28, 31. *See also* Internet
Wonderland Club, 11, 66
World Wide Web (WWW), 16–17, 20. *See also* Internet

Youth Self Report (YSR), 74–75

About the Authors

Professor RICHARD WORTLEY is director of the Jill Dando Institute of Security and Crime Science at University College London. He began his career as a prison psychologist before becoming an academic and is a former chair of the Australian Psychological Society's College of Forensic Psychologists. Recent books include *Preventing Child Sexual Abuse: Evidence, Policy and Practice* (with Stephen Smallbone and William Marshall) and *Psychological Criminology: An Integrative Approach*.

STEPHEN SMALLBONE is a professor in the School of Criminology and Criminal Justice at Griffith University and an Australian Research Council Future Fellow. His publications include *Preventing Child Sexual Abuse: Evidence, Policy and Practice* (with William Marshall and Richard Wortley) and *Situational Prevention of Child Sexual Abuse* (with Richard Wortley).